D1646183

Poitou-Charentes Lifeline

by
Val Gascoyne

SURVIVAL BOOKS • LONDON • ENGLAND

First published 2004

All rights reserved. No part of this publication
may be reproduced, stored in a retrieval system or
recorded by any means, without prior written
permission from the author.

Copyright © Val Gascoyne 2004
Cover photograph: Roger Moss (:www.picturefrance.com)

Survival Books Limited, 1st Floor,
60 St James's Street, London SW1A 1ZN, United Kingdom
☎ +44 (0)20-7493 4244, 🖷 +44 (0)20-7491 0605
✉ info@survivalbooks.net
🖳 www.survivalbooks.net
To order books, please refer to page 334.

British Library Cataloguing in Publication Data.
A CIP record for this book is available
from the British Library.
ISBN 1 901130 23 1

Printed and bound in Finland by WS Bookwell Ltd

ACKNOWLEDGEMENTS

A huge thank-you to Chris, who was always there with support, and Barnaby, who was convinced that his mum was just a mirage when he woke in the night – thank you both for your understanding; I promise to be more organised next time. Writing this book has taught me many things, of which one is to have great sympathy for the editor who receives a manuscript from a new author, so a huge thank-you to Joe Laredo, who must have gone into shock when faced with this book but still managed to drag my work kicking and screaming into a state suitable for publication. Thanks also to his wife and colleague, Kerry, for her help with the editing and proofreading, as well as the layout of the text. I'm grateful to Roger Moss for his permission to use the cover photograph. A final thank-you to Jim Watson for his superb illustrations, maps and cover design.

OTHER TITLES BY SURVIVAL BOOKS

The Alien's Guide To Britain; The Alien's Guide To France; The Best Places To Live In France; The Best Places To Live In Spain; Buying, Selling & Letting Property; Foreigners In France: Triumphs & Disasters; Foreigners In Spain: Triumphs & Disasters; How To Avoid Holiday & Travel Disasters; Costa Del Sol Lifeline; Dordogne/Lot Lifeline; Renovating & Maintaining Your French Home; Retiring Abroad; Rioja And Its Wines; The Wines Of Spain

Living And Working Series

Abroad; America; Australia; Britain; Canada; The Far East; France; Germany; The Gulf States & Saudi Arabia; Holland, Belgium & Luxembourg; Ireland; Italy; London; New Zealand; Spain; Switzerland

Buying A Home Series

Abroad; Britain; Florida; France; Greece & Cyprus; Ireland; Italy; Portugal; Spain

Order forms are on page 334.

What Readers & Reviewers Have Said

If you need to find out how France works, this book is indispensable. Native French people probably have a less thorough understanding of how their country functions.

Living France

This book is a Godsend – a practical guide to all things French and the famous French administration – a book I am sure I will used time and time again during my stay in France.

Reader

I would recommend this book to anyone considering the purchase of a French property – get it early so you do it right!

Reader

Let's say it at once: David Hampshire's *Living and Working in France* is the best handbook ever produced for visitors and foreign residents in this country. It is Hampshire's meticulous detail which lifts his work way beyond the range of other books with similar titles. *Living and Working in France* is absolutely indispensable.

Riviera Reporter

I found this a wonderful book crammed with facts and figures, with a straightforward approach to the problems and pitfalls you are likely to encounter. It is laced with humour and a thorough understanding of what's involved. Gets my vote!

Reader

I was born in France and spent countless years there. I bought this book when I had to go back after a few years away, and this is far and away the best book on the subject. The amount of information covered is nothing short of incredible. I thought I knew enough about my native country. This book has proved me wrong. Don't go to France without it. Big mistake if you do. Absolutely priceless!

Reader

If you're thinking about buying a property in France, Hampshire is totally on target. I read this book before going through the buying process and couldn't believe how perfectly his advice dovetailed with my actual experience.

Reader

About Other Survival Books on France

In answer to the desert island question about the one how-to book on France, this book would be it.

THE RECORDER

It's just what I needed! Everything I wanted to know and even things I didn't know I wanted to know but was glad I discovered!

READER

There are now several books on this subject, but I've found that this book is definitely the best one. It's crammed with up-to-date information and seems to cover absolutely everything.

READER

Covers every conceivable question concerning everyday life – I know of no other book that could take the place of this one.

FRANCE IN PRINT

An excellent reference book for anyone thinking of taking the first steps towards buying a new or old property in France.

READER

Thankfully, with several very helpful pieces of information from this book, I am now the proud owner of a beautiful house in France. Thank God for David Hampshire!

READER

I saw this book advertised and thought I had better read it. It was definitely money well spent.

READER

We bought an apartment in Paris using this book as a daily reference. It helped us immensely, giving us confidence in many procedures from looking for a place initially to the closing, including great information on insurance and utilities. Definitely a great source!

READER

A comprehensive guide to all things French, written in a highly readable and amusing style, for anyone planning to live, work or retire in France.

THE TIMES

THE AUTHOR

Originally from Hertfordshire, Val Gascoyne worked as a retail manager before returning to college to qualify as an administrator and going on to run her own secretarial business for five years. Having spent most of her earnings on travelling, she eventually moved to France for fresh challenges, a calmer life and French neighbours. There she set up Purple Pages (see below). This book and its companion, *Dordogne/Lot Lifeline*, are a development of that activity and are the first Val has written for Survival Books.

Purple Pages
Grosbout, 16240 La Forêt de Tessé, France
☎ 05 45 29 59 74, UK ☎ 0871-900 8305
🖳 www.purplepages.info

This company produces tailored directories, unique to each family, which are the result of exhaustive research and contain everything you could possibly need to know about an area – from when the dustmen call and where the nearest English-speaking doctor is to be found to facilities and services for specific medical needs or sporting passions.

CONTENTS

3 Charente-Maritime 149

4. Deux-Sèvres 221

5. Vienne 273

Index 328

Order Forms 334

Important Note

Every effort has been made to ensure that the information contained in this book is accurate and up to date. Note, however, that businesses and organisations can be quite transient, particularly those operated by expatriates (French businesses tend to go on 'for ever'), and therefore information can quickly change or become outdated.

It's advisable to check with an official and reliable source before making major decisions or undertaking an irreversible course of action. If you're planning to travel long-distance to visit somewhere, always phone beforehand to check the opening times, availability of goods, prices and other relevant information.

Unless specifically stated, a reference to any company, organisation or product doesn't constitute an endorsement or recommendation.

Barrel-making, Arciac

Author's Notes

- Times are shown using the 12-hour clock, e.g. ten o'clock in the morning is written 10am and ten in the evening 10pm.

- Costs and prices are shown in euros (€) where appropriate. They should be taken as guides only, although they were accurate at the time of publication.

- Unless otherwise stated, all telephone numbers have been given as if dialling from France. To dial from abroad, use your local international access code (e.g. 00 from the UK) followed by 33 for France and omit the initial 0 of the French number.

- His/he/him/man/men (etc.) also mean her/she/her/woman/women (no offence ladies!). This is done simply to make life easier for both the reader and, in particular, the author, and isn't intended to be sexist.

- Warnings and important points are shown in **bold** type.

- The following symbols are used in this book: ☎ (telephone), 🖹 (fax), 🖥 (internet) and ✉ (email).

- British English is used throughout. French words and phrases are given in italics in brackets where appropriate and are used in preference to English where no exact equivalents exist.

- If there isn't a listing for a particular town under a given heading, this facility or service wasn't available in or near that town at the time of publication. For facilities and services that are available in most towns or are provided on a regional basis and are therefore not listed individually in the department chapters, see **Chapter 1**.

Île d'Yeu

INTRODUCTION

If you're thinking of living, working, buying a home or spending an extended holiday in the Poitou-Charentes region of France, this is **the book** for you. *Poitou-Charentes Lifeline* has been written to answer all those important questions about life in this region that aren't answered in other books. Whether you're planning to spend a few months or a lifetime there, to work, retire or buy a holiday home, this book is essential reading.

An abundance of tourist guides and information is available about Poitou-Charentes, but until now it has been difficult to find comprehensive information about local costs, facilities and services, particularly in one book. *Poitou-Charentes Lifeline* fills this gap and contains accurate, up-to-date, practical information about the most important aspects of daily life in the Poitou-Charentes region. If you've ever sought a restaurant that's open after 10pm, a 24-hour petrol station or something to do with your children on a wet day, this book will become your 'bible'.

Information is derived from a variety of sources, both official and unofficial, not least the hard-won experiences of the author, her friends, family and colleagues. *Poitou-Charentes Lifeline* is a comprehensive handbook and is designed to make your stay in the region – however long or short – easier and less stressful. **It will also help you save valuable time, trouble and money, and will repay your investment many times over!** (For comprehensive information about living and working in France in general and buying a home in France, this book's sister publications, *Living and Working in France* and *Buying a Home in France*, written by David Hampshire, are highly recommended reading.)

The Poitou-Charentes region is a popular holiday destination and a wonderful place to live: it enjoys relatively mild winters and long, hot summers; its unspoiled countryside, enchanting villages and beautiful coastline are one of France's best-kept secrets; the delicious local cuisine (the best of country fare and delicious seafood) and wine are a magnet for foodies; and the relaxed lifestyle and quality of life attracts an increasing number of foreigners. I trust this book will help make your life easier and more enjoyable, and smooth the way to a happy and rewarding time in Poitou-Charentes.

Bienvenue en Poitou-Charentes!   Val Gascoyne
                                                                April 2004

Saintes

1

Introducing Poitou-Charentes

This chapter is divided into three sections: Section 1, below, provides a general introduction to the Poitou-Charentes region and a brief description of each of its four departments and their main towns; Section 2, beginning on page 26, contains information about getting to (and from) the region and getting around by public transport once you're there; Section 3, beginning on page 45, lists useful general information in alphabetical order – detailed information relating to each department is contained, under similar headings, in **Chapters 2** to **5**.

OVERVIEW

Stretching from the Atlantic coast in the west towards the Massif Central in the east, Poitou-Charentes has enormous variety: from small farming communities to bustling seaside towns and even an island where motor vehicles are banned. Whether you walk along the ramparts in Angoulême, stroll around the marina at La Rochelle or visit the futuristic theme park of Futuroscope, you're never far away from a wealth of culture and history.

This is a region full of châteaux and waterways, mills and vineyards – among the last, of course, those of the world famous Cognac. The area can

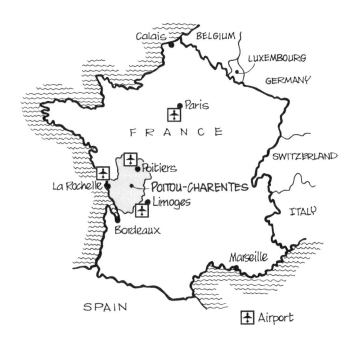

be explored by water, by bicycle or on foot, with no shortage of comfortable accommodation and traditional cuisine to greet you at the end of each day. For those who enjoy photography, there's an endless supply of subjects, from wildlife to picturesque villages, from spectacular sunsets over the sea to bustling markets, each season bringing with it a change of scenery.

The tasty traditional cuisine is enhanced by an abundance of local produce, while an assortment of festivals and venues across the region ensure that the evenings can be just as fulfilling as the days.

In each department, a selection of main towns has been made and facilities and services in these towns highlighted, although others are included where appropriate. The selected towns are geographically

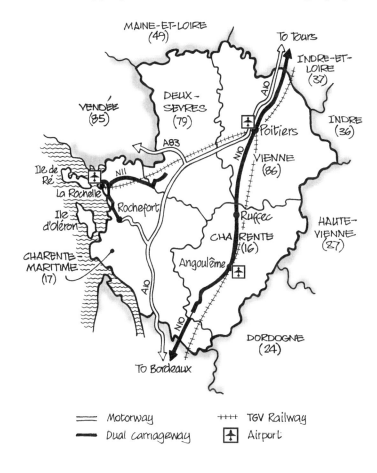

spread, so at least one of them should be reasonably close wherever you choose to stay or live.

The selected towns are as follows:

Charente (16)

- **Angoulême**
- **Chalais**
- **Cognac**
- **Confolens**
- **Ruffec**

Charente-Maritime (17)

- **Jonzac**
- **La Rochelle**
- **Rochefort**
- **Royan**
- **St Jean d'Angély**
- **Saintes**

Deux-Sèvres (79)

- **Melle**
- **Niort**
- **Parthenay**
- **Thouars**

Vienne (86)

- **Civray**
- **Châtellerault**
- **Loudun**
- **Montmorillon**
- **Poitiers**

Charente

This department is named after the Charente river, which is 360km (225mi) long and flows through the departments of Vienne, Charente and Charente-Maritime on its way to the Atlantic coast at Rochefort. Along the way the river powers watermills to produce walnut oil and flour and even to cut stone. In the rolling countryside in the south-west of Charente lies Cognac, a town surrounded by acres of vines stretching far into the distance, from which come the famous drink of the same name and the regional specialty, Pineau des Charentes – an aperitif resembling Normandy's Pommeau.

Angoulême

The capital of Charente is steeped in history, with buildings dating from 16th and 18th centuries. The *mairie* was once a castle, two of whose towers remain. Angoulême is a walled town built on a hill with a parapet walkway giving views over the town and the Charente Valley.

Angoulême is home to the national comic strip centre and hosts the International Cartoon Festival every January, regularly attracting over

200,000 people. As you travel through the city you will see many walls decorated to reflect this event: look out for the butcher standing with a dog outside his shop and the bandits in the windows.

Chalais

Situated in the south of Charente, Chalais lies near the border of three other departments and is ideally located to explore the coasts of Charente-Maritime as well as those north of Bordeaux, whilst only a few miles south is the department of Dordogne (featured in the companion volume in this series, *Dordogne/Lot Lifeline*). In the centre of Chalais is a wonderful statue of a woman drinking water from the flowing fountain while the magnificent château looks down on the town.

Cognac

Undoubtedly most famous for the production of the eponymous drink, which is produced, distilled and matured in cellars on the banks of the river Charente, Cognac is a colourful town, which has been awarded 'three flowers' in the national urban flower competition. There are tours of the cellars and distilleries to give visitors an insight into the history, production and maturing of Cognac. There's also the château where François I was born. Jarnac, the birthplace of former French President François Mitterrand, is close by.

Confolens

This is a medieval town on the banks of the river Vienne that hosts a famous international folk festival every summer. Many timbered houses line the steep and narrow streets of the hillside, the top of which affords a magnificent view over the town.

Ruffec

Ruffec is a small town in the north of Charente, close to the borders of Deux-Sèvres and Vienne. It lies on the N10, a major road running from Poitiers down past Bordeaux. Ruffec was the home of the Duc de Saint-Simon and there are still remains of his castle and walls to be seen. To one side of the town centre, the old quarter, with its cobbled streets and ancient buildings, leads down to the river.

Charente-Maritime

This department is located on the Atlantic coast and includes the offshore islands of Aix, Oléron and Ré. The seaside resorts of Rochefort and Royan are steeped in maritime history and boast ancient fortifications as well as fishing harbours and yachting marinas. To the north, La Rochelle has the largest marina on the European Atlantic coast, with moorings for 3,500 yachts. If you prefer to look at the sea rather than sail on it, there are enough restaurants and cafes overlooking the marina to give you a change every night for many weeks.

Inland is the unique Marais Poitevin, where waterways replace paths and country roads. Further south, ancient towns with colourful markets offer modern water parks and thermal spas. Good food and drink are produced in abundance in this department, with oysters and cheese, Cognac and Pineau.

Jonzac

Built on a spur of rock encircled by the River Seugne, Jonzac is now a spa town with a 15th century château and battlements, and a former convent that's home to an archaeological museum and is the setting for the Saintonge-Québec summer university. There's also a brand new casino and a West Indian water park with wave pool and Caribbean beach huts.

La Rochelle

Founded in the 10th century on a rocky platform in the middle of marshlands, La Rochelle was a fishing village that became a major port as early as the 11th century. The old harbour was built from around the 13th century, some of the 14th-and 15th-century towers still standing.

More modern attractions include a magnificent aquarium and many varied museums and an abundance of restaurants and cafes alongside the old port. In the summer evenings, the roads around the old port are closed to traffic and a fair takes over the streets with entertainment going on until the early hours. La Rochelle is a major sailing centre and hosts the largest floating boat show in Europe.

Rochefort

Rochefort is in the heart of Charente-Maritime, only a few miles from the coast and the islands. There's a strong naval tradition in Rochefort, where great naval dockyards were created in the 17th century. There's a garden by the dockyard containing all the plants brought back by travellers from overseas. The surrounding area can be explored by bicycle, on horseback or on foot and you can discover many museums detailing its maritime heritage.

Royan

Royan, at the mouth of the Gironde, is a large seaside resort, which launched the fashion for sea bathing in the 19th century. The town was almost totally destroyed in 1945 and now boasts post-war innovations in architecture, including Notre Dame church, built in 1955, whose daring lines dominate the seafront. The five beaches sheltered from westerly breezes are a paradise for swimmers and those who enjoy building sandcastles; the most famous, 'Grande Conche' has more than 2km (1.25mi) of sand.

Saint Jean d'Angély

Saint Jean d'Angély is situated on the banks of the River Boutonne where, after the fall of the Roman Empire, the dukes of Aquitaine chose to settle. During the last hundred years the town has become prosperous owing to the development of local industries: shoes, biscuits, Cognac, wood and high quality agricultural products. In the east of the department, Saint Jean enjoys a pleasant micro-climate, and the nearby countryside is calm and restful.

Saintes

Saintes is more than 2,000 years old and was the capital city of one of the Gallic tribes, the Santons. It was converted to Christianity early in its history and became a town with a strong religious vocation. On the eve of the French Revolution modern town planning brought a new dimension to the town with the creation of wide avenues, and in the 19th century the railway and its workshops turned the right bank into a new centre of activity. Today, Saintes is a cultural and tourist centre with its amphitheatre, Roman baths, boat trips and the recently renovated Gallia Theatre in the centre of town. The old quarter, which leads down to the river, is a pedestrian area full of small shops and bistros.

Deux-Sèvres

This department is one of great variety, with the magnificent Château d'Orion in the north and the forest of Chizé in the south. The wetlands of the Marais Poitevin on the border with Charente-Maritime offer a maze of waterways, the best way to discover which is by water; there's even a floating market in the summer.

Melle

Melle is a town full of history, including no fewer than three Roman churches and a silver mine. 'The path of discovery' leads you on a 6km (3.75mi) walk past over 1,000 varieties of trees and shrubs from all over the world. In the centre of the town is a distinctive pink and grey bridge, while a selection of traditional restaurants and the indoor market cater for most gastronomic tastes.

Niort

Originally a Gallic village, Niort has been modernised whilst managing to retain relics of its glorious history. The impressive Donjon is a reminder of the fortifications that Henry II Plantagenet had erected, and the legend of the dragon that was struck down by Jacques Allonneau is represented by the fantastic and unmistakable serpents that dominate rue Ricard off the main square – in total they're 200m long and weigh 12 tonnes. The streets are full of medieval character and contain many churches and temples.

Tucked into a bend in the river Sèvre, Niort is also a commercial town, although trees and gardens help to create a feeling of 'countryside in the town' and the Green Corridor provides a relaxing and natural walk along the river as it leaves the town, with gardens and play areas making it appealing to all ages.

Parthenay

In the Middle Ages Parthenay was one of the major fortresses in the Poitou region and the town still has over 100 half-timbered houses. The historic houses along the cobbled streets of the St Jacques district are home to various sculpture and enamelling workshops. Parthenay also leads the way in technology, being the first town in France to be an internet service provider, thereby allowing free internet access throughout the town.

Thouars

Thouars is a beautiful town built on a spur of rock, encircled by the river Thouet. On the left bank the imposing château looks down over the old town with its timbered houses on steep narrow streets leading up to the old square. On Friday mornings, the main town is dominated by a bustling market; its theatre, cinema and nightclub cater for all tastes in the evening.

Vienne

Vienne is a peaceful department with an important place in French history. It boasts a highly acclaimed architectural heritage, including many buildings in the Romanesque style. In contrast the Futuroscope theme park is as famous for its architecture as for its films and technology.

Châtellerault

Châtellerault became famous in the Middle Ages for crafts such as the production of cutlery and rope, but during the industrial revolution these trades were replaced by a munitions factory, which continued to operate until the 1960s. This building, called 'La Manu', now houses the Auto Moto Vélo museum and offers various leisure activities.

The river Vienne runs through the centre of Châtellerault, where there are four public gardens. To the east of the river is a network of narrow streets with a variety of small shops and restaurants leading to the boulevard Blossac, the town's main commercial thoroughfare. To the south of the town are a lake and a forest.

Civray

A bustling market town, with the 12th century St Nicolas church in its centre, Civay is best explored on foot – especially when the large Tuesday market closes the town centre to traffic. Since Roman times the town has been known as a stopping point for travellers and it now has a wide variety of accommodation, including a holiday village and campsite by the river Charente, which runs through the centre. The ring road is now complete and so Civray can maintain the tranquillity of a country town.

Loudun

Situated at the most northerly point of the department, Loudun isn't far from the Loire valley but still has many of the Romanesque buildings for which Poitou-Charentes is famous. Perhaps most famous for its 'devils' (written about by Aldous Huxley, among others), Loudun has much historic interest. Sainte Croix, a church of amazing architecture with frescoes dating from the end of the 13th century, has become a venue for various cultural events. La Tour Carrée is a square tower built ten centuries ago from whose summit (over 30m/100ft high) you can look out over Loudun and the surrounding area.

Montmorillon

Classified as a town of both art and history, Montmorillon has distinctive architecture, including a gothic bridge, timbered buildings and 12th century funeral chapel, as well as an abundance of floral colour. The church of Notre Dame was built in the tenth century and looks down on the steep tiny streets of the old quarter, now known as the Cité de l'Écrit. Recognised as one of the 15 communities in Europe that specialises in all aspects of books, Montmorillon attracts over a 150,000 visitors each year.

Poitiers

The regional capital, which is situated on a tall rocky outcrop, has been inhabited for over 2,000 years and wherever you go you're surrounded by history. The town boasts over 100 churches and, if you take a stroll through the large pedestrian area, you will come across an 11th century palace nestling among the shops. In more recent years, it's the Futuroscope theme park that has attracted many visitors to Poitiers and, with constantly updated films, games rooms and technology, it continues to retain its unique quality.

During the summer months, there's a series of events in the town centre, including concerts, shows and bands, all of which can be enjoyed from one of the many street cafés. Nestling in the side streets is an assortment of internationally acclaimed restaurants.

GETTING THERE & GETTING AROUND

Getting There By Air

There are several airlines that fly direct to the region, whose international airports are La Rochelle, Limoges and Poitiers. A wider choice of routes is available to the Paris airports, from where you can complete your journey by train.

Although budget airlines can offer good fares, the scheduled airlines also offer some good prices and are sometimes cheaper than the budget airlines if you're booking either late or well in advance.

The following tables list direct routes from England, Scotland and Ireland (North and South) that were in service in early 2004. These are intended only as a guide, as airline services are constantly changing, and you should check with the relevant airports or airlines (see below) for the latest information.

England

From	To	Airline
Birmingham	Paris	British Airways & Air France
Bristol	Paris	Air France
Leeds	Paris	British Midland
Liverpool	Paris	Easyjet
Luton	Paris	Easyjet
London Heathrow, Gatwick & City	Paris	British Airways & Air France
London Heathrow	Angoulême, with two stops	Air France, BMI & British Airways

London Luton	Paris	Easyjet
London Stansted	Poitiers, La Rochelle & Limoges	Ryanair
Manchester	Paris	Air France
Newcastle	Paris	Easyjet & Air France
Southampton	Paris	Air France

Scotland

From	To	Airline
Aberdeen	Paris	Air France
Edinburgh	Paris	British Airways, British Midland & Air France
Glasgow	Paris	British Airways, British Midland & Air France

Ireland

From	To	Airline
Dublin	Paris	Ryan Air & Air France

Contact details for the airlines listed above are as follows:

Airline	Website	UK ☎	French ☎
Air France	www.airfrance.com	0845-359 1000	08 20 82 08 20
British Airways	www.britishairways.com	0870-850 9850	
Easyjet	www.easyjet.com	0870-600 0000	
Ryan Air	www.ryanair.com	0871-246 0000	08 99 70 00 07

The following websites may help you to find low-cost flights with scheduled airlines:

- www.cheapflights.co.uk
- www.ebookers.com
- www.expedia.co.uk
- www.flightline.co.uk
- www.travelocity.co.uk

Plane & Helicopter Hire

Aéro Charter Darta	Aéroport de Nantes Atlantique	☎ 02 40 84 84 84
Air Angoulême	Aérodrome, Champniers Private planes and helicopters to hire	☎ 05 45 69 81 92

Atlantique Air Assistance	Les Comboitures 🖳 *www.atlantiqueairassistance.fr*	☎ 02 41 63 05 50
Jean-Philippe Jaillais	84 rue Gambetta, Thouars	☎ 05 49 96 08 54
Locavia France	5 rue S-Lieut Raymond Collard, Biard All destinations in Europe.	☎ 05 49 37 28 36
On Top Aviation	L'Aérodrome, Missé	☎ 05 49 96 20 94

Car Hire

The larger towns have several car hire companies, one of which is listed below for each of the selected towns. The websites of the 'big five' companies are as follows:

- Avis   🖳 *www.avis.fr*
- Budget   🖳 *www. budget.fr*
- Car'Go   🖳 *www.cargo.fr*
- Europcar   🖳 *www.europcar-atlantique.com*
- Hertz   🖳 *www.hertz-grand-ouest.com*

Airport-Based Car Hire

Angoulême	ADA Location, 19 place Gare	☎ 05 45 92 65 29
Limoges	Avis, 1ter avenue Général de Gaulle	☎ 05 55 33 36 37
Poitiers	Car'Go, 4 rue Carreau	☎ 05 49 38 18 33
La Rochelle	Europcar, 158bis boulevard Joffre	☎ 05 46 41 09 08

Charente

Angoulême	Go Car, avenue de Mal de Lattre de Tassigny	☎ 05 45 37 39 49
Cognac	Europcar, 51 avenue d'Angoulême, Châteaubernard	☎ 05 45 82 32 43
Confolens	Garage Soulat, 12 avenue Général de Gaulle	☎ 05 45 84 00 27
Ruffec	Europcar, 56 avenue Célestin Sieur	☎ 05 45 31 58 58

Charente-Maritime

Jonzac	Europcar, Garage Martin, route Pons	☎ 05 46 48 74 00
La Rochelle	Avis, 166 Boulevard Joffre	☎ 05 46 41 13 55
	Espace Autoplus, place de Verdun Offers electric vehicles for hire.	☎ 05 46 34 02 22
Rochefort	Budget, La Fayette Auto, 56 avenue du 11 Novembre	☎ 05 46 87 18 00
Royan	Europcar, 13 place Docteur Gantier	☎ 05 46 05 20 88
St Jean d'Angély	Europcar, Central Garage, ZI Point du Jour	☎ 05 46 59 29 47
Saintes	Budget, 45 avenue de la Marne	☎ 05 46 74 28 11

Deux-Sèvres

Melle	Europcar, Garage Guibert, 33 avenue du C. Bernier	☎ 05 49 29 16 38
Niort	Avis, 89 rue de la Gare	☎ 05 49 24 36 98
Parthenay	Hertz, Station Shell, 20 boulevard Georges Clémenceau	☎ 05 49 64 41 55
Thouars	Europcar, 52 avenue Victor Leclerc	☎ 05 49 96 30 31

Vienne

Civray	Boudrin Location, route Limoges, Savigné	☎ 05 49 87 00 55
Châtellerault	Avis Location, 24 avenue Adrien Treuille	☎ 05 49 23 18 18
Loudun	ADA, Garage Boilaive, 47 avenue Val de Loire	☎ 05 49 98 52 52
Montmorillon	Hyper U, 2 avenue de Provence	☎ 05 49 84 08 42
Poitiers	Europcar, 48 boulevard de Grand Cerf	☎ 05 49 58 25 34

Taxis

Charente

Angoulême	Angoulême Radio Taxis, La Gare	☎ 05 45 95 55 55
	Gouinaud Martine Taxis, 23 rue Clérac à Sillac	☎ 05 45 61 17 66
	Taxi 16, 112 Bellegarde	☎ 05 45 39 94 47
Chalais	Taxi Aubeterre, bois Billaud	☎ 05 45 98 18 53
Cognac	Action Auto Taxi, 107 avenue Victor Hugo	☎ 05 45 82 55 20
	Taxi 2000, 43 boulevard Javrezac	☎ 05 45 82 40 05
	Taxi Giraud, 7 rue de Pons	☎ 05 45 35 35 00
Confolens	Géron, ZI Croix St Georges	☎ 05 45 84 02 72
	Bouty, Rond Pont avenue Général de Gaulle	☎ 05 45 85 37 02
Ruffec	PM, 29 rue Général Leclerc	☎ 05 45 31 07 94
	Taxi Ruffecois, 65 route d'Aigre	☎ 05 45 31 23 21
	Beck Taxi, 46 rue Gambetta	☎ 05 45 31 30 80

Charente-Maritime

Jonzac	Dezauzier et Fils, 21 avenue Victor Hugo	☎ 05 46 48 30 73
	Taxi Fabrice Paul	☎ 05 46 32 45 13
La Rochelle	ABC Radio Taxi, 11 Square du Poitou	☎ 05 46 42 22 00
	Abeilles Radio Taxis Rochelais, 60 rue Thiers	☎ 05 46 41 55 55
	Taxi Dompierrois, 10bis rue Soleil Couchant	☎ 05 46 68 14 08
	Dompierre-sur-Mer	☎ 06 80 72 60 08

Rochefort	Allo Taxi Radio, rue Docteur Paul Peltier	☎ 05 46 99 07 64
	Taxi Station Centre, Place des Martyrs	☎ 05 46 99 03 74
	Taxi Tonnacquois, Tonnay Charente	☎ 05 46 87 64 34
Royan	Abord Taxi, 22 rue Eugene Pelletan	☎ 05 46 05 78 03
	Taxis Radio Royannais, rue Clouzit	☎ 05 46 39 88 88
St Jean d'Angély	Brochard Jérôme Taxi, 47 rue Treille Marc Galliot, 24 rue Rosiers	☎ 06 09 65 63 65 ☎ 05 46 32 15 06
	Taxi Sarrazin, 2 rue Guy Cassou de St Mathurin	☎ 05 46 59 04 44
	Dautel François , 81 faubourg Taillebourg	☎ 05 46 33 63 24
Saintes	Abbaye Taxis, 3 route Gémozac	☎ 05 46 74 24 24
	Alfa Taxi, Gare de Saintes	☎ 05 46 92 99 22
	Roos Frantz Taxis, Place de la Gare	☎ 05 46 91 15 15

Deux-Sèvres

Melle	Roger Flageul, 11 rue Desfontaines	☎ 05 49 29 76 93
	Sarl Barré, St Martin lès Melle	☎ 05 49 29 14 70
Niort	Radio Niortais, place Martin Bastard	☎ 05 49 24 60 00
	Taxi Bohin, 4 rue Papillons	☎ 05 49 24 20 87
	Taxi Niortais Damien Ecale, 55 rue Equarts	☎ 05 49 73 10 52
Parthenay	Sureau Jean-Marie, 130 avenue Prés Wilson	☎ 05 49 64 04 43
	Taxi Services, 21 rue des Tanneurs	☎ 05 49 71 22 70
	Bonnifait Michenot, 16 avenue Victor Hugo	☎ 05 49 94 00 11

Thouars	Taxi Clisson, 5 rue Minacle, St Jacques	☎ 05 49 96 12 15
	Taxi La Vallée du Thouet, 1 boulevard R. Vouhé	☎ 05 49 66 44 36
	Baudouin Taxi, 1 place Gare	☎ 05 49 66 20 75

Vienne

Civray	Amb/Taxi Sud Vienne, 6 rue Chemin Vert	☎ 05 49 87 00 35
	Savigné Taxi, Champagné Lureau, Savigné	☎ 05 49 87 30 36
Châtellerault	B. Gaillard Taxi, 37 Résid Forêt Viennoise	☎ 05 49 23 08 29
	Allo Artisan Taxi, 35 rue Molière, Naintré	☎ 05 49 90 29 22
	Allo Châtel'Taxis, 103 route Pleumartin	☎ 05 49 85 99 99
Loudun	Bisson Taxi, 1 bd 11 novembre 1918	☎ 05 49 98 04 50
	Jean-Claude Cotilleau, 15 place Portail Chaussé	☎ 05 49 98 04 70
Montmorillon	Taxi Jean-Marie, 27 route de Lussac	☎ 05 49 91 12 52
	Bujon René, 18 place St Martial	☎ 05 49 84 07 66
Poitiers	Artisans Gie Radio Taxis, 22 rue Carnot	☎ 05 49 88 12 34
	Chartier Bernard, 155bis rue Faubourg du Pont Neuf	☎ 05 49 42 57 00
	Maillochaud Laurent, 7 chemin Botte Molle	☎ 05 49 60 75 99 ☎ 05 49 60 13 08

Trains

If you're flying in to Paris Charles de Gaulle, it's possible to get to Poitou-Charentes by train, as described below.

From Charles de Gaulle Airport

There are trains direct from Charles de Gaulle airport to the two stations below, from where you can connect to other stations across the region. Note that many train carriages don't allow the use of mobile phones. The sign of a sleeping mobile indicates that all phone calls need to be taken in the area connecting the carriages.

Angoulême	Four direct *TGV*s a day, with a journey time of three hours.
Poitiers	Seven direct trains a day, taking two and a half hours.

The *TGV* is operated by the SNCF   ☎ 08 92 35 35 35
💻 *www.voyages-sncf.com*

The above website has an English option and enables you to look up and book train travel both to and within France.

Getting There By Car

Channel Crossings

Travelling to Poitou-Charentes from the UK by car you have the option of crossing the channel by Eurotunnel, which is a quick crossing but a long drive on the French side, or by ferry, which takes longer but involves less driving through France, unless you cross to Calais, which is slightly further from the region than the Channel Tunnel terminal. The most popular routes for those travelling to the region are to Calais, Caen, Cherbourg, Dieppe and St Malo, and the main carriers are detailed below. The routes into St Malo provide the shortest drive once in France. There are also crossings from Weymouth to St Malo via Guernsey or Jersey between mid-March and the beginning of November, but these routes require a change of vessel on the relevant island.

Route	Journey Time
Dover/Calais by Channel Tunnel	35 minutes
Dover/Calais by Seacat	1 hour
Dover/Calais by standard ferry	1 hour 15 minutes
Newhaven/Dieppe by Seacat	Around 2 hours
Portsmouth/Caen by fast ferry	3 hours 30 minutes
Portsmouth/Caen by standard ferry	6 hours daytime
	7 hours 30 minutes overnight
Poole/Cherbourg by ferry	2 hours 15 minutes daytime
	6 hours 15 minutes overnight
Dublin & Rosslare/Cherbourg by ferry	18 hours
Portsmouth/St Malo by ferry	9 hours daytime
	11 hours 30 minutes overnight
Poole/St Malo by Seacat	4 hours 35 minutes

Dover/Calais

Eurotunnel: 💻 *www.eurotunnel.co.uk*   *UK* ☎ 0870-535 3535

Lines open Mondays to Fridays 8am to 7pm, Saturdays 8am to 5.30pm, Sundays 9am to 5.30pm.

There are two or three crossings per hour during the day and less frequent crossings during the night.

Property Owners' Club   *UK* ☎ 0870-538 8388
Five return crossings must be purchased initially, at £129 each for long-stay or £99 for short-stay – an excellent saving if you want to travel at peak times, as the tickets are vastly cheaper than an ordinary peak-time fare, but on the other hand you don't get a discount for travelling at 6am in the middle of winter! The tickets are 'fully flexible'. There's an initial administration fee of £30 plus an annual membership fee of £35. Membership of the Property Owners' Club allows you to use the Club Class check-in and entitles you to a 20 per cent discount off bookings for friends and relatives.

Seacat: Hoverspeed (🖳 *www.hoverspeed.com*)   *UK* ☎ 0870-240 8070
                                                         France ☎ 03 21 46 14 54
The Seacat operates from mid-March to mid-December, hourly from 5am to 8pm in high season.

Ferry: P&O Ferries (🖳 *www.poferries.com*)   *UK* ☎ 0870-520 2020
                                                         France ☎ 01 55 69 82 28

Sea France (🖳 *www.seafrance.co.uk*)   *UK* ☎ 0870-571 1711
                           France ☎ 03 21 46 80 00 or ☎ 08 25 82 60 00
Crossings all year, at least one every hour in high season.

Newhaven/Dieppe

Seacat: Hoverspeed (🖳 *www.hoverspeed.co.uk*)   *UK* ☎ 0870-240 8070
                                                         France ☎ 03 21 46 14 54
This service operates from the beginning of April to the first week in October, offering up to two crossings a day, depending on the time of year and day of the week.

Frequent User membership is free but you need to provide three booking references from the previous six months as proof of regular travel. Membership entitles you to a discount of 20 per cent.

Portsmouth/Caen

Fast Ferry: P&O Ferries (🖳 *www.poportsmouth.com*)   *UK* ☎ 0870-520 2020
                                                         France ☎ 01 55 69 82 28

This fast ferry operates from April to September with an average of two crossings a day.

Standard Ferry: Brittany Ferries
(🖳 *www.brittany-ferries.co.uk*)   *UK* ☎ 0870-366 5333
                                                                    France ☎ 08 25 82 88 28
These ferries operate all year with at least two sailings a day.

Property Owners' Travel Club   *UK* ☎ 0870-514 3555
Brittany Ferries' Property Owners' Travel Club offers savings of up to 33 per cent on passenger and vehicle fares and three guest vouchers for friends, providing up to 15 per cent savings on standard fares. There's a one-off registration fee of £35 and a £40 annual membership fee.

Poole/Cherbourg

Ferry: Brittany Ferries (🖳 *www.brittany-ferries.co.uk*)   *UK* ☎ 0870-366 5333
                                                                    France ☎ 08 25 82 88 28
This service runs from mid-February to mid-November, with at least one daytime crossing every day.

For details of the Property Owners' Travel Club, see above.

Dublin & Rosslare/Cherbourg

Ferry: P&O Irish Sea (🖳 *www.poirishsea.com*)   *UK* ☎ 0870-242 4777
                                                                    from ROI ☎ 1800-409049
This is an 18-hour service from Dublin, some ships travelling via Rosslare. Phone lines are open Mondays to Fridays from 7.30am to 10.30pm, and Saturdays and Sundays from 7.30am to 8.30pm.

Portsmouth/St Malo

Ferry: Brittany Ferries (🖳 *www.brittany-ferries.co.uk*)   *UK* ☎ 0870-366 5333
                                                                    France ☎ 08 25 82 88 28
There's at least one daytime crossing every day from January to mid-November. Overnight sailings depart at 8.30pm to arrive at 8am the next day.

For details of the Property Owners' Travel Club, see above.

Poole/St Malo

Seacat: Condor Ferries (🖳 *www.condorferries.co.uk*)   *UK* ☎ 0845-345 2000
Office open Mondays to Fridays from 8.30am to 7.30pm, Saturdays 8.30am to 5.30pm, and Sundays 9am to 5pm in summer; Mondays to Fridays

8.30am to 5.30pm, and Saturdays and Sundays 9am to 5pm in winter. This service operates from the end of May to the end of September.

Frequent Traveller Membership entitles you to a 20 per cent discount on all Channel crossings and a 10 per cent discount between the Channel Islands and France. Individual annual membership costs £66 plus a £20 for a spouse.

Booking

As an alternative to booking direct with the ferry company, you can use one of several companies that will help you to obtain the cheapest fare. These include:

🖳 *www.ferrycrossings-uk.co.uk*	UK ☎ 0871-222 8642
🖳 *www.cheap4ferries.co.uk*	UK ☎ 0870-700 0138
🖳 *www.ferry-crossings-online.co.uk*	

Suggested Routes

Suggested routes to the most central main town in each department from each port are described below. These are based on an average driving speed of 120kph (75mph) on motorways and 80kph (50mph) on other roads, and costs are based on fuel at €1.10 per litre and fuel consumption of 30mpg in towns and 40mpg on the motorway. Toll charges given are approximate, as tolls on many motorways south of Paris vary according to the day of the week and the time.

From Calais

Depending on the time of you 'hit' Paris, your journey time can vary by anything up to one and half hours. Times to avoid are 7 to 10am and 3 to 7pm (not least because your chance of being involved in a crash are even higher at those times than at others!). If you aren't familiar with driving on the Paris ring road (*périphérique*) and other motorways near Paris, pay attention to the signposts, as the junctions are close together and you have little warning of the next one. In fact, if you aren't familiar with driving on the Paris ring road, you might be better advised to choose another route!

● **Calais ➔ Angoulême**

Suggested Route	**Summary**
A 26 to Béthune	Distance: 735 km (460mi)
A1 to Paris	Time: 7 hours, 10 minutes
A3 southbound towards Paris	Cost: €60 plus tolls (€47)

A86 towards Bordeaux (around Paris)
A186 towards Bordeaux (around Paris)
A10 past Tours to Poitiers
N10 south to Angoulême

● **Calais ➔ Poitiers**

Suggested Route   **Summary**
A 26 to Béthune   Distance: 625km (390mi)
A1 to Paris   Time: 5 hours, 45 minutes
A3 southbound towards Paris Cost: €50 plus tolls (€45)
A86 towards Bordeaux (around Paris)
A186 towards Bordeaux (around Paris)
A10 past Tours to Poitiers

● **Calais ➔ Niort**

Suggested Route   **Summary**
A 26 to Béthune   Distance: 700km (438mi)
A1 to Paris   Time: 6 hours, 20 minutes
A3 southbound towards Paris Cost: €56 plus tolls (€50)
A86 towards Bordeaux (around Paris)
A186 towards Bordeaux (around Paris)
A10 past Poitiers
Just before Niort take the A83
N11 into Niort

● **Calais ➔ Saintes**

Suggested Route   **Summary**
A 26 to Béthune   Distance: 760km (475mi)
A1 to Paris   Time: 6 hours, 50 minutes
A3 southbound towards Paris Cost: €60 plus tolls (€55)
A86 towards Bordeaux (around Paris)
A186 towards Bordeaux (around Paris)
A10 past Poitiers and on to junction 35,
  Saintes

From Dieppe

● **Dieppe ➔ Angoulême**

Suggested Route   **Summary**
N27 ➔ A151 ➔A150 towards Rouen Distance: 625km (390mi)
A13 to Paris   Time: 6 hours, 40 minutes

Périphérique east (around Paris)   Cost: €50 plus tolls (€30)
A6 towards Nantes
A10 past Orléans to Poitiers
N10 south to Angoulême

● **Dieppe ➜ Niort**

Suggested Route   **Summary**
N27 ➜ A151 ➜A150 towards Rouen   Distance: 590km (370mi)
A13 to Paris   Time: 5 hours, 55 minutes
Périphérique east (around Paris)   Cost: €48 plus tolls (€20)
A6 towards Nantes
A10 past Poitiers to junction 32
N11 into Niort

● **Dieppe ➜ Poitiers**

Suggested Route   **Summary**
N27 ➜ A151 ➜A150 towards Rouen   Distance: 510km (320mi)
A13 to Paris   Time: 5 hours, 15 minutes
Périphérique east (around Paris)   Cost: €40 plus tolls (€28)
A6 towards Nantes
A10 to Poitiers

● **Dieppe ➜ Saintes**

Suggested Route   **Summary**
N27 ➜ A151 ➜A150 towards Rouen   Distance: 650km (405mi)
A13 to Paris   Time: 6 hours, 20 minutes
Périphérique east (around Paris)   Cost: €52 plus tolls (€25)
A6 towards Nantes
A10 to junction 35, Saintes

From Caen

● Caen ➜ **Angoulême**

Suggested Route   **Summary**
N158 from Caen towards Falaise   Distance: 450m (280mi)
Continue on N158 to Sées   Time: 5 hours, 20 minutes
N138 to Alençon   Cost: €35 plus tolls (€17)
A28 past Le Mans, exit at Ecommoy
N138 past Tours to the A10
A10 to Poitiers
N10 south to Angoulême

● **Caen ➜ Niort**

Suggested Route
A84 past Avranches to Rennes
N137 to Nantes
Ringroad west around Nantes,
    in the direction of the airport
A83 to Niort

Summary
Distance: 430km (270mi)
Time: 4 hours, 55 minutes
Cost: €35 plus tolls (€20)

● **Caen ➜ Poitiers**

Suggested Route
N158 from Caen towards Falaise
Continue on N158 to Sées
N138 to Alençon
A28 past Le Mans, exit at Ecommoy
N138 past Tours to the A10
A10 to Poitiers

Summary
Distance: 335km (210mi)
Time: 4 hours, 5 minutes
Cost: €27 plus tolls (€15)

● **Caen ➜ Saintes**

Suggested Route
N158 from Caen towards Falaise
Continue on N158 to Sées
N138 to Alençon
A28 past Le Mans, exit at Ecommoy
N138 past Tours to the A10
A10 to junction 35, Saintes

Summary
Distance: 470km (295mi)
Time: 5 hours, 10 minutes
Cost: €38 plus tolls (€28)

From Cherbourg

● **Cherbourg ➜ Angoulême**

Suggested Route
N13 to Valognes
D900 to Coutances
D971/D973 to Avranches
A84 towards Rennes
N137 to Nantes
Ringroad west around Nantes, in the direction of the airport
A83 past Niort to the A10
A10 to junction 34, St Jean d'Angély
D939 to Angoulême

Summary
Distance: 570km (355mi)
Time: 7 hours, 5 minutes
Cost: €46 plus tolls (€13)

● **Cherbourg ➜ Niort**

Suggested Route
N13 to Valognes
D900 to Coutances
D971/D973 to Avranches
A84 towards Rennes
N137 to Nantes
Ringroad west around Nantes, in the direction of the airport
A83 to Niort

Summary
Distance: 465km (290mi)
Time: 5 hours, 25 minutes
Cost: €37 plus tolls (€8)

● **Cherbourg ➜ Poitiers**

Suggested Route
N13 to Valognes
D900 to Coutances
D971/D973 to Avranches
N175 to join A84 towards Fougères
D155 to Fougères
N12 to Ernée
D31 to Laval
D21 Sablé-sur-Sarthe
D306 to join A11 southbound
A85 to junction 3, Saumur
N147 south to Poitiers

Summary
Distance: 450km (280mi)
Time: 6 hours, 10 minutes
Cost: €37 plus tolls (€20)

● **Cherbourg ➜ Saintes**

Suggested Route
N13 to Valognes
D900 to Coutances
D971/D973 to Avranches
A84 towards Rennes
N137 to Nantes
Ringroad west around Nantes, in the direction of the airport
A83 past Niort to the A10
A10 south to junction 35, Saintes

Summary
Distance: 535km (335mi)
Time: 6 hours, 15 minutes
Cost: €43 plus tolls (€15)

From St Malo

● **St Malo ➜ Angoulême**

Suggested Route
N137 to Nantes
Ringroad west around Nantes,
    in the direction of the airport
A83 past Niort to the A10

Summary
Distance: 430km (270mi)
Time: 5 hours
Cost: €35 plus tolls (€13)

A10 to junction 34, St Jean d'Angély
D939 to Angoulême

● **St Malo ➜ Niort**

Suggested Route
N137 to Nantes
Ringroad west around Nantes,
   in the direction of the airport
A83 to Niort Summary

Summary
Distance: 330km (205mi)
Time: 3 hours, 20 minutes
Cost: €25 plus tolls (€8)

● **St Malo ➜ Poitiers**

Suggested Route
N137 to Nantes
Ringroad west around Nantes,
   in the direction of the airport
A83 past Niort to the A10
A10 to Poitiers

Summary
Distance: 400km (250mi)
Time: 4 hours, 15 minutes
Cost: €30 plus tolls (€13)

● **St Malo ➜ Saintes**

Suggested Route
N137 to Nantes
Ringroad west around Nantes,
   in the direction of the airport
A83 past Niort to the A10
A10 south to junction 35, Saintes

Summary
Distance: 400km (250mi)
Time: 4 hours, 10 minutes
Cost: €32 plus tolls (€15)

Télépéage

If you're travelling regularly on French motorways, it's worth considering Télépéage. This involves a one off fee of €30 for the disc that fits to your windscreen, then €20 a year. An invoice is sent out monthly and you can arrange to pay by direct debit from a French bank account, in which case there's no charge for the disc.

With the standard contract there's no discount on tolls, but you no longer have to queue to pay, as you can use a dedicated lane. In fact, you don't even need to wind down your window as you go through a toll point. The same disc can be used on all French motorways. There are contracts that give discounts of up to 20 per cent on tolls, but these are primarily for commuters.

Apply online (💻 *www.cofiroute.fr* – click on 'liber-t' in the French-language version) or go to the office at any toll point – usually near the kiosks.

Getting There By Rail

Eurostar

⌨ *www.eurostar.co.uk*

UK ☎ 08705-186186
France ☎ 08 92 35 35 39

The Eurostar travels from Waterloo (London) and Ashford to Lille and Paris, from where you can travel to Poitou-Charentes. Lille is the easier route, if available, as you just change platforms rather than having to cross Paris to get a connecting train south from Montparnasse. To Lille, there are nine trains per day Mondays to Fridays, more on Saturdays (journey time 2 hours); to Paris, there are one or two trains per hour (journey time 3 hours). Below are details of the routes to each main town in Poitou-Charentes.

	From Lille	**From Paris**
Charente		
Angoulême	Direct – 4 hours	Direct – from two and a half hours
Chalais	Change at Angoulême	Change at Angoulême
Cognac	Change at Angoulême	Change at Angoulême
Ruffec	Change at Poitiers	Direct – two and a half hours

(There's no railway station at Confolens.)

Charente-Maritime		
Jonzac	Change at Bordeaux	Change at Bordeaux
La Rochelle	Change at Poitiers	Direct – 3 hours
Rochefort	At least two changes required	Change at La Rochelle or Nantes
Royan	Change at Angoulême	Change at Angoulême or Niort
Saintes	Change at Angoulême	Change at Angoulême or Niort
St Jean d'Angély	At least two changes required	Change at Niort

Deux-Sèvres		
Niort	Change at Poitiers	Direct - from two and a quarter hours
Parthenay	Change at Poitiers	Change at Poitiers
Thouars	At least two changes required	Change at Tours

(There's no railway station at Melle.)

Vienne		
Châtellerault	Change at Poitiers	Direct – from one and a half hours

Loudun	At least two changes required	At least two changes required
Montmorillon	Change at Poitiers	Change at Poitiers
Poitiers	Direct – from two and a quarter hours	Direct – from one and half hours

Getting Around

Buses in the region are primarily to serve the schools and colleges and so the routes pass not only the schools but in many cases railway stations as well. Unfortunately, this also means that there's drastic reduction (if not a total cessation) in services on some routes during school holidays. Timetables are usually displayed at bus stops.

Charente

General   Cars Thorin, avenue Paul Mairat,
           Mansle   ☎ 05 45 22 20 05
           This company operates bus routes from Ruffec to Angoulême
           and from Ruffec to Champagne-Mouton.

           Cars Les Rapides du Poitou   ☎ 05 49 46 27 45
           Operates a service from Ruffec to Poitiers via Civray.

Angoulême Citram/STGA, place du
           Champ de Mars   ☎ 05 45 65 25 25
           Local bus routes to and around Angoulême. The kiosk is open
           for tickets and timetables from 1 to 6pm Mondays to Fridays
           and from 9am to 12.30pm Saturdays.

Cognac   Citram/Transcom   ☎ 05 45 82 01 99
           Local buses in and around Cognac.

Ruffec   Le Rurabus   ☎ 05 45 30 38 43
           Operated by the Centre Social et Culturel du Ruffécois, this
           local bus service is available only on Wednesdays to residents
           of the communes of Ruffec and Nanteuil-en-Vallée. A return trip
           to anywhere in the Ruffec/Nanteuil-en-Vallée area costs €7.60
           and you must book by calling the above number.

Charente-Maritime

General   Aunis Saintonge, 2 rue Terriers, Saintes ☎ 05 46 97 52 00
           This company runs many bus services across the department,
           including routes to the Ile d'Oléron and Royan; some services
           don't operate in the school holidays.`

           Océars, place de Verdun, Rochefort   ☎ 05 46 99 23 65
           This company runs bus routes in the central area of Charente-

Maritime. As with Aunis Saintonge, the timetable changes according to school holidays.

Citram, place de Verdun, Rochefort   ☎ 05 46 82 31 30
Various routes, including one between Rochefort and St Jean d'Angély and two around Rochefort town (buses are known as 'Le Petit Bleu').

La Rochelle   Autoplus, place de Verdun
Yellow bicycles available all year (from May to September the pick-up point is on Quai Valin). Free for the first two hours.

Espace Autoplus, place de Verdun   ☎ 05 46 34 02 22
Electric vehicles for hire.

Le Passeur
A permanent ferry service between the old harbour (vieux port) and the Ville en Bois, where it's easier to park. Operates from 7.45am to midnight at peak periods. The crossing takes only two or three minutes.

There's also a water bus service between the old harbour and the marina (Port des Minimes) from March to September – a 20-minute trip.

Ré Bus Aunis Saintonge
The company runs a bus service from the station and Place de Verdun to all the villages on Ile de Ré.

Deux-Sèvres

General   RDS, place de la Gare, Parthenay   ☎ 05 49 94 08 72
This local bus company covers Deux-Sèvres, with routes from Thouars and Parthenay in the north through Niort and Poitiers to Chef Boutonne and Sauzé Vaussais in the south.

Niort   Tan, Le Kiosque, place de La Brèche,
Niort   ☎ 05 49 24 50 56
&
8 rue Paul Sabatier (head office)   ☎ 05 49 09 23 45
This company operates a comprehensive bus network around the city. Full details and timetables are available from both the kiosk and the tourist office. The kiosk is open from Mondays to Fridays between 7.30am and 12.30pm and from 1.30 to 6.30pm and on Saturdays from 9.30am till noon.

Vienne

There are various bus routes across Vienne, and Poitiers has a local service. Timetables are displayed at bus stops, at Poitiers railway station and at tourist offices, or can be obtained from the offices listed below.

Châtellerault	STAO, 5 rue Bernard Palissy	☎ 05 49 02 23 23
	TAC, 103 route de Pleumartin and Le Kiosque, boulevard Blossac	☎ 05 49 93 16 54
Poitiers	Espace Bus, 8 rue du Chaudron d'Or	☎ 05 49 88 23 41
	Société des Transports Poitevins (STP), avenue de Northampton	☎ 05 49 44 77 00

GENERAL INFORMATION

Accommodation

Châteaux

Bienvenue au Château
🖥 *www.bienvenue-au-chateau.com*
This website is available in English and gives details of château accommodation in western France.

Gîtes And Bed & Breakfast

Tourist offices have lists of bed and breakfast facilities (B&B) in the area and may display one in their window. Some communes have *gîtes* available for rent via the *mairie*.

Internet Booking

The following websites have both *gîte* and B&B accommodation listed and bookings are made direct with the owners via the site, where contact details are given.

🖥 *www.frenchconnections.co.uk*
French Connections.

🖥 *www.pour-les-vacances.com*
Pour Les Vacances – a British site for B&B accommodation.

🖥 *www.holidayhomes-france.co.uk*
Holiday Homes France – for both *gîtes* and B&B.

Hotels

National Chains

The following hotels can be found throughout France:

Formule 1	🖳 *www.hotelformule1.com*	☎ 08 92 68 56 85
Hôtel de France	🖳 *www.hotel-france.com*	☎ 01 41 39 22 23
Hôtel Première Classe	🖳 *www.hotelpremierclasse.fr*	☎ 08 25 00 30 03
Ibis Hotels	🖳 *www.ibis.hotel.com*	☎ 08 92 68 66 86
Mercure	🖳 *www.mercure.com*	☎ 08 25 88 44 44
Novotel	🖳 *www.novotel.com*	☎ 08 25 88 44 44

Administration

Regional Capital

Poitiers is the capital of the Poitou-Charentes region as well as the capital of the department of Vienne.

Conseil Régional de Poitou-Charentes,
15 rue Ancienne Comédie, Poitiers   ☎ 05 49 55 77 00

Préfectures

The *préfecture* is the administrative centre for each department and is located in the department's main city. You may need to contact or visit the *préfecture* or *sous-préfecture* (see below) if you apply for a residence permit, register ownership of a new car or apply for planning permission.

Charente	7 rue Préfecture Angoulême 🖳 *www.charente.pref.gouv.fr*	☎ 08 21 80 30 16
Charente-Maritime	38 rue Réaumur, La Rochelle 🖳 *www.charente-maritime.pref.gouv.fr*	☎ 05 46 27 43 00
Deux-Sèvres	4 rue du Guesclin, Niort 🖳 *www.deux-sevres.pref.gouv.fr*	☎ 05 49 08 68 68
Vienne	1 place Aristide Briand, Poitiers 🖳 *www.vienne.pref.gouv.fr*	☎ 05 49 55 70 00

Sous-Préfectures

Charente

| Cognac | 362 rue Jean Taransaud | ☎ 05 45 82 00 60 |
| Confolens | 1 rue Antoine Babaud Lacroze | ☎ 05 45 84 01 44 |

Charente-Maritime

| Jonzac | 4 rue Château | ☎ 05 46 48 02 11 |

Rochefort	21 rue Jean Jaurès	☎ 05 46 87 08 08
St Jean d'Angély	28 place Hôtel de Ville	☎ 05 46 32 24 87
Saintes	12 place Synode	☎ 05 46 92 37 00

Les Deux-Sèvres

Bressuire	4 place Hôtel de Ville	☎ 05 49 80 49 80
Parthenay	2 rue Citadelle	☎ 05 49 94 03 77

Vienne

Châtellerault	2 rue Choisnin	☎ 05 49 86 79 80
Montmorillon	1 boulevard Strasbourg	☎ 05 49 91 12 44

Town Halls (Mairies)

All French towns have an *hôtel de ville*, which is the equivalent of a town hall, and most villages have a *mairie*, which has no equivalent in the UK (and certainly isn't a 'village hall'!). To avoid confusion, we have used the French word *mairie* to apply to both town hall and *mairie* unless otherwise specified.

Although town halls are usually open Mondays to Fridays, the opening hours of mairies vary greatly and in small communes they may be open only two or three hours each week at set times (usually on two days). There's usually a function room (*une salle des fêtes* or *salle polyvalente*), attached to the town hall/*mairie* or close by. Notice boards at the town halls/*mairies* are used for formal notices, while local shops usually display a variety of posters for local events.

The 'mayor' of a town or village is *Monsieur* or *Madame le Maire* (yes, even a female mayor is '*le Maire*'!). The *Maire* is the equivalent of a British mayor but is usually more accessible and has more immediate authority in the community. If you buy or rent a property in a small community, you should visit the *mairie* at the earliest opportunity to introduce yourselves to the Maire.

If you're considering making any alterations to your house or boundaries, it's **essential** to contact the *Maire* **before** undertaking any work or even drawing up plans. Full details of the required procedures are described in **Renovating & Maintaining Your French Home** (see page 334).

The town hall/*mairie* should also be your first port of call if you need any advice, as they're a mine of useful information and, if they haven't got what you need, will either get it for you or point you in the right direction.

Banks

The majority of French banks close for lunch and are open Saturday mornings. Banks are rarely open on Mondays and in small towns may be open only in the mornings or even just a few sessions a week. Below are the names of the most commonly found banks, with a web address and a contact number (if available) to allow you to find the branch closest to you.

Banque Populaire   🖳 *www.banquepopulaire.fr*   ☎ 05 55 45 33 00

BNP Paribas   🖳 *www.bnpparibas.net*   ☎ 08 20 82 00 01
To find your nearest branch click on 'toutes les agences et leurs régions'.

Banque Tarneaud   🖳 *www.tarneaud.fr*   ☎ 08 10 63 28 28
Open Mondays to Fridays 7.30am to 10pm, Saturdays 9am to 5pm.

Caisse d'Epargne   🖳 *www.caissedepargne.com*   ☎ 05 49 44 50 00

Crédit Agricole   🖳 *www.creditagricole.fr*
To find your nearest branch, on the front page of the site use the box in the top right corner with the map of France. There are some English pages available on this website.

Charente office   ☎ 05 45 20 49 60
Charente-Maritime/Deux-Sèvres office   ☎ 05 46 98 17 17
Vienne office   ☎ 08 10 81 68 17

The Charente-Périgord division of this bank has an English-language help line open Mondays to Fridays 10am to 5pm ☎ 05 45 20 49 60

Crédit Lyonnais   🖳 *www.creditlyonnais.fr*   ☎ 08 21 80 90 90
There's an English option on the website.

Crédit Mutuel   🖳 *www.cmso.com*   ☎ 08 21 01 10 12
To find your nearest branch click on '*où nous trouver*'.

Société Générale   🖳 *www.societegenerale.fr*   ☎ 05 49 55 57 00
To find your nearest branch on the website go to '*trouver une agence*'.

English-Language Bank

Britline   15 esplanade Brillaud de Laujardière, 14050 Caen Cedex   ☎ 02 31 55 67 89
🖳 *www.britline.com*

Britline is based at the Caen (14) branch of Crédit Agricole. Some of its forms are printed in English, although most forms and its newsletter are in French. However, an English-speaking teller always answers the phone.

Note that branches of Crédit Agricole in Poitou-Charentes (and elsewhere) aren't familiar with dealing with Britline and, as it's in a different department, you cannot pay in cheques at your local branch. To pay a cheque into your Britline account you need to post it to Britline at the above address. Withdrawals, however, are possible through any Crédit Agricole cash machine. As more and more Crédit Agricole branches have English-speaking staff, you may find opening an account locally more advantageous.

General Information

French banking is quite different from banking in the UK. The most noticeable differences are the following:

- French cheques are laid out differently (the amount **precedes** the payee), and you must state the town where the cheque was written. Note also that, when writing figures, a comma is used in place of a decimal point and a point or space instead of a comma in thousands, e.g. €1.234,56 or €1 234,56.
- You must usually press a button or even enter a code to gain access to a bank.
- Most banks have open-plan desks with receptionists, who handle minimal amounts of cash, most cash transactions being carried out by machine.
- Some banks don't have any cash at the counter. When withdrawing money, you're given a card, which you take to a cash machine to obtain the money. This system doesn't always enable you to withdraw the exact amount you want, e.g. €20 or €40, but not €30.
- Receipts aren't always issued when paying in money without a paying-in slip, so ask for a paying-in book (or simply ask for a receipt – *un reçu*).
- When you open an account, you will be given copies of your *relevé d'identité bancaire* (normally called *un RIB* – pronounced 'reeb'), which contains all your account details. As you will need to provide a *RIB* when setting up a direct debit or an account (e.g. with a shop) and when asking anyone (e.g. an employer) to pay money into your account, it's wise to take extra copies.
- There are no cheque guarantee cards, although many shops now insist on identification with cheques.
- Cheques are guaranteed for payment in France, but if you write a cheque without sufficient funds in your account (unless you have an authorised overdraft facility) it may result in a registered letter being sent by the bank demanding that funds are paid into the account within 30 days. If this happens again within 12 months, the account will be closed and you will be unable to hold any account in France for a year and will be blacklisted for three years. **You have been warned!**
- It's wise to keep at least €30 in your account at all times to cover any unexpected charges. For example, some banks charge to transfer money

between accounts of the same bank while others charge you each time you access your account online.
● If your cheque book is lost or stolen, irrespective of which bank you use, call ☎ 01 42 41 22 22 between 8am and 11pm.

Opening a French bank account will provide many benefits – not least the provision of a debit card (*une carte bleue*), which has a microchip and requires you to enter a four-digit PIN rather than sign a receipt. Such a card enables you to use automated petrol pumps (see page 60) and will save you embarrassment and hassle in shops where the staff are unfamiliar with UK credit cards and either won't accept them or don't know how to 'swipe' them. Most *cartes bleues* can be used all over Europe.

Moneo

Moneo is a system designed to eliminate the need to carry small change. A Moneo card has an initial cost of €8 and is then 'charged' with up to €100 and can be used to buy a newspaper, a loaf of bread or even a bar of chocolate in shops, cafés, newsagents and bakeries displaying the Moneo sign, of which there's an increasing number. The card can be used for purchases up to €30 and, once the credit is used, it can be re-charged at banks and post offices. Cards are ordered from your bank and you must have a French bank account to obtain one.

Business Services

Employment Agencies

Agence Nationale pour l'Emploi (ANPE)
🖳 *www.anpe.fr*

This is the national employment agency, which has a main office and several smaller offices in each department. The main offices are as follows:

Charente	6 rue Père Joseph Wresinski, Angoulême	☎ 05 45 38 63 00
Charente-Maritime	7 avenue Porte Neuve, La Rochelle	☎ 05 46 67 40 08
Deux-Sèvres	Carrefour Atlantique, avenue Léo Lagrange, Niort	☎ 05 49 28 75 00
Vienne	44 boulevard Pont Achard, Poitiers	☎ 05 49 88 86 90

Independent companies include the following:

Adecco	🖥 *www.adecco.fr*
Manpower	🖥 *www.manpower.fr*
Vedior Bis	🖥 *www.vediorbis.com*

Communications

Telephone
Fixed Line Telephone Services

Telephone installations must be carried out by France Télécom, but telephone services are also available from a number of other operators, some of which are listed below.

| France Télécom | 🖥 *www.francetelecom.fr* | ☎ 1014 |

The website has an English option and France Télécom has an English-language help line (☎ 00 800 44 33 22 11).

One.Tel	🖥 *www.onetel.fr*	☎ 08 25 92 55 55
Tele2	🖥 *www.tele2.fr*	☎ 08 11 24 00 10
Primus Telecom	🖥 *www.as24telecom.com*	☎ 05 53 05 47 82

An excellent English-language service provided by Andrew Martin.

These companies can prove to be cheaper than France Télécom, especially for international calls, which are often the same tariff day and night, but you should always compare before deciding. France Télécom's standing charge is payable for the line, even if you use another service provider.

Mobile Telephones

Mobile phone (*portable* or, increasingly, *mobile*) shops are found in most town centres, and hypermarkets sell a good selection of handsets and connection packages. Reception in rural areas can be poor, with some quite large areas having no reception at all. There are just three service providers in France: Bouygues, Orange and SFR. Note that SFR has an English-language customer service if you dial ☎ 4357 (H-E-L-P!) from an SFR phone or ☎ 01 55 82 55 82 from a land line. If your mobile phone is lost or stolen, contact the appropriate number below:

Bouygues	☎ 08 00 29 10 00
Orange	☎ 08 25 00 57 00
	from abroad ☎ +33 6 07 62 64 64
SFR	☎ 06 10 00 19 00
	from abroad ☎ +33 6 10 00 19 00

Public Telephones

These are located all over towns and villages and in railway stations, bars and cafés. The new kiosks are Perspex and usually accept only cards;

however, if there's a group of three or more kiosks, one may accept coins. All public phones allow international calls and there's a button with a double flag symbol, which you can press for the telephone display to appear in different languages.

Telephone cards are available from post offices, railway stations, cafés, banks and anywhere you see the sign *Télécarte en vente ici*. Cards don't have a standard design, as they're used for advertising. You often need a telephone card for internet access at a public facility such as the post office.

Telephone Directories

Directories are no longer available from France Télécom stores. If you don't have a directory or would like a copy for a neighbouring department, they can be obtained by phoning ☎ 08 10 81 07 67 and cost between €7.50 and €12 depending on size. The line is often busy, so keep trying: choose option 2, then hold until the message finishes and (eventually) you will be put through to an operator.

Directories usually incorporate both yellow pages (*les pages jaunes*) and white pages (*l'annuaire* or *les pages blanches*) in a single book, back to back, although you may order them separately. All listings in the residential section are alphabetical order within each commune, so you need to know the name of the commune where the person you want to call lives.

Special Rate Phone Numbers

Special rate numbers normally start with 08 or 09 (mobile numbers start 06). Numbers beginning 09 are charged at high rates and are to be avoided if possible. The cost of calls to numbers beginning 08 varies greatly (see below), and you're advised to be wary of numbers for which the charge isn't specified. You should also avoid numbers starting with 00, as calls may be routed via another country. Common 08 prefixes include the following:

● 0800, 0805, 0809 – free call (known as *numéros verts*);
● 0810, 0811 – local call rates (known as *numéros azur*);
● 0836 – calls vary from free to €1.35 plus 34 centimes per minute;
● 0899 79 – €1.35 for connection plus 34 centimes per minute.

Internet

There are a number of internet service providers (ISPs) in France, and the following websites can help you to choose the best provider for you.

🖳 *www.club-internet.fr*
🖳 *www.francenet.fr*
🖳 *www.illiclic.com* (operated by La Poste)
🖳 *www.freesurf.fr*

⌨ *www.wanadoo.fr* (operated by France Télécom and available in English)
⌨ *www.worldnet.fr*

The best way to get connected is to go to a public internet access provider (see below) and use this access to register an address and obtain the dial-up numbers, etc. so that you can then go online at home. Note that software may need to be installed in your computer. You can register with Wanadoo by phone (☎ 08 10 28 32 83), when you will be given the necessary access codes and phone numbers immediately.

Wanadoo offers various packages for internet use, which can work out cheaper than paying per minute if you use the internet for more than a few hours a month.

Public Internet Access

All France Télécom stores have internet access, as do many post offices. Public places that offer access usually require a telephone card.

Broadband

High-speed or lines or broadband (*le haut-débit*) are gradually becoming more widely available, although not often in rural areas. However, the French government plans to have high speed lines available throughout the country, including rural areas, by 2006. To find out if broadband is currently available where you are, go to ⌨ *www.francetelecom.fr* and on the front page click on '*Tout sur l'ADSL*', then click the red label/box, '*L'ADSL chez vous?*', enter your phone number and it will tell you straight away if high-speed lines are available to you.

There are various tariffs available for high-speed connections, for example Wanadoo and France Télécom offer ADSL packages, usually entailing a set fee plus a monthly payment. Offers are changing all the time and are frequently advertised on TV and on the relevant web sites. More information can be obtained from ⌨ *www.francetelecom.fr* and ⌨ *www. adsl-france.org*.

Useful Web Addresses

The following is a selection from the myriad websites accessible:

⌨ *www.voila.fr* – A French search engine.
⌨ *www.pagesjeunes.fr* – This site has the option at the bottom to convert the language to English.
⌨ *www.meteoconsult.com* – Weather site. (Alternatively call ☎ 08 99 70 11 11 and press '1' for the weather forecast in English.)
⌨ *www.surf-report.com* – 24-hour weather forecasts for coastal areas.
⌨ *www.service-public.fr* – The official gateway to the French civil service.

🖳 *www.google.com* – Although this is an English-language search engine, when foreign web sites are located it gives you the option of translating the web page into English – the results are never less than entertaining!

Television & Radio

Whether your television (TV) set will work in France is dependent on which model you have. Most televisions bought in the UK in the last few years should work in France, as most now have the capability to pick up both Secam and PAL signals. If you buy a television in France, you may find that it's sold without a stand.

If you're learning French, watching French TV with subtitles is a good idea. If subtitles are available, they can be found on Teletext 888. If you have a TV guide, the programme may have a symbol of an ear to show that it has subtitles, which are generally for the hard of hearing but will do just as well for foreigners!

It's possible to get British television in France but a satellite dish is needed and you must ensure that you're aware of the legalities before proceeding. There are various British suppliers and installers of satellite who will give you all the information you need, including the following company, which has a comprehensive website:

Big Dish Satellite	Mouriol, Milhaguet, 87440 Marval 🖳 www.bigdishsat.com ✉ *office@bigdishsat.com*	☎ 05 55 78 72 98

Licence

To watch TV in France you need a licence, costing €116.50 for colour and €74.31 for black and white. This fee covers all the television sets that you own in France, even if in different locations such as a caravan or holiday home. As in the UK, when a television set is purchased, the shop must inform the authorities and a television licence bill will duly arrive (unlike the UK, it takes several months!).

If you bring a British TV into France that's capable of receiving French programmes, you should notify the Centre Régional de la Redevance Audiovisuelle within 30 days.

CRRA	🖳 *www.service-public.fr*	☎ 01 49 70 40 00

Radio

There's a variety of national and local stations that can be received in the region, some of which are detailed below.

Station	FM Frequency	Description
Accords	94.7/96.8/104.1	Easy listening, current hits and golden oldies – these frequencies are for the areas surrounding Poitiers, Angoulême and Confolens respectively.
Allouette	91.6/105.7	Easy listening and current hits
Bleu Point	106.4	Easy listening and current hits
Culture	96.4	Talk radio and mainly classical music
Europe 2	106.6	Current hits
Forum	89.1/91.7/102.6	Easy listening and current hits
Inter	93.8/99.4	Talk radio and easy listening
MFM	98.4	Easy listening and local information every half hour
Mixx FM	99.9 100.3	Current hits aimed at a teenagers/ youngsters
Nostalgie	98.7	Golden oldies
Rire	88.6	Comedy and humour
Sky Rock	103.1	Current hits aimed at a teenagers/ youngsters

Entertainment

Cinemas

Some French cinemas show English-language films in their original version, i.e. in English with French subtitles. These are identified by the letters *VO* (*version originale*) next to the title. (*VF* indicates that a film has been dubbed into French.)

Festivals

There are many annual festivals in this region, just a small selection of which are listed in this book. Dates vary each year, so just the month has been given. A *Fêtes et Festivals* brochure, giving precise dates, is available from tourist offices.

Music

There's a substantial classical orchestra in Poitou-Charentes, which plays all over the region, under the direction of Jean-François Heisser (☎ 05 49 55 91 10). Note that this topic is listed under **Leisure Activities** in the following chapters.

Video & DVD Hire

DVDs are widely available and are usually viewable in English, but check the back of the case before buying or renting: there will be a Union Jack and/or the words *Sous-titres* (sub-titles) and *Langues* (languages) with '*Anglais*' in the list that follows. Some video shops also hire out DVD players (*lecteurs*).

Medical Facilities & Services

Ambulances

Ambulances are operated privately in France. If an ambulance has been agreed or requested by a doctor or medical establishment, the cost can be reclaimed if you're registered with the French social security system. In the event of a medical emergency dial ☎ 15.

Doctors

French doctors and dentists have flexible working hours and doctors may have an 'open surgery' during the week, or even at certain times every day, when no appointment is necessary; you just go and wait your turn.

You don't need to register with a doctor or dentist when you arrive in France; simply call when you need an appointment. There's a charge each time you visit or they visit you (more expensive in the evenings) which is partially reclaimable if you're registered with French social security or if you're on holiday from the UK and have an E111 form. **Remember to keep all receipts, including those of any prescriptions and the labels from any medicines prescribed, to send with your claim.**

If you intend to be in France for a long period or indeed permanently, it's recommended to ask your UK doctor for a print-out of your medical record. He may not be able to give you copies of the actual written records, but should be willing to provide a print-out (although you will probably be charged – £50 or more), which you should take to a French doctor on your first visit.

An E111 is valid indefinitely, but if it's more than a year old it may be harder to get the paperwork sorted out. They're free from post offices in the UK, so if you aren't living permanently in France it's advisable to renew yours regularly.

When you go to a doctor or dentist in France, he will give you a form with details of the treatment given, their details and reference number. Ensure that you give your British address if you intend to reclaim these costs with your E111. This form should be attached to your E111 and sent to the nearest Caisse Régionale Assurance Maladie Centre Ouest (CRAMCO – see **Health Authority** on page 58).

Emergencies

In the event of an emergency, dial one of the following numbers:

Any medical emergency
SAMU (*Service d'Aide Médical d'Urgence*)   ☎ 15

Police   (see also below)
Gendarmes   ☎ 17

Fire or accident not requiring medical help (see below)
Sapeurs-Pompiers   ☎ 18

The *SAMU* are often the first on the scene in the event of an accident, but you should call the police first and they will contact the *SAMU*.

A number of other useful emergency numbers are listed below.

Poisoning
Centre Anti-Poisons (Bordeaux)   ☎ 05 56 96 40 80

Gas leak
Gaz de France   Charente   ☎ 08 10 16 16 00
(EDF)   Charente-Maritime   ☎ 05 46 43 43 43
                   Deux-Sèvres   ☎ 05 49 28 30 31
                   Vienne   ☎ 05 49 47 89 00

Electricity problems
Électricité de   Charente   ☎ 08 10 33 30 16
France (EDF)   Charente-Maritime   ☎ 08 10 33 30 17
                   Deux-Sèvres   ☎ 08 10 33 3079
                   Vienne   ☎ 08 10 33 30 86

Lost or stolen bank card
                   Banque Populaire   ☎ 08 25 08 24 24
                   BNP Paribas   ☎ 08 25 03 24 24
                   Banque Tarneaud   ☎ 08 25 00 59 59
                   Caisse d'Epargne   ☎ 08 92 68 32 08
                   Crédit Agricole*   ☎ 08 00 81 08 12
                   Crédit Lyonnaise   ☎ 08 21 80 90 90
                   Crédit Mutuel   ☎ 05 56 24 28 28
                   Société Général   ☎ 08 25 07 00 70
                   * includes Britline (see page 48)

Other emergency numbers are listed in the front of the yellow pages.

Fire Brigade

The fire brigade (*sapeurs-pompiers* or *pompiers*) have a high level of medical training and are one of the first on the scene of any accident, often carrying out medical procedures until the arrival of the *SAMU*. In rural areas, *pompiers* are often 'reserves' and are called to duty by a siren giving three short, very loud blasts.

You can also call the fire brigade if you have a bee or wasp swarm. In the summer, such swarms are common and the *pompiers* get very busy, but they will still usually come the same day, although it may be late! You pay them directly, around €30, for the service.

Health Authority

The Caisse Régional Assurance Maladie Centre Ouest (CRAMCO) is the organisation that deals with medical claims and expenses. You must contact CRAMCO in order to join the French social security system. Before you can join this system you need to have applied for or be in possession of a residence permit (*titre de séjour*, more commonly known as a *carte de séjour*, although strictly this is just one type of *titre de séjour*). Ambiguous new regulations came into force in January 2004, which can be interpreted to mean that EU nationals no longer require a *titre de séjour*; you should apply for one nevertheless, as the application procedure ensures that you meet the criteria for residence.

CRAMCO representatives pay regular visits to certain towns (usually to the *mairie*), in which case you can meet them in person and ask any questions you may have. Otherwise, you will need to contact one of the CRAMCO offices listed below:

Angoulême	30 boulevard Bury (main office)	☎ 05 45 95 76 13
Cognac	48 rue Marc Marchadier	☎ 05 45 83 88 90
Confolens	La Mairie, place Hôtel de Ville	
	Tuesdays and Wednesdays 9.30am to 12.15pm	
Ruffec	La Mairie, place des Martyrs	
	Tuesdays 9am to 12.30pm and 1.45 to 3.15pm, Wednesdays 9am to 12.30pm.	

Police

There are two main types of police in France: *police nationale* and *gendarmes*. The *police nationale* is under the control of the Interior Ministry and deals with 'general' crime, mostly in urban or semi-urban areas. They're most commonly seen in towns and are distinguished by the silver buttons on their uniforms. At night and in rain and fog they often wear white caps and capes.

The *gendarmerie nationale* is part of the army and under the control of the Ministry of Defence, although it's also at the service of the Interior Ministry. *Gendarmes* deal with serious crime on a national scale and all crime in rural areas where there's no *police* station. They're also responsible for motorway patrols, air safety, mountain rescue, etc.

Gendarmes wear blue uniforms and traditional caps (*képis*) and have gold buttons on their uniforms. Gendarmes include police motorcyclists (*motards*), who patrol in pairs.

In addition to the above, most cities and medium-size towns have their own police force, *police municipale* or *corps urbain*, who deal mainly with petty crime, traffic offences and road accidents. They're usually based at the *mairie*.

All French police are armed with guns.

Some of the smaller *gendarmeries* are being merged with others and a rural station may be open only limited hours, but the local number will always be put through to the station that's on duty.

Motoring

Accidents

In the event of an accident involving two or more cars, it's normal for the drivers to complete an accident report form (*constat à l'amiable*), which is provided by French insurance companies. This is completed by all drivers involved, who must agree (more or less) on what happened. You can write in English or any other language and it's important that you check the particulars (e.g. address) of the other driver(s) listed on the form against something official, such as their driving licence. Take care when ticking the relevant boxes that the form cannot be added to or changed later and be sure that you're happy that you understand what has been written by the other driver(s). A *constat à l'amiable* isn't mandatory, and you can refuse to complete one if the other driver(s) disagree with your interpretation of what happened.

Car Insurance

It isn't necessary to have an insurance 'green card' (although some insurance companies issue one as a matter of course), but you must notify your insurance company of your dates of travel. Insurance for British registered cars abroad is becoming more difficult, many British insurance companies cutting the length of time they're allowing a car to be abroad, so check carefully with your insurance company. If you're bringing your car to France permanently but cannot re-register it (e.g. if it's a lease car or has been modified), there are some French companies that will insure your car, but only for a maximum of 12 months. **However, you should read the small print, as cover may be effective only for six or three months or even one month.**

AGF Assurfinance   💻 *www.agf.fr*
AXA Assurance   💻 *www.axa.fr*

Azur Assurances	🖥 *www.azur-assurances.fr*
GAN Assurances	🖥 *www.gan.fr*
MAAF Assurances	🖥 *www.maaf.fr*
Mutuel du Mans Assurances	🖥 *www.mma.fr*

Car Repairs & Service

Most privately owned petrol stations service and repair cars and some of the large chains, such as Shell and Esso, have a workshop attached. Even small towns will have a repair garage of some description. However, if your car is damaged, you must contact your insurer **before** having any repairs carried out and the insurer may specify certain garages to carry out the repairs.

Petrol Stations

Petrol stations in France are generally open much shorter hours than in the UK, although there are some that are manned 24 hours a day, where a British credit card can be used for payment. Otherwise, if a station has a '24/24' sign, this means that petrol can be bought using automated pumps that will only take a credit or debit card with a microchip and a four-digit code, such as French bank cards.

Petrol stations in Poitou-Charentes that are open long hours are listed below.

Charente

Shell   RN10, Barro   ☎ 05 45 30 36 65
                      (just south of Ruffec, on the northbound carriageway)
                      Open 24 hours.

Charente-Maritime

Saintes   Esso, 3 avenue Salvador Allende   ☎ 05 46 93 20 27
                      (on the main road running north up to the hospital from the
                      southern ring road)
                      Open 24 hours.

Tonnay Charente Total, 109 avenue Aunis La Vigerie   ☎ 05 46 83 79 54
                      (east of Rochefort)
                      Cash desk open 6am to11pm.

Vienne

Poitiers   Elf, RN10, Jaunay Clan   ☎ 05 49 52 03 33
                      (north of the town, near Futuroscope)
                      Open 24 hours.

                      Shell, avenue John Kennedy   ☎ 05 49 01 61 82

(to the east of the city, off the south east ring road)
Open 24 hours.

Couhé   Esso, RN10, Vivonne   ☎ 05 49 42 43 53
                       (on the N10 southbound, just north of the town)
                       Open 24 hours.

Rules & Regulations

When driving in France, you must have the following in your car at all
times:

- Vehicle registration document or, if you're driving a leased or hired car,
  a letter of authority and a VE103 Hired Vehicle Certificate from the
  leasing or hire company;
- Your driving licence;
- Vehicle insurance documents;
- A warning triangle;
- Spare bulbs.

It's also advisable to carry a fire extinguisher and a first-aid kit.

Note also the following general rules and regulations:

- The wearing of seatbelts is compulsory and includes passengers in rear
  seats when seatbelts are fitted. You (or any of your passengers) can be
  fined up to €90 for not wearing a seatbelt. Children must be
  accommodated in approved child seats, and children under ten cannot
  ride in the front of a vehicle unless it has no back seat.
- Failure to dip your lights when following or approaching another
  vehicle can cost you up to €750 and a penalty point on your licence if
  you have a French licence. French licenses (*permis de conduire*) work in
  reverse, with points given with the licence that you can then lose.
- French traffic lights usually have a small set of lights at eye level, which
  are handy if you can't see the main lights (there are rarely lights on the
  far side of a junction). If the amber light (either a normal round light or
  an arrow shape) is flashing, you may continue (in the direction
  indicated, if an arrow shape) but must observe any relevant priority
  signs. If you jump a red light, you can be fined €300!
- Watch out for a triangular sign with a red border displaying a large
  black X. This means that you **don't** have priority at the next junction
  (which may not be a crossroads) but **must** give way to the right,
  however minor the joining road is.
- Always come to a complete stop at junctions when required to (i.e. by a
  STOP sign) and ensure that your front wheels are behind the white line.
  Failure to stop behind the line can cost you €750.
- **Beware of moped riders.** French people are allowed on mopeds from

the age of 14, and many youngsters pull out and weave around traffic without looking or indicating; even French motorists give them an extremely wide berth when overtaking!

● The name sign as you enter a village or town marks the start of the urban speed limit (see below) and the name crossed through as you leave marks the end.

● Parking in towns with parking meters is often free between noon and 2pm (times vary).

● And finally, don't assume that a British licence plate will prevent you from being stopped. From autumn 2004, tickets for motoring offences such as illegal parking and speeding will be sent for payment to the country in which a car is registered.

Further details of French driving regulations can be found in *Living and Working in France* (see page 334).

Speed Limits

Speed limits in France vary according to road conditions, as shown below. When visibility is below 50m (165ft) for any reason (e.g. rain or fog), you must not exceed 50kph (32mph) on **any** road. Speeds shown are in kilometres per hour with miles-per-hour equivalents in brackets.

Type Of Road	Speed Limits	
	Dry Road	Wet Road
Motorway	130 (81)	110 (68)
Dual-Carriageway	110 (68)	100 (62)
Single-Carriageway	90 (56)	80 (50)
Town	50 (32)	50 (32)

Note: The above limits apply unless otherwise indicated (e.g. lower limits sometimes apply in built-up areas).

If you're caught exceeding a speed limit by 40kph (25mph), your driving licence can be confiscated on the spot.

Pets

General Information

France is a nation of dog-lovers, although French people's attitude towards other pets and animals in general can be alarmingly indifferent (sometimes also to dogs). The following information may be of use to those importing a pet or buying a pet in France.

- Many restaurants will provide food and water for dogs, some even allowing dogs to be seated at the table! Hotels may provide a rate for pets to stay.
- It's common practice to have third party insurance in case your pet (or child!) bites someone or causes an accident; the majority of household insurance policies include this, but you should check.
- Dogs must be kept on leads in most public parks and gardens in France and there are large fines for dog owners who don't comply.
- There have been no reported cases of rabies in central or southern France for ten years, but if you intend to put a cat or a dog into kennels or a cattery, it must be given a rabies vaccination.
- Rural French dogs are generally kept more as guard dogs than as pets and often live outdoors. Vicious dogs are (usually) confined or chained, but in a small community other 'pet' dogs may be left to wander around the village or hamlet.
- In towns and cities, the use of 'poop scoops' are required and dedicated bins are provided in streets and parks.
- Dogs aren't welcome on the majority of beaches and, if you're staying on a campsite, they must be vaccinated against rabies and wear a collar at all times.
- On trains, pets under 6kg (13lb) which can be carried in a bag are charged around €5, but larger ones must be on a lead and wear a muzzle and will be charged half the normal second-class fare.
  - Some Mercure and Formule 1 hotels accept dogs (see page 45).

Horse Dentists

Vets in France don't deal with horses' teeth and there are specific equine dentists, listed in the appropriate chapter.

Horse Feed

The feed you need is obviously dependent on how your horses are used and what their current feeding regime is. In any case, until you've established your new suppliers, it's wise to bring over with you any specific feeds.

Your local agricultural Co-Op (look out for huge hoppers, sometimes in the middle of nowhere, which may be marked 'Civray') will sell sacks of feed and often pony nuts. Some have started selling only 'high-performance' nuts, so check carefully. Maize and barley are often available.

A local farmer may be your best source of feed, which is usually sold as whole grain or as flour (farine), although some farmers will crush grain for you. An alternative used locally for horses that have come from the UK is whole-grain barley soaked for 24 hours. Your local farmer will also be the best source of hay and straw. See also **Riding Equipment** on page 65.

Spillers exports horse feeds to France; to find your nearest supplier visit Spillers' website at 🖳 *www.spillers-france.com* or contact one of the following:

SA Sodiva	7 rue de la Roberdière, 35000 Rennes 🖳 *www.coopagr-bretagne.fr*	☎ 02 99 59 87 05
A. Vigala-Nord	rue du Canal, St Nicholas les Arras, 62052 St Laurent Blangy ✉ *savigala@nordnet.fr*	☎ 03 21 60 40 40

Identification

All dogs in France must be tattooed or microchipped with an identity number, enabling owners to quickly find lost pets and also preventing a rabies or other vaccination certificate from being used for more than one dog. Tattoos used to be done inside the ear but it may now be done inside the animal's back leg.

The costs of the two procedures are similar, although charges aren't fixed and vary considerably according to the veterinary practice – between around €25 and €75 for tattooing and from €35 to €70 for microchipping.The numbers are kept in a central computer by SPA (see below). If you lose your pet, contact the nearest SPA office.

Pet Parlours

Although many dogs are used as guard dogs, there are many that are domestic pets, and a large number of 'pet parlours' (*salon de toilettage de chiens et chats*) are to be found in France.

Pet Travel

Pet Passport Scheme

The Department for Food, Agriculture and Rural Affairs (DEFRA) operates a 'pet passport' scheme (known as PETS) for the benefit of owners wishing to take their pets abroad and bring them back to the UK. Full details of the requirements for re-entry into the UK are available from the DEFRA helpline or website (☎ +44 (0)870-241 1710, 🖳 *www.defra.gov.uk*). The helpline is accessible from both England and France and the lines are open from 8.30am to 5pm (UK time) Mondays to Fridays. Alternatively, a company called Dogs Away offers a free eight-page booklet to guide you through the process (☎ +44 (0)20-8441 9311, 🖳 *www.dogsaway.co.uk*).

Crossing the Channel through the Tunnel reduces the possibility of stress for your pets, as you can remain with them. Some ferry companies may allow you to check your pet on the car deck during the crossing, but this isn't always easy and can make the pet more distressed when you leave it again.

If applying for a pet passport in France, always ensure that you have in your possession the *carte de tatouage* before you start the pet passport process, as unless you have this card, which has your name and address as the registered owner, the registration of the microchip (*puce*) will be refused, along with the rabies vaccination, blood test, etc.

Sea Crossings

Hoverspeed   *UK* ☎ 0870-240 8070
Each pet is charged £18 each way. Bookings aren't possible on line and must be made by phone.

Brittany Ferries   *UK* ☎ 0870-366 5333
Brittany Ferries issues a specimen copy of the certificate needed so that you can check that the French vet has the correct one. In an emergency, this copy is valid.

Eurotunnel   *UK* ☎ 0870-535 3535
The check-in desk for pets at Coquelles is to the right of the check-in lanes. Animals are checked in before entering the Eurotunnel site. A single journey costs £30 per animal; guide dogs for the disabled are free. You can book via the website but are advised to book by phone, as a limited number of pets are allowed per train.

Riding Equipment

Gamm Vert   🖳 *www.gammvert.fr*
These garden centres sell horse feed and some basic equipment, depending on the size of the store. The website gives both location and opening hours of your nearest store.

Décathlon   🖳 *www.decathlon.fr*
These large sports stores carry a wide selection of riding accessories and equipment, including the hire of clippers (*tondeuses*), which are available for half or full days.

SPA

The Société pour la Protection des Animaux (SPA) is an organisation similar to the RSPCA in the UK but it isn't a national scheme, so you must contact your departmental office with any complaints or questions. Details are included in the following chapters.

Veterinary Clinics

Most veterinary surgeries are open from Mondays to Saturdays, usually closing for lunch. There are often open surgeries as well as appointments. Where a vet's name isn't given there's more than one vet at the surgery.

Many vets will deal with horses and other equines but generally those that are used for riding out rather than eventing or competitions.

Places To Visit

Beaches

Many towns and villages have a *plan d'eau*, which can be a lake or part of a river. It may be just for fishing and relaxing beside or there may be a beach, playground, crazy golf and more. Details of all such facilities are given in the following chapters.

Churches & Monuments

Churches of interest are signposted from main roads and motorways and can be easily identified, e.g. *Église XIVème Siècle* =14th century church.

Cognac, Pineau & Wine Producers

There are vast numbers of producers in this region and we've listed only a selection, both large and small.

Professional Services

As many architects also offer a project management and general building services, they have been listed under **Architects & Project Managers** in the **Tradesmen** sections.

Religion

Catholic Churches

Churches can be found in most communities, and services in the villages are generally held in rotation with other churches in the parish. Notices are displayed on church doors or just inside giving details of the forthcoming services. In some small villages, the church doesn't have regular services but is used only on special occasions once or twice a year.

Restaurants

There are so many restaurants in the region that we've been able to give only a selection to get you started on your gastronomical voyage of discovery. It's usual for restaurants of all types to offer set menus (*menu*), which are dishes put together by the chef that complement each other and may change daily. In smaller restaurants, this may be all that's available, although there's usually a choice of two or three dishes for each course.

Routiers

These restaurants can be found on main roads and have a circular logo – half red, half blue. They're usually alongside lorry parking areas and provide meals for drivers which have a reputation for being good quality and good value, the restaurants themselves being clean and tidy. You may be seated canteen style and find yourself next to a 'trucker' but you will get a four-course meal, sometimes with wine included in the price (it's the coffee you have to pay extra for!). Prices vary, but around €10 is usual.

Rubbish & Recycling

Dustmen

The collection of household rubbish (*ramassage*) varies not only between departments but also within areas of each department. It may be collected once or twice a week, and there may be separate collections (e.g. weekly or fortnightly) for recyclable waste, which must be put in special bags (see **Recycling** on page 68).

In towns, you may find 'wheelie bins' in the street. If so, you're responsible for putting your rubbish sacks in the bins, which are then emptied once or twice a week. If there's more than one type of wheelie bin, the other(s) are for recycling (see **Recycling** on page 68).

Rural areas may also have wheelie bins, with one or two for each group of houses. If there are no bins, rubbish should be put in bin bags and left at the edge of the road, although you're advised to hang them up out of reach of marauding dogs, cats and wildlife; **dustmen won't go down drives or onto property**. Dustmen often come very early, so bags need to be put out the night before.

If collection day falls on a bank holiday, rubbish is generally collected the day **before** rather than the day after – or the collection may simply be cancelled.

The best way to find out what happens in your commune is to speak to your neighbours or enquire at the *mairie*.

In most areas, separate taxes are payable by homeowners for rubbish collection and many French people are fiercely protective of the services for which they pay. You're therefore strongly advised not to put rubbish into a wheelie bin if you're driving a car registered in another department; the same applies if you try to use a rubbish tip in a different department or even a different commune (see **Rubbish Tips** below).

Metal Collection

If the previous occupiers kindly left their old fridge or bedstead in the garden, your *mairie* should be able to put you in touch with your local 'rag and bone man' or arrange for them to be taken away. In some communes, there's a regular (e.g. quarterly) *récupération des objects encombrants*, the dates of which you should be advised in advance.

Recycling

Somewhat belatedly, the French have gone in for recycling in a big way, but recycling systems vary greatly with the region and the department, some areas having no facilities at all whilst others collect recyclable waste from outside your house. Whatever the system, the colour coding is always the same:

● **Blue** – Paper and card, including catalogues and junk mail, but not window envelopes.
● **Yellow** – Packaging, cans (including aerosol cans), tins, drinks cartons and plastic milk bottles but not plastic bags or the thin plastic that encloses junk mail or six-packs of bottles of water or other products.
● **Green** – All clear and coloured glass except drinking glasses and light bulbs; no corks or lids.

Here is a summary of some of the systems currently in place in Poitou-Charentes:

● Blue and yellow bags distributed free (usually available from the *mairie*) and collected at the same time as your household rubbish;
● Yellow bags only distributed (again the bags are free and available from the *mairie* if there are none at the property), in which case all recyclable material (except glass) is put in the same bag, and collected once a fortnight or once a week, often on a different day from non-recyclable rubbish;
● Blue containers for your paper and card distributed, which you put by the road and which are emptied at the roadside, leaving the container behind;
● Glass collected from outside your house, usually in conjunction with the blue containers but in a rigid container, such as a strong box, supplied by you and also emptied at the roadside, leaving the container behind;
● A series of collection banks, usually green for glass, blue for paper and yellow for plastic and packaging, near the *mairie*;
● Large mesh cages, just for plastic bottles, often found at rubbish tips (see below);

● A series of wheelie bins with different coloured lids beside the bins for non-recyclable rubbish or a different coloured wheelie bins supplied to each house.

There are many designs of kitchen bin in France that have two or three compartments for the different types of waste. Note that polystyrene cannot be recycled; if you have a large quantity, such as packaging from a household appliance, you can dispose of it at a tip (see below).

Batteries

Batteries can be recycled in most supermarkets, where you will find tal, clear Perspex/black plastic containers on a chipboard plinth in the foyer or by the customer service desk. Car batteries can be recycled at the rubbish tip (see below).

Clothes & Shoes

Recycling containers for clothes and shoes can often be found in supermarket car parks.

Glass

If glass isn't collected from outside your house, you need to use a bottle banks. If there isn't one locally, they can usually be found in supermarket car parks, at the rubbish tip or in public car parks or lay-bys.

Printer Cartridges

Printer ink cartridges can also be recycled, sometimes in supermarket entrance foyers and sometimes at the *mairie* or library. Toner cartridges can be recycled at the rubbish tip.

Rubbish Tips

Every town and many large villages have a rubbish tip (*déchetterie*); even small communes may have a *décharge*, which is primarily for garden rubbish but may also be used for building rubble.

Déchetteries are clearly marked in towns and outlying areas by a symbol of a hand holding three arrows. Here you can dispose of large metal objects, such as bikes and cookers, as well as oil, glass, paper, clothes and batteries, although you may not be allowed to dispose of household rubbish bags, which should be put out for collection at your house.

Some tips accept a limited quantity of building rubble each day from individuals; if they suspect that you're a tradesman, you will be refused. Some rubbish tips issue a pass to all residents who want to use the tip (available from your *mairie*). If you don't have a card and are driving a car registered in another department (or country), you may be asked where you live or even be prevented from using the tip at all.

Schools

If you're planning to put your children into French school, the first place to go is your *mairie*. They will give you details of the relevant school for your child's age, both private and state schools. The school week for junior and infant schools is generally Mondays, Tuesdays, Thursdays and Fridays. Some areas also have lessons on Wednesday mornings, as do most secondary schools (*collèges*). There's no school on Saturdays in this region and no school uniform.

Enrolment

To register your children at a school, you must go and see the head teacher and he will tell you whether there are places and the relevant start date. Take the following with you:

- Details of all vaccinations since birth, which will be entered in your child's *livre de santé* if he has one;
- The name and address of his last school (if appropriate);
- A copy of his last school report and/or any results you have from any academic tests;
- Evidence of school insurance, which is compulsory in France (see below). At your first meeting, it will be sufficient to say that you've applied for the insurance.
- If your child previously attended a French school, the *Certificat de Radiation*, which is proof that all contact and dealings have terminated with the previous school. A closing report from a UK school may be accepted.

French schools don't usually provide stationery and can have a long list of stationery and equipment that you must provide, so ask for a copy.

Transport

There's a comprehensive network of school buses (*car/bus scolaire*), which collect children in rural areas. An application form for a bus pass can be obtained from the school or the *mairie* and you will need to provide two passport-size photographs. The cost, if any, depends on where you live, how many school-age children there are in the family and what schools they go to.

Holidays

Schools in France are divided into three groups for their holidays so that spring half term and Easter holidays are staggered, which prevents ski and other resorts from becoming overcrowded. Poitou-Charentes schools are in Group B. You may also find that there's no half-term break between the Easter and summer holidays. Calendars are distributed by a wide variety of organisations giving the school holiday dates for the three groups. If a school operates a four-day week, it will give you a list of holiday dates, which may vary by a day or two from the 'official' dates to make up the statutory hours per term.

Insurance

All children must have insurance to attend school in France. Insurance is provided by a number of companies, but Mutuelles Assurances Eléves (MAE) is the most popular and is very good. The most comprehensive cover is €24.00 and covers your child for all eventualities, both in and out of school and cover for use of all French medical facilities. Contact details for MAE are given below. Whichever insurer you use, you must provide the school with a certificate to prove that your child is covered.

Mutuelles Assurances Eléves, 10 rue Eugène Thomas,
17000 La Rochelle   ☎ 05 46 41 06 40

Mutuelles d'Assurances   🖥 *www.mae.fr*   ☎ 08 20 00 00 70
Helpline open from 9am to noon and from 1 to 5.30pm Mondays to Fridays.

Mutuelles d'Assurances, Résidence de l'Epid'Or,
60 boulevard Chabasse, 16000 Angoulême   ☎ 05 45 92 68 87

Extra Tuition

If your child wants or needs extra help, but not structured lessons, it's worth contacting the local college, as it may be able to recommend a student who is happy to come to your house and spend time with your child going over class notes or lessons. Not only is this cheaper than a qualified teacher but a younger person may be less daunting for children.

Shopping

General Information

Opening Hours

When available, the opening hours of various shops have been included, but they're liable to change; check before travelling long distances.

Many small businesses are staffed only by the family and as a result you may find that the village shop or even the town co-op may close completely for two weeks while the proprietor goes on holiday.

Shop opening hours can change from summer to winter, particularly when school starts in September: Not only does the merchandise seem to change overnight, but shops that were open all day (*sans interruption*) and on Sunday mornings are suddenly closed for two hours at lunchtime and not open on Sundays at all. Other shops may change their lunchtime closure and close completely on Mondays.

The information in this section relates to shopping in general; details of shops in each department can be found in the following chapters.

Mobile Shops

In rural communities there are various mobile shops, all of which sound their horns loudly as they go through the village. These may include a bakery (*boulangerie*), a butcher's (*boucherie*), a grocery (*épicerie*) and a fishmonger's (*poissonnerie*).

Alcohol

There aren't as many off-licences (*caves*) in France as in England, as the hypermarkets and supermarkets sell the majority of alcoholic drinks. The specialist shops listed under this heading sell table wine by the litre, usually starting at just over €1 per litre, but you must take your own container. Suitable containers with taps on can be bought at DIY stores or large supermarkets.

Bakers'

Bakeries (*boulangeries*) are usually small family-run businesses that close one day a week and often on Sunday afternoons. They also run delivery vans, going through local villages and hamlets from two to seven days a week, depending on the area.

British Groceries

Many supermarkets are now introducing some 'high demand' British produce to their international sections, e.g. Golden Syrup and HP Sauce. Stock varies with demand and the size of the shop, so keep a look out, especially in hypermarkets and popular tourist areas.

Expatdirect.co.uk   💻 *www.expatdirect.co.uk*   ☎ +44 (0)7980-265553
Supplies British produce at supermarket prices: 30kg of goods delivered anywhere in France for £14.95.

Chemists'

Even small towns will have a chemist's (*pharmacie*) but they may be open limited hours, such as Tuesdays to Fridays and every other Saturday and Monday. Outside normal opening hours a notice should be displayed giving the address of the nearest duty chemist (*pharmacie de garde*). Alternatively, the *gendarmes* hold a list of duty chemists; dial ☎ 17.

Chemists are trained to give first aid and can also carry out procedures such as taking blood pressure. They can be asked advice on many ailments and without a prescription can give a wider variety of medicines than are available over the counter in the UK. Chemists are also trained to distinguish between around 50 types of mushroom and toadstool and to identify local snakes in order to prescribe the correct antidote for poisoning.

DIY

There are many DIY (*bricolage*) stores in the region, most towns having at least one of the following:

Weldom   💻 *www.weldom.com*
Bricomarché   💻 *www.bricomarche.com*
Castorama   💻 *www.castorama.fr*
Mr Bricolage   💻 *www.mr-bricolage.fr*

Equipment & Tool Hire

To hire equipment or tools you generally need to take some identification, *e.g.* a household bill, and must pay a deposit, by cheque or debit card. Note that this topic is listed under **Domestic Services** in the following chapters.

Frozen Food

There are frozen food (*surgelés*) shops that deliver to homes and frozen food producers that only sell direct, orders being placed by phone, via the internet or with the driver. The two largest companies that both have shops and do home deliveries are:

Picard Surgelés 💻 *www.picard.fr*
Thiriet Glaces   💻 *www.thiriet.com*

Garden Centres

The most commonly found garden centres (*jardineries*) are Gamm Vert and Jardiland, the latter being a large store most commonly found on retail parks.

Gamm Vert   🖥 *www.gammvert.fr*
Jardiland   🖥 *www.jardiland.fr*

Key Cutting & Heel Bars

Key cutting kiosks and heel bars (*cordonneries*) may be found in a hypermarket complex, outside supermarkets or as independent stores in the high street.

Kitchens & Bathrooms

Specialist shops selling kitchen and bathroom furniture and fittings can often be found in large retail parks.

Markets

Some markets and fairs take place in the centre of towns and villages and can cause streets to be closed; as they're often situated on car parks, parking can become difficult. Food markets in France are well worth a visit if you haven't experienced them before (and aren't squeamish), but do check the prices, particularly at indoor markets, which are sometimes more expensive than you might expect.

Newsagents'

Many general newsagents' (*maison de la presse* or simply *presse*) sell British daily newspapers and even British magazines and paperbacks. They can order specific magazines or publications, such as the *TV* and *Radio Times*, on request.

Publications

Le Charentais Annonce, *Gazette de Saintes*, *Le 16*, *Le 17*, *Le 79* and *Le 86* are just some of the local 'classified' newspapers, which include advertisements for local events, items for sale, cars, etc. They're free and can be found in most newsagents as well as *tabacs*, bakeries and other shops.

The two weekly newspapers listed below are designed and written for expatriates and can be delivered anywhere in the world. An annual subscription costs between £75 and £90.

The Guardian Weekly   🖥 *www.guardian.co.uk*   ☎ +44 (0)870-066 0510
Condenses the best of *The Guardian*, *The Observer*, *Le Monde* and *The Washington Post* and adds bespoke articles.

The Weekly Telegraph   🖥 *www.expat.telegraph.co.uk* ☎ +44 (0)1454 642464
Condenses *The Daily* and *Sunday Telegraph* and adds bespoke articles.

Organic Food

Organic produce (*produits biologiques/bio*) is widely available in supermarkets and hypermarkets. Organic shops are becoming more popular but tend to appear and disappear rapidly.

Passport Photographs

Kiosks can usually be found in the entrance to supermarkets and in hypermarket centres.

Post Offices

French post offices offer a wide range of facilities, including cash machines, internet access and automated postage machines that can operate in English.

Retail Parks

As in the UK, retail parks tend to be on the outskirts of cities and large towns and in France there tends to be a hypermarket at the centre.

Second-Hand Goods

Brocantes come in all shapes and sizes and are a cross between an antique shop and a second-hand shop. You can find them in most towns and along main roads. *Brocantes* can be the source of some good bargains. *Dépôts-vente* (a cross between a pawnshop and a charity shop) are also a good source of second-hand goods. They sell on behalf of the public for a commission of around 20 per cent.

Supermarkets & Hypermarkets

French supermarkets advertise heavily on roadside hoardings, often giving directions and distance in minutes, but be aware that these directions can just stop, leaving you lost and apparently a great deal more than '5 mins' away from the store. They often advertise at the side of a competitor's store, when their store is actually in the next town.

The most common supermarkets in this region are listed below; the websites will give you the location of the store nearest to you.

Leclerc	💻 *www.e-leclerc.com*
Intermarché	💻 *www.intermarche.com*
Champion	💻 *www.champion.fr*
Super U	💻 *www.super-u.com*

Hypermarkets (*hypermarchés*) are one of the best sources of electrical goods and general household items. There doesn't seem to be the quantity of specialist electrical stores in France as there is in the UK and it's quite normal to buy your new washing machine from Géant or Auchan. Hypermarkets tend to be situated in a retail park on the outskirts of towns and cities and the buildings themselves are often small shopping precincts with a variety of shops and services.

Note the following general points regarding French super- and hypermarkets:

- Very few supermarkets open on Sundays – occasionally on Sunday mornings but never in the afternoon – and no hypermarkets open on Sundays.
- Opening hours can change from summer to winter, with a longer lunchtime closure and slightly later evening opening in summer.
- Larger stores may open all day Mondays to Fridays, others only on Fridays and Saturdays, closing for lunch the rest of the week, the smallest stores closing for lunch every day.

Swimming Pool Equipment

Once summer arrives, supermarkets and DIY stores are stocked with pool equipment and accessories, from chlorine and pumps to covers and steps.

Sports

General information relating to certain sports is given below (in alphabetical order). A selection of the activities available in each department is provided in the following chapters; full details are available from tourist offices and *mairies*. Not surprisingly, large towns have the widest range of facilities.

Note that many 'physical' sports require a licence. The relevant club will have the forms and a medical may be required, which your doctor can carry out as a standard consultation.

Golf

The following website provides full details in English of all the clubs in Poitou-Charentes as well as across France: 🖥 *www.golflounge.com/fr*.

Horse Riding

Local tourist offices have copies of *Topo Guides*, which give details of the routes in the area suitable for horse riding. Your local horse yard is the best place to enquire about competitions, as not all yards are competitive. Those that are will be involved in many events, both regional and local, throughout the year.

Snooker, Pool & Billiards

French billiards is a highly skilful (and, some say, tedious) game played with just three balls on a table without pockets. Snooker and pool are also widely played. Many bars and cafés have pool tables, and some also snooker and/or billiard tables.

Tourist Offices

Tourist offices hold details of local events throughout the year and are a good source of general information and local guide books. Regional and general tourist office details are listed below. Details of departmental offices are given in the following chapters; opening hours are current but may change slightly from year to year.

Comité Régional du Tourisme   ☎ 05 49 50 10 50
🖳 *www.poitou-charentes.vacances.com*

Maison Poitou-Charentes, 68–70 rue du
Cherche-Midi, Paris   ☎ 01 42 22 83 74

Office de Tourisme de Paris, 25 rue des Pyramides,
Paris (main office)   ☎ 08 92 68 30 00
🖳 *www.paris-touristoffice.com*

Tradesmen

Almost every commune has a tradesman (*artisan*) of some description, from carpenter (*menuisier*) or builder (*maçon*) to electrician (*électricien*) or plumber (*plombier*).

One way to find out what local tradesmen there are is to look through the phone book in the residential listing for your commune; tradesmen will have their profession next to their name and address. The best way, however, is to ask at the *mairie*; it's likely that the *Maire* will even give you a personal introduction.

Builders

Using local French tradesmen has the advantage that they know the materials they will be working with, are familiar with the systems in place in your property and, as they live locally, will have a reputation to maintain. The increasing influx of Britons to rural France means that more and more French artisans are working for and with the British, which in turn is making them more willing to communicate in a mixture of French and English, drawings and sign language. (see also Translators & Teachers below).

Registered builders in France have their work guaranteed for ten years and must be fully insured to cover any accident or damage to themselves, you or your property. To check whether a tradesman is registered to work in France, go to 🖥 *www.cofacerating.fr*, click on the Union Jack at the top and go to 'For more information on ... companies"; this takes you to a form where you enter the tradesman's telephone number. If he's registered, the company information will appear; a big red cross indicates that he isn't registered.

Should you decide to use an un-registered tradesman – either French or British – you should be aware that, if there's an accident, you will be personally and financially liable; you will have no warranty on the work carried out and you won't be able to claim the low tax rate (5.5 per cent instead of 19.6 per cent) available until the end of 2005 for renovation work. You could have additional problems if you need to make an insurance claim involving the work (e.g. in the case of a flood or subsidence).

Note, however, that tradesmen's insurance doesn't cover them for all trades, but only for the skills for which they're registered; for example, your builder may offer to sort out your electrics, but he may not be registered as an electrician and hence not insured for that work.

Just as you would in the UK, ensure that you have got several quotes, if possible have seen some work already done and that you are happy with the tradesman. Further details of finding and supervising builders in France can be found in **Renovating and Maintaining Your French Home** (see page 334).

Planning Permission

If you want to make any alterations to your home – even painting the window frames a different colour – you must first visit the *mairie*, as there are strict regulations (which vary from commune to commune) governing what can and cannot be done and a strict procedure that must be followed for certain types of work. This is too a complex subject to describe here. For full details, refer to **Renovating and Maintaining Your French Home** (see page 334).

Translators & Teachers

French teachers and translators in each department are listed under this heading in the following chapters. See also **Schools** on page 70.

Translation

If you have a small amount of text that you need translated, the Altavista website (🖥 *www.altavista.com*) can translate up to 150 words from a variety of different languages. This is not an accurate translation and should never be relied on for legal or professional purposes, but it will give you the gist of the information. This and the Google site (🖥 *www.google.com*) can also translate websites.

Utilities

Electricity

In France electricity bills are in two parts: consumption and a monthly standing charge (*abonnement*). Electricity consumption is charged according to one of a range of tariffs. The standing charge is related to how much power (calculated in kilowatts or kW) you have available to you at any time: the more power you have available, the higher the standing charge. Your consumption charge is also related to the amount of power you have available, the charge per unit being higher the more power is available.

On the back of your electricity bill (*votre facture en détail*) it will say what your standing charge is per month (…€/*mois*). Under *montant à prélever* it will give you your existing allowance of kW at any one time, e.g. '*puissance 6kW, code 024*'. At the bottom of the reverse side of your bill you will find the cheap rate hours (*heures creuses*), which are usually from 1 to 7am and from noon to 2pm.

If you use more than the power available, the trip switch is triggered and you will be thrown into darkness and left to fumble for a torch. To prevent repeated 'tripping' of the system, you must ensure that your allowance of power is sufficient to cover your expected maximum power consumption at any one time (e.g. running the dishwasher, washing machine and cooker all at once), although this will cost you more.

An alternative is to install a piece of equipment called a *délesteur*, which is a tiny computer wired into your system: when the system is overloaded, it automatically switches off apparatus in order of priority (pre-determined by you, e.g. hot water tank, tumble drier, but not lights, alarm or plug sockets).

Like most other utility bills, electricity bills are normally issued bi-monthly in France. As your meter will be outside the property and accessible from the street (you mustn't block access to it), it will usually be read without your knowing it. If a reading hasn't been possible, your electricity bill will be estimated (indicated by an *E* alongside the figures). If the estimate is higher than the actual reading, you can take your bill to your local office (listed in subsequent chapters) and you will be sent an amended bill.

Gas

Gas (*gaz*) can be natural, butane or propane. If you aren't on mains gas (which is generally available only in larger towns and residential areas), you will need a tank (*citerne*), which provides propane gas, or bottles to provide butane. If you use gas only for cooking, bottles are sufficient; if you have gas central heating, a tank is essential. The main difference between natural and propane gas is that propane burns much hotter (take care when trying to simmer milk!) and appliances designed for natural gas will need to have the injectors changed to a smaller size. If the appliance is new, it should come with two sizes of injector (the larger size, for natural gas, is usually the one that comes fitted).

If there's already a tank at the property, you will be required to pay a deposit for it and, when it has been filled up, the price of a full tank of gas, irrespective of how much was left in it. The gas company will credit the previous owners with what was left in the tank. The deposit can be as much as €1,000 and a tank full of gas as much as €800, so you should take this into account when negotiating the price of the property. Instead of a deposit, you can chose to pay a monthly charge for the tank.

You can monitor your gas consumption using the gauge on a tank and re-order when it drops to the red line. You may find that the gas company will come automatically when they believe you should be due for a refill. Gas bottles don't have gauges but can simply be shaken to ascertain how much gas is left.

You don't always have to pay immediately when your tank is refilled. The driver may give you a delivery note stating the quantity delivered, the price per unit and the total due. If the bill is large, you may be able to send two cheques, one dated a month after the other, but check with your supplier first.

Water

Water in France is supplied by a variety of organisations, from national companies to individual communes – in the latter case with bills sent from by the *mairie*.

Wood

To find a local supplier of firewood, ask a neighbour or at the *mairie*, as many farmers in the region supply suitable wood. When ordering wood, you need to specify how much you want in an arcane measure called a *stère*, which is roughly 0.6 cubic metres (many people erroneously believe it's one cubic metre) or 500kg of wood. You may also need to specify whether it's for burning now or in a few years and whether it's for a large open fire or a log burner. Wood for log burners is slightly more expensive, as it has to be cut smaller. You can of course order the longer length and cut your own for the log burner. Electric and petrol chainsaws (*tronçonneuses*) are available from all DIY stores from the autumn onwards and can also be hired from certain outlets. Depending on the age and type of wood, expect to pay around €20 to €25 per cubic metre.

Six cubic metres should be enough for a winter if you're only using fires and log burners for cold days or just evenings, for example. If fires are your only source of heating, you will need more, depending of course on how many fires you have and whether you have a wood-burning cooker.

Wood varies in suitability for use on an open fire. Good and unsuitable woods are listed below.

Good Woods

● Apple tree (*pommier*) – produces a good scent;
● Ash (*frêne*) – burns well and produces plenty of warmth whether green or brown, wet or dry;
● Beech (*hêtre*) – almost smokeless;
● Chestnut (*châtaignier*) – needs to be aged;
● Oak (*chêne*) – must be old and dry;
● Pear tree (*poirier*) – produces a good scent.

Unsuitable Woods

● Birch (*bouleau*) – bright and fast burning;
● Elm (*orme*) – doesn't burn well;
● Fir (*sapin*) – bright and fast burning;
● Poplar (*peuplier*) – fast burning and produces a bitter smoke.

Chimney Sweeps

It costs around €45 to have a chimney swept (*ramonage*). The chimney sweep (*ramoneur*) may ask you to sign a form in order for him to charge you the lower rate of VAT (5.5 per cent instead of 19.6 per cent). Although you're no longer legally required to have your chimney swept regularly, if there's a fire which started in the hearth and you're unable to produce a receipt showing that your chimney has been swept recently, you may have difficulty claiming on insurance (check your policy). If using a fire or log burner throughout the winter, you're recommended to have a chimney swept at least once a year anyway.

Château Rochefoucauld

2

Charente

This chapter provides details of facilities and services in the department of Charente (16). General information about each subject can be found in **Chapter 1**. All entries are arranged alphabetically by town, except where a service applies over a wide area, in which case it's listed at the beginning of the relevant section under 'General'. A map of Charente is shown below.

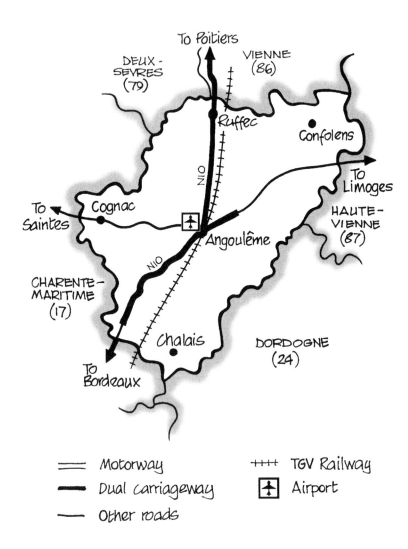

Motorway

Dual carriageway

Other roads

TGV Railway

Airport

Accommodation

Camping

Angoulême	Camping de Bourgines, Parc Bourgines	☎ 05 45 92 83 22

(north of the Charente river in the north of the town)

Chalais   Camping Municipal, route de Ribérac,
               Aubeterre sur Dronne   ☎ 05 45 98 60 17
               (down by the river)
               This three-star campsite has a beach, bathing and, in July and
               August, lifeguards.

Cognac   Camping Municipal Chatenay,
               Le Chatenay   ☎ 05 45 32 13 32
               (on the east side of the town)

Confolens   Camping Municipal des Ribiers,
               21 avenue St Germain   ☎ 05 45 85 35 27
               (alongside the river)

Ruffec   Camping de Réjallant   ☎ 05 45 31 29 06
               (south of the town near the Charente river)

Châteaux

La Rochefoucauld Château de La Rochefoucauld   ☎ 05 45 62 07 42
               (north-east of Angoulême)
               This château has been in the same family for over 1,000 years
               and is considered one of the most beautiful in France. There
               are two double bedrooms, both with en-suite facilities with
               prices from €170 per night including breakfast.

Jarnac   Château Saint Martial   ☎ 05 45 83 38 64
               (just east of Cognac)
               This early 19th century chateau is situated in the centre of
               Jarnac within a park on the banks of the Charente river. There
               are five double rooms, each with private bathroom. English is
               spoken and the chateau is open all year round. Rooms from
               €100 to €119, including breakfast.

Gîtes And Bed & Breakfast

General   Gîtes de France, 17 place Bouillaud,
               Angoulême   ☎ 05 45 69 48 64
               🖳 www.gitescharente.com
               Bookings can be made by phone or via the internet.

Hotels

Hotels have only been listed for the towns that have a limited number. Angoulême and Cognac have a wide selection, including national chains such as those given on page 45.

Chalais	Hôtel de France et de l'Angleterre, 66 avenue de la Gare Double rooms from €25 per night.	☎ 05 45 98 10 03
	La Cagouille, 50 rue de Bordeaux Double rooms from €26 per night.	☎ 05 45 98 14 68
Confolens	Mère Michelet, 17 allée Blossac Double rooms from €39 per night.	☎ 05 45 84 04 11
	Hôtel Emeraude, 20 rue Emile Roux €29 to €39 per room per night.	☎ 05 45 84 12 77
Ruffec	La Toque Blanche, rue Général Leclerc (in the centre of town) €45 for a double room.	☎ 05 45 30 30 30

Bars & Nightlife

A booklet called *Sortir* (🖳 *www.sortir16.net*) published every month gives comprehensive details of fairs, concerts, nightlife and everything else happening in Charente. Available free from tourist offices, libraries, etc.

Angoulême	In the old quarter between the Hôtel de Ville and the covered market are many bars and brasseries that are open until the early hours, including some of the following:	
	L'Art Brut Café, 25 rue d'Aguesseau Dinner and live shows every Saturday night.	☎ 05 45 92 03 71
	Au Bureau, 8 rue R. Poincaré Concerts every Thursday evening (except July and August), karaoke and disco at weekends. Open 7am to 2am, brasserie non-stop 11am to 1am.	☎ 05 45 94 31 31
	Blues Rock Café, 19 rue Genève Open from 11am to 2am. Themed evening on Wednesdays.	☎ 05 45 94 05 98
	Bowling d'Angoulême, 528 route de Bordeaux	☎ 05 45 67 00 66

🖥 *www.bowling-angouleme.fr*
Bowling, video arcade, snack bar, snooker, all air-conditioned.
Open Mondays to Saturdays 11am to 2am, Sundays 1pm to
2am.

La Giraffe, 23 rue Cloche Verte   ☎ 05 45 90 91 20
(in the old side streets down from the Hôtel de Ville)
Bar/café. Open until 2am.

L'Hacienda, 6–8 rue de Genève   ☎ 05 45 39 08 95
Live acts held at this café/bar.

The Kennedy Irish Pub, 3 rue de Beaulieu   ☎ 05 45 94 12 41
Live music, including jazz and blues. Thursday concerts
starting at 9.30pm, Saturday evening jazz or blues music.
'Outdoor' seating in covered archway.
Darts and pool. Open every day 4pm to 2am.

La Nef, rue Louis Pergaud   ☎ 05 45 25 97 00
🖥 *www.dingo-lanef.com*
Music club with piano and jazz music and frequent concerts.

Barbezieux Fair Play, 6 boulevard Chanzy   ☎ 05 45 78 87 43
Café, bar, brasserie with karaoke every Wednesday afternoon
and Saturday evening, and occasional concerts.

La Part Des Anges, 85 rue Victor Hugo   ☎ 05 45 78 32 26
Nightclub.

Chalais Les Couleurs, 1 rue du Four Banal   ☎ 05 45 98 07 63
(in the town centre)
Restaurant with live shows and bands; forthcoming events are
advertised locally. Open until 1am.

Bar du Marché, avenue de La Gare   ☎ 06 79 25 86 15
Hosts bands and holds themed evenings. British owned.

Paradise Club, place Champ de Foire,
Brossac   ☎ 05 45 98 75 02
(north-west of Chalais) Nightclub.

Cognac Le Pilou Pilou, rue du 14 Juillet   ☎ 05 45 81 07 39
(opposite the tourist office)
Club/bar. Open Tuesdays to Saturdays 6.30pm to 1.30am.

La Maison Blanche, Pont St Jacques   ☎ 05 45 36 51 17
(on a little 'island' in the river Charente)
Open Fridays to Sundays midnight to dawn.

	West Rock, 9a place de Cagouillet	☎ 05 45 32 17 28

West Rock, 9a place de Cagouillet ☎ 05 45 32 17 28
💻 *www.westrock.org*
(a short walk from place Francois I)
Holds live shows and concerts.

La Rochefoucauld Bar ManzAna, avenue de la Gare ☎ 05 45 70 71 49
💻 *www.ifrance.com/manzanaconcert*
Concert/band venue.

Ruffec La Cigale ☎ 06 70 20 40 52
(off the N10 at the junction marked to Salles de Villefagnan,
D27; aim towards the vivid green and white storage tanks and
carry on towards Chenon and it's on the right). There are tea
dances here every Sunday from 3 to 8pm and evening dances
with an orchestra.

Iguana Bar, La Chèvrerie ☎ 05 45 31 15 76
(signposted off the D26 north-west out of Ruffec)
British-run pub with bar food, ale and darts.

Le Moulin Enchanté Discotheque,
Condac ☎ 05 45 31 26 24
(on the road to Confolens)
€5 entry.

Verteuil-sur- Dixieland Café, 46 rue des Halles ☎ 05 45 31 40 35
Charente (south of Ruffec)
French, Italian and 'Tex-Mex' cuisine, shaded beer garden at
the rear. Piano bar every Tuesday evening, shows and themed
evenings. Open Tuesdays to Sundays noon to 2am in summer,
4pm to 2am in winter.

Business Services

Computer Services

General K. Humphreys Chez Bouchet,
Montalembert ☎ 05 49 07 53 46
✉ *humphreyskeith@aol.com*
This Briton deals with computer problems, hardware, software
and upgrades, covering northern Charente, southern Vienne
and eastern Deux-Sèvres.

Angoulême Bureau Centre, Rond Point Girac ☎ 05 45 65 82 40
Mondays to Saturdays 9am to 12.30pm and 1.30 to 7pm for
sales, service and supplies for all makes of PC.

Chalais Techni-Services, 2 rue de Barbezieux ☎ 05 45 95 45 90
(opposite the 'lady' fountain)

Mondays and Saturdays 9am to noon and 3 to 7.30pm,
Tuesdays to Fridays 3 to 7.30pm.

Cognac   IFF, 130 Aristide Briand   ☎ 05 45 35 21 21
                All day Tuesdays to Saturdays and Monday afternoons.
                Training, upgrades and PCs made to measure, including home
                installation.

Ruffec   Nord Charente Informatique,
                4 place Général de Gaulle   ☎ 05 45 31 12 46
                (at the lights at the bottom of the hill from Leclerc)
                Closed Mondays.

Computer Training

Angoulême   MJC Louis Aragon, place Victoria   ☎ 05 45 61 29 56
                Introduction and training Tuesday evenings.

Chalais   College, 34 route d'Angoulême   ☎ 05 45 98 16 42
                Workshops on Monday evenings.

Confolens   Micromut, 8 rue Fontaine des Jardins
                Practical help with IT, internet, etc. Meetings on Monday
                evenings at Communauté des Communes du Confolentais.

Employment Agencies

(see page 50)

Communications

Fixed Telephones

General   France Télécom: Dial 1014 or go to
                🖳 *www.francetelecom.fr*
                Local shops are listed below.

Angoulême   43–45 rue Marengo
                (in the town centre)

                Géant Centre, Champniers
                (north of the town)

Cognac   4 rue du 14 juillet

Internet Access

Angoulême   Espace Franquin, boulevard Berthelot   ☎ 05 45 37 07 33
                Tuesdays to Fridays 9am to 6pm, Saturdays 2 to 6pm.

	La Poste, Place Francis Louvel	☎ 05 45 90 41 00

Café, Bande Dessinée,
121 rue de Bordeaux   ☎ 05 45 38 65 65
Tuesdays to Fridays 10am to 6pm, weekends 2 to 6pm.

Chalais   Techni-Services, 2 rue de Barbezieux   ☎ 05 45 95 45 90
(opposite the 'lady' fountain) Mondays and Saturdays 9am to
noon and 3 to 7.30pm, Tuesdays to Fridays 3 to 7.30pm.

Médiathèque, 37 rue Barbezieux   ☎ 05 45 98 67 00
Mondays 9am to noon, Wednesdays 9am to 6pm, Thursdays 2
to 6pm, Fridays 2 to 7pm, Saturdays 9am to 6pm. €2.50 per
hour.

Cognac   Alpha, 33 rue du Canton   ☎ 05 45 36 10 63
Mondays to Fridays 8.30am to 7pm, Saturdays 8.30 to
12.30pm. English spoken.

I@I, rue Aristide Briand   ☎ 05 45 36 60 95
Mondays to Fridays 9am to noon and 1.30 to 5pm. ADSL.

Confolens   La Poste, place Hôtel de Ville   ☎ 05 45 85 47 00
Access using a card purchased at the post office.

Ruffec   Centre Social Internet Access,
place Aristide Briand   ☎ 05 45 30 38 43
(to the left of La Poste)
Mondays to Fridays 9am to 12.30pm and 2 to 6pm, closed
Thursday mornings.

Nord Charente Informatique   ☎ 05 45 31 12 46
4 place Général de Gaulle
(at the lights at the bottom of the hill from Leclerc)
Closed Mondays.

Mobile Telephones

All France Télécom shops sell mobile phones.

Angoulême   Phone Shop/SFR, Géant, Champniers   ☎ 05 45 37 47 47
SFR, 18 place Marengo   ☎ 05 45 22 81 21
Open Mondays to Saturdays.

Chalais   Odyssée Telecom, avenue de La Gare   ☎ 05 45 78 61 46
Closed Tuesdays.

Cognac   Espace SFR, rue Aristide Briand   ☎ 05 45 35 58 88
Open Mondays to Saturdays 9.30am to 7pm.

| Ruffec | Odyssée Télécom, 8 place des Martyrs de l'Occupation | ☎ 05 45 31 12 63 |

Closed Mondays.

Domestic Services

Baby Sitting & Crèches

| Angoulême | Centre Information Jeunesse, Espace Franquin, 1ter boulevard Bethelot | ☎ 05 45 37 07 30 |

🖳 *www.info-jeunesse16.com*
Open Tuesdays to Saturdays.

Curtain Making

| General | Carol Weekes 'Les Petites Pommes', Les Hâtes, Couture | ☎ 05 45 90 88 36 |

✉ *dacawe@wanadoo.fr*
Curtains made to measure for addresses in Poitou-Charentes.

Equipment & Tool Hire

Angoulême	3 ETP, 19 rue Pierre Levée	☎ 05 45 61 03 72
Confolens	SJL, Zone du Max Felix	☎ 05 45 29 51 50
Ruffec	Loc.Ve.Mat, avenue Célestin Sieur	☎ 05 45 31 22 37

Garden Services

| Angoulême | Mag-Paysag, 15 place du Docteur Barret | ☎ 05 45 38 15 80 |

Design and maintenance, automatic watering systems and garden stonework.

| Melle | Garden Maintenance Services, Champs-Viron, La Couarde | ☎ 05 49 06 03 53 |

🖳 *www.silkwarner.com/garden*
British-run company offering grass cutting, garden clearance and maintenance within a 60km (37mi) radius of Melle.

Launderettes

| Angoulême | Lavomatique, 19 rue Monlogis |

Open every day from 7am to 9pm.

| Cognac | Lavomatic, Parc du Fief du Roy, Châteaubernard |

Open every day from 7am to 9pm.

| Ruffec | Laverie Automatique, place Aristide Briand |

Open every day from 7am to 9pm.

Septic Tank Services

Aigre   Dutartre, Marcillac-Lanville   ☎ 05 45 21 57 43
                         (south of the town)
                         Emptying of tanks and blockage clearance.

Angoulême   Assaini-France, ZI Ma Campagne,
                         Les Chaumes de Crage   ☎ 05 45 67 95 10

Châteauneuf   Sanitra Fourrier, 23 rue Général
-sur-Charente   de Gaulle   ☎ 05 45 66 26 70
                         Other units at Angoulême and Cognac.

Entertainment

This section is not intended to be a definitive guide but gives a wide range
of ideas for the department. Prices and opening hours were correct at the
time of publication, but it's best to check before travelling long distances.

Cinemas

Angoulême   Cinéma CGR, 30 rue St Roch   ☎ 05 45 38 03 62
                         🖳 *www.cgrcinemas.com*
                         11 screens – four accessible to disabled people.

Chalais   Le Théâtre, rue de la Courtillère   ☎ 05 45 98 10 61

Cognac   Cinéma CGR Pathé, 57 avenue
                         Victor Hugo   ☎ 05 45 36 22 11
                         Seven screens.

Confolens   Cinéma Le Capitole, 3 place Emile Roux ☎ 05 45 84 00 47

Ruffec   Cinéma Family, 5 rue Plaisance   ☎ 05 45 31 18 96
                         Shows English-language films once a month.

English Books

Verteuil-sur-   The Book Stop, 1 rue des Halles   ☎ 05 45 89 03 65
Charente   (just south of Ruffec in northern Charente)
                         For buying, exchanging and selling English-language books.
                         Tuesdays 3 to 8pm, Wednesdays to Saturdays 11am to 4pm.

English-language books can be borrowed from the following libraries.
Note that Ruffec library will return to 1 rue Raoul Hediart when major
building work is complete, in 2005/06.

	Mon	Tue	Wed	Thu	Fri	Sat
Angoulême rue Jean Jaurès ☎ 05 45 95 31 32	closed	9.30–12.30 1.30–6.00	9.30–6.00	1.30–6.00	9.30–12.30 1.30–6.00	9.30–12.00 1.30–5.00
Chalais 37 rue Barbezieux ☎ 05 45 98 67 00	9.00–12.00	closed	9.00–6.00	2.00–6.00	2.00–7.00	9.00–6.00
Cognac 10 rue Minage ☎ 05 45 36 19 50	closed	1.30–6.00	10.00–6.00	closed	1.30–6.00	10.00–12.30 1.30–5.00
Ruffec Place du Jumelage ☎ 05 45 31 32 82	closed	closed	10.00–12.00 2.00–6.00	10.00–12.00 2.00–6.00	2.00–6.00	10.00–12.00 2.00–6.00

Festivals

January — Angoulême
Festival International de la Bande Dessinée ☎ 05 45 97 86 50
🖳 *www.bdangouleme.com*
An international festival dedicated to cartoons, with exhibits by world famous cartoonists and the chance to participate in workshops.

May (Ascension weekend) — Aubeterre
Faites de l'Art
The streets of Aubeterre are full of painters and artists.

April (around second week) — Cognac
International crime film festival ☎ 05 45 35 60 00

July (four days) — Cognac
Music Festival ☎ 05 45 36 11 81
🖳 *www.bluespassions.com.*
Swing, gospel, soul, funk, rhythm and blues. Over 250 musicians playing some 80 concerts in the heart of the town.

Roumazières-Loubert
Lumières de l'Histoire au Château
de Peyras ☎ 05 45 71 25 25
A sound and light show at the 6th–8th century château. Medieval meals are available.

July/August (four days) — Mainfonds & Aubeville
Coupe d'Europe de Montgolfières ☎ 05 45 64 02 87
These two villages are the take-off point for over 60 hot air balloons from all over the world.

August (one week)	Confolens Festival de Confolens 🖳 *www.festivaldeconfolens.com* Five hundred artists from five continents all meet for this celebration of tolerance, openness and friendship.	☎ 05 45 84 00 77

August (around 15th)	Chalais International show jumping competition at the foot of the château.	

September (third weekend)	Angoulême Circuit des Remparts Vintage car rally, including a race around the ramparts.	☎ 05 45 94 95 67

November	Angoulême Festival of Games 🖳 *www.ludo-angouleme.com* A huge show, with a hall for younger children and their activities and a second full of professional remote control cars, the latest game consoles, and all things electronic. Entrance fee around €5.	☎ 05 45 94 75 61

November (three days)	Angoulême Gastronomades – Food in the Media This three-day festival is dedicated to food and wine, with produce and publications from all over the world.	☎ 05 45 95 16 84

Theatres

Angoulême	Théâtre d'Angoulême, avenue Maréchaux 🖳 *www.theatre-angouleme.org* (in the centre of the town) Plenty of parking in the surrounding roads.	☎ 05 45 38 61 61

Cognac	Théâtre Atypique, place Robert Schumann Large theatre with many different shows, including classical concerts, musicals and opera.	☎ 05 45 82 32 78

Rouillac	La Palène, boulevard Encamp 🖳 *www.lapalene.unireseau.com* (north-west of Angoulême)	☎ 05 45 96 80 38

Video & DVD Hire

Angoulême	Point Video, 171 rue de Périgueux Rentals also available 24 hours a day via external dispenser.	☎ 05 45 95 29 91

Chalais   There's a 24-hour video dispenser beside Intermarché.

Cognac   Gammes Video, 31 boulevard
                 Denfert Rochereau   ☎ 05 45 83 97 61
                 Mondays to Saturdays 11am to 8pm. There's a 24-hour
                 dispenser for DVDs and videos.

Confolens   ALFA Vidéo, 5 rue Ferrandie   ☎ 05 45 84 20 51
                 Mondays to Saturdays 3 to 8pm and Saturday mornings 9am
                 to 12.15pm.

Ruffec   New Vidéo, 51 rue de la République   ☎ 05 45 30 37 34
                 Mondays 3.30 to 8pm, Tuesdays to Saturdays 10am to
                 12.30pm and 3 to 8pm.
                 DVD players for hire. There's a 24-hour dispenser outside.

Leisure Activities

This section isn't intended to be a definitive guide but gives a wide range
of ideas for the department. Prices and opening hours were correct at the
time of publication, but it's best to check before travelling long distances.

Art Classes

Angoulême   MJC Louis Aragon, place Victoria   ☎ 05 45 61 29 56
                 A variety of classes for adults and children all week.

Cognac   Centre d'Animation, 9a place de
                 Cagouillet   ☎ 05 45 32 17 28
                 Painting, drawing and collage for six to ten-year-olds;
                 watercolours, pastels and oil painting for adults.

Ruffec   Ecole d'Arts Plastiques   ☎ 05 45 31 24 48
                 Contact Mr Delage for details of current courses.

Ballooning

Angoulême   10 impasse Paul Bert, Gond-Pontouvre ☎ 05 45 69 14 74
                 ✉ *messolo.alain@ wanadoo.fr*
                 All year, subject to weather.

Bike Hire

Angoulême   Jamain Frères, 137 rue de Basseau   ☎ 05 45 25 44 44
                 Closed Saturday afternoons and Monday mornings.
                 Bikes from €15.25 per day and €60 per week.

Boat & Train Rides

Angoulême   River Cruises   ☎ 05 45 95 16 84
Cruises with or without dining, always with heating and drinks
available. The vessel, 'l'Angoumois', travels up the Charente as
far as Trois Palis and you can have the opportunity to discover
the paper mill and the chocolate factory. Information and
bookings at the tourist office in Angoulême.

Cognac   Barge Cruise   ☎ 05 45 82 10 71
A cruise up the river Charente from the Salle-Verte quay
aboard a replica of a traditional timber barge that used to carry
barrels of cognac and wine down the river. The cruise lasts
around 95 minutes.

Le Petit Train De Cognac,
place François I   ☎ 02 40 62 06 22
A tourist train running through the town every day, mid-May to
the end of September.

Jarnac   River Cruise (embark under the bridge) ☎ 05 45 82 09 35
An 80-minute trip aboard the 'Chabot', July and August 11am,
3pm, 4.30pm and 6pm. Times on request out of season or see
the board by the bridge.

Boat Hire

General   Charentes Croisières, 4 rue Haute
de l'Écluse, Fléac   ☎ 05 45 91 38 18
💻 www.charente-croisieres.com
Rent a houseboat for up to 12 people.

Angoulême   Charente Croisières, impasse de
l'Ecluse, Fléac   ☎ 05 45 91 38 18
💻 www.charente-croisieres.com
(west of the town)
Boat hire one way or return to Saintes, weekend, mid-week or
full week.

Randonnée Fluviale, 9 impasse des
Boilevins, Fléac   ☎ 06 87 55 20 49
(west of the town)
Boat hire for 90 minutes or a whole week. Open every day in
July and August, weekends and bank holidays April to June,
September and October, by appointment at other times of year.

Cognac   Locaboat Plaisance   ☎ 05 45 36 63 66
(on the quai opposite Hennessy)

Bridge

Angoulême   84 rue Montauzier   ☎ 05 45 91 30 71
Sessions from Mondays to Wednesdays 2.30 to 6.30pm and
on Mondays 8.30pm to 00.30am. Groups on Fridays 2 to 5pm,
lessons for beginners on Mondays 8.30pm.

Chalais   Ancienne Mairie de St Christophe   ☎ 05 45 98 12 17
Tuesday and Friday afternoons and Wednesday evenings.

Cognac   Bridge Club de Cognac, 72 rue de Pons ☎ 05 45 82 00 58

Confolens   Club de Bridge de Confolens   ☎ 05 45 85 35 60
Meetings at Ancien Collège Emile Roux.
Tournaments Tuesdays and Fridays at 8pm; beginners
welcome!

Ruffec   Club de Bridge   ☎ 05 49 87 02 30
Meetings at the Espace F. Mitterand (behind Le Syndicat
d'Initiative) in Civray, 15 minutes north-east of Ruffec.
Fridays from 8.15pm and Wednesdays from 2pm, September
to June inclusive. Regular tournaments.

Children's Activity Clubs

Angoulême   Baby Gym, MJC Louis Aragon,
place Victoria   ☎ 05 45 61 29 56
Wednesdays: three to four-year-olds at 4.15pm, five to six-
year-olds at 3.30pm.

Confolens   Centre Social Culturel, Château d'Assit,
2 rue St Michel   ☎ 05 45 84 00 43
This centre runs a crèche and organises leisure activities for
children from 3 to 14 on Wednesdays during term and every
day during school holidays. It also co-ordinates a wide variety
of local courses and sports in the town, from yoga to French
classes. Mondays to Fridays 9am to noon and 2 to 6.30pm.

Ruffec   Halte-Garderie Municipal,
Square André Brothier   ☎ 05 45 31 21 62
Tuesdays to Thursdays 8.30am to 6pm, Fridays 8.30am to
5pm.

Centre Social et Culturel, place
Aristide Briand   ☎ 05 45 30 38 43
Held at Ecole Méningaud.
Child care and leisure activities for children from 4 to 12.
Wednesdays during term and every day during school holidays
7.30am to 7pm. From €5.50 to €15.50 per day depending on
the activities.

Parent and Toddler Group   ☎ 05 45 30 00 63
Contact Alison Beavan for more information.

Circus Skills

Angoulême   MJC Louis Aragon, place Victoria   ☎ 05 45 61 29 56
Circus skills taught to all from five-year-olds upwards.
Wednesdays and Saturdays.

Crazy Golf

Cognac   Parc François I
(in the north of the town centre bordering the river Charente)

Dancing

Angoulême   Foyer des Jeunes, avenue du Général
de Gaulle, Gond-Pontouvre   ☎ 05 45 68 18 78
Folk dancing on Wednesday evenings.

Modern Jazz, place Victoria   ☎ 05 45 61 29 56
A wide range of classes from introduction for four-year-olds to
advanced adult classes.

Chalais   ☎ 05 45 98 72 53
Folk dancing for adults Wednesday evenings.

Cognac   Centre d'Animation, 9a place Cagouillet   ☎ 05 45 82 17 28
Classical dance, ballet and modern jazz.

Confolens   Salle du Moulin   ☎ 05 45 84 17 11
Every Wednesday evening there's a variety of classical dance
classes, including beginners'.

Ruffec   Centre Social et Culturel, place
Aristide Briand   ☎ 05 45 30 38 43
Oriental dance classes every Friday morning 10am to noon.
First session free.

Drama

Angoulême   La Grand Font, place Henri Chamarre   ☎ 05 45 93 22 22
Tuesday evenings.

Chalais   ☎ 05 45 98 27 92
Contact P. Boisseau for current information.

Cognac   Centre d'Animation, 9a place de
Cagouillet   ☎ 05 45 32 17 28
Courses for children and adults with an end-of-year show.

French & English Conversation

Cognac   Club Franco-Anglais de Conversation,
                51 rue d' Angoulême   ☎ 05 45 82 35 30
                This group welcomes French and English-speakers for
                conversation and cultural exchange in both languages.
                Meetings on first and third Tuesdays of the month 6.30 to 8pm.

Flying

Angoulême   Aéroclub Angoulême, Brie-Champniers   ☎ 05 45 69 88 22
                💻 *www.perso.wanadoo.fr/aeroclub-angouleme*
                Trial flights, lessons and flying school.

Cognac   Ailes Cognaçais, Aéro Club   ☎ 05 45 82 13 51
                Flying school, training, sightseeing flights and competitions.

Villefagnan   Ouest Hélicoptère, La Serpaudrie   ☎ 05 45 30 09 10

Gyms & Health Clubs

Angoulême   Club Top-Forme, 22 rue Guy Ragnaud   ☎ 05 45 92 18 74
                Fitness and cardio training.

Cognac   Espace Pleine Forme, 9 rue St Pierre   ☎ 05 45 82 33 67
                Fitness gym, massage, sauna and beauty centre.

Karting & Quad Bikes

Angoulême   Formula Kart Speedway, Champniers   ☎ 05 45 37 44 00
                Introductions and driving school. Open July and August from 2
                to 7pm.

Cognac   Passion Kart Indoor, Nercillac   ☎ 05 45 83 22 60
                (just east of Cognac)

La Rochefoucauld Société M.G.Kart, Chez Glaude   ☎ 05 45 63 55 57
                (just east of La Rochefoucauld)
                A large circuit.

Lakes & Beaches

Aubeterre-sur- Centre de Loisirs
Dronne   There's a beach down by the camp site, with a playground,
                volleyball pitch, trees for shade and a lifeguard in the summer.
                Dogs are allowed, but not on the beach or in the water.

Chabanais   Lac de Lavaud (south of the town)   ☎ 05 45 65 26 69
                A large lake with two centres:
                Site de 'La Guerlie', Pressignac   ☎ 05 45 89 35 97

This beach is on the north shore with a life guard in attendance in July and August. In season there are also pedalos, waterskiing for children, mini-golf and horse riding. There's also a bar/restaurant on this side of the lake.

Centre Nautique 'Terres de Charente', Verneuil   ☎ 05 45 65 30 62
On the south shore of the lake this watersports centre offers sailing, windsurfing, canoeing/kayaking, rowing and bike hire.

Ruffec   Aire de Réjallant, Condac
A park area based around a series of islands and bridges over the branching Charente. Playing in the river is possible among the islands, there is a small games area and sandy beach. There are picnic tables, an outdoor ping pong table, ice creams and a restaurant.

St Yrieix   Lac St Yrieix – Plan d'Eau de La Grande Prairie   ☎ 05 45 37 40 61
(signposted from the N10 on the west side of Angoulême)
A vast lake with a large sandy beach, spacious play area for children, café/bar with ice creams and drinks, small karting circuit, crazy golf, a large area that is popular with kite flyers and a path around the whole area suitable for both walking and cycling. There's also a sailing centre with windsurfing, canoeing and sailing.

Music

Angoulême   CSCS – MJC Sillac, 40 rue Pierre Aumaître   ☎ 05 45 91 76 11
Jazz group for over 16s, Thursday evenings.

CSCS Rives de Charente, 5 quai du Halage   ☎ 05 45 94 81 03
Introduction to music for four to six-year-olds.

Cognac   Centre d'Animation, 9a place Cagouillet   ☎ 05 45 32 17 28
Musical workshops and singing courses.

Big Band.   ☎ 06 80 24 86 22
Amateur jazz orchestra.

Ruffec   l'Atelier du Musicien, le Bourg, Benest   ☎ 05 45 31 80 23
Although based in Benest (between Ruffec and Confolens), musical workshops are held at a variety of locations including Ruffec. Classes given include piano, clarinet, flute and violin.

Centre Social et Culturel, place Aristide Briand   ☎ 05 45 30 38 43
Electronic music workshops on Wednesday afternoons.

	Music Ruffec, rue de La République	☎ 05 45 31 03 78

Children's and adult lessons available.

Photography

Angoulême   14 rue Marcel Paul   ☎ 05 45 95 17 89
Wednesday evenings 7 to 9pm.

Pottery

Angoulême   CSCS Rives de Charente, 5 quai du Halage ☎ 05 45 94 81 03
Adult courses Tuesday and Thursday afternoons.

Rollerskating & Skate Boarding

Angoulême   CSCS – CAJ, La Grand Font,
place Henri Chamarre   ☎ 05 45 93 22 22
11 to 16-year-olds Saturdays 10am to noon.

Le Fox Roller Club, 3 impasse Tati   ☎ 05 45 95 53 97

Roller Hockey, Les Patineurs
d'Angoulême   ☎ 05 45 61 41 83

Terrain de rink hockey, boulevard
Jean Moulin   ☎ 05 45 61 55 40
There's a free skate park in the centre of the town, at the side
of the station between the Gare de Marchandises and the
boulevard du 8 Mai 1945.

Brie   Large, free skate park opposite the *déchetterie*, which is
clearly signposted from the main roads.

Scouts & Guides

Cognac   Contact Olivier Marzio   ☎ 05 45 83 14 32
For 8 to 19-year-olds.

Social Clubs & Organisations

Rotary Clubs

Angoulême   Rotary Club Angoulême Val de Charente, 86 avenue du
Général de Gaulle, Soyaux   🖥 *www.france-adot.org*

Cognac   Restaurant Domaine du Breuil,
104 rue Robert Daugas   ☎ 05 45 35 32 06

Town Twinning

Cognac   Comité de Jumelage de Cognac,

	59 rue Aristide Briand	☎ 05 45 35 29 22

Twinned with Perth in Scotland.

Confolens	Comité de Jumelages, la Mairie, l'Hôtel de Ville	☎ 05 45 84 00 15

Twinned with Pitlochry in Scotland.

Stamp Collecting

Confolens	Société de Philatelie et de Cartophilie de Confolens	☎ 05 45 85 33 44

Meetings every Sunday 10am to noon.

Cognac	Cercle Philatélique de Cognac, Parking Jules Ferry	☎ 05 45 32 14 15

Tea Dancing

Ruffec	La Cigale	☎ 06 70 20 40 52

(off the N10 at the junction marked to Salles de Villefagnan, D27; aim towards the vivid green and white storage tanks and carry on towards Chenon and it's on the right)
There are tea dances here every Sunday from 3 to 8pm and evening specials with an orchestra.

Tree Climbing

Tusson	Association L'Araignée	☎ 06 81 15 65 20

Ruffec	Association L'Araignée, Mairie de Les Adjots	☎ 05 45 29 59 89

Explore the canopy of the forests using 'monkey bridges', aerial runways, rope ladders and more. Safety equipment provided!

Vintage Cars

Angoulême	Club de Vieilles Roues Charentaises	☎ 05 45 68 28 30

Outings, shows and competitions.

Cognac	Retromobile Club Cognaçais, 53 rue d'Angoulême	☎ 05 46 94 01 21

For the passionate and aspiring owners of vintage cars. Various outings, rallies and exhibitions and advice on restoration.

Walking & Rambling

General	22 boulevard de Bury, Angoulême	☎ 05 45 38 94 48

An information centre that provides details of walking routes in Charente. Tourist offices have local guide books and data sheets for walkers.

| Angoulême | Randonneurs de La Charente | ☎ 05 45 61 30 59 |

| Chalais | | ☎ 05 45 98 18 77 |

Organised walks every Wednesday and Sunday.

| Cognac | Les Randonneurs du Cognaçais | ☎ 06 23 25 12 15 |

Long walks every Sunday with shorter walks on alternate
Monday and Saturday afternoons.

| Confolens | Oxygène | ☎ 05 45 84 24 27 |

Departing from outside the *mairie* on Wednesdays and Fridays
at 7.15pm for walks of about an hour. Sunday at 9am for longer
walks and Thursdays at 7.30pm for newcomers.

Yoga

| Angoulême | Amicale Laïque d'Angoulême, 14 rue Marcel Paul | ☎ 05 45 95 17 89 |

Monday and Wednesday evenings. Adults only.

| Ruffec | Salle de Danse, place Aristide Briand | ☎ 05 45 91 59 54 |

(under the Salle Culturel)
Wednesdays at 8.15pm.

Medical Facilities & Services

Ambulances

In the event of a medical emergency dial 15.

Angoulême	☎ 05 45 92 46 35
Chalais	☎ 05 45 98 28 11
Cognac	☎ 05 45 32 19 30
Confolens	☎ 05 45 84 02 72
Ruffec	☎ 05 45 31 07 94

Doctors

English-speakers may like to contact the following doctors.

| Angoulême | Dr Travaillé, 27 rue Trois Fours | ☎ 05 45 95 04 88 |

| Chalais | Groupe Médical, 8 rue Champ de Foire, Montmoreau | ☎ 05 45 24 06 06 |

(just north of Chalais)

| Cognac | Dr Provost, 137 rue Haute de Croulin | ☎ 05 45 82 37 70 |

| Confolens | Dr Guillebaud, 2 route Villevert | ☎ 05 45 84 20 53 |
| Ruffec | Dr Stavros Sokolakis, 9 rue de le République | ☎ 05 45 31 05 08 |

Dentists

English-speakers might like to contact the following dentists.

Angoulême	Dr Plazer, 3 place Victor Hugo	☎ 05 45 95 95 78
Chalais	Dr Blanca, 10 avenue de l'Aquitaine, Montmoreau (just north of Chalais)	☎ 05 45 60 33 68
Cognac	Dr Pedeutour, 2 rue Planat	☎ 05 45 82 60 77
Confolens	Cabinet Dentaire Mutualiste, rue Croix Saint Georges	☎ 05 45 85 47 20
Ruffec	Dr Lambert, 29 place Martyrs de l'Occupation	☎ 05 45 31 27 80

Emergency Services

Fire Brigade

Dial 18.

Gendarmerie Nationale

Some of the smaller *gendarmeries* are being merged with others and may be open limited hours, but the local number will always put you through to the station that is on duty.

Angoulême	boulevard Artillerie	☎ 05 45 37 50 00
Chalais	43 rue Barbezieux	☎ 05 45 98 10 09
Cognac	57 rue Bellefonds	☎ 05 45 82 01 86
Confolens	9 rue Juillet	☎ 05 45 84 04 55
Ruffec	15 boulevard Général Pinoteau	☎ 05 45 31 00 46

Health Authority

Local offices of the Caisse Régional Assurance Maladie Centre Ouest (CRAMCO) are listed below.

Angoulême	30 boulevard Bury (main office)	☎ 05 45 95 76 13
Cognac	48 rue Marc Marchadier	☎ 05 45 83 88 90
Confolens	La Mairie, place Hôtel de Ville Tuesdays and Wednesdays 9.30am to 12.15pm	
Ruffec	La Mairie, place des Martyrs Tuesdays 9am to 12.30pm and 1.45 to 3.15pm, Wednesdays 9am to 12.30pm.	

Hospitals

All the hospitals below have an emergency department.

Angoulême	Hospitalier Camille Claudel, St Michel (south of the city off the N10 – a large pink building)	☎ 05 45 67 59 59
Cognac	Standard Hôpital, rue Montesquieu	☎ 05 45 36 75 75
Confolens	Hôpital Labajouderie, rue Hôpital	☎ 05 45 84 40 00
Ruffec	15 rue Hôpital (near the swimming pool)	☎ 05 45 29 50 00

Motoring

Breakers' Yards

Brie	Aadra, RN141, Les Rassats (just north of Angoulême)	☎ 05 45 65 90 02
Confolens	Confolens Pièces Auto, 23 avenue St Germain	☎ 05 45 29 68 12
	Maine de Boixe Casse Auto 16, RN10 (off the RN10 between Ruffec and Angoulême)	☎ 05 45 20 73 13
Ruffec	Deal Christian, Les Gallais	☎ 08 00 80 11 68

Car Dealers

| Angoulême | Audi/VW, Olympe Autos, ZA Les
Montagnes, Champniers | ☎ 05 45 69 44 44 |
| | Alfa Romeo, Les Montagnes,
Champniers | ☎ 05 45 69 18 20 |

BMW, Laujac Automobiles,
51 rue Saint-Antoine   ☎ 05 45 69 38 88

Chrysler/Jeep, Patrick Launay,
Les Montagnes, Champniers   ☎ 05 45 25 51 00

Citroën, DAC, ZA Les Montagnes,
Champniers   ☎ 05 45 69 44 00

Fiat, Goutard SA, 69 bd Besson Bey   ☎ 05 45 95 59 81

Ford, GPS Automobiles, Les
Montagnes, Champniers   ☎ 05 45 22 22 77

Honda, 93 route Paris, Gond Pontouvre ☎ 05 45 68 70 55

Land Rover, Vogue Automobiles,
Les Montagnes, Champniers   ☎ 05 45 69 05 03

Mazda, route Paris, Gond Pontouvre   ☎ 05 45 68 37 52

Mercedes, Patrick Launay, Les
Montagnes, Champniers   ☎ 05 45 95 69 10

Nissan, Delage, Les Montagnes,
Champniers   ☎ 05 45 94 94 94

Peugeot, SCAA, Les Montagnes,
Champniers   ☎ 05 45 90 05 05

Renault, Garage Benoit Menard,
352 rue de Périgueux   ☎ 05 45 95 19 60

Rover, Vogue Automobiles, Les
Montagnes, Champniers   ☎ 05 45 69 05 03

Seat, 93 route Paris, Gond Pontouvre   ☎ 05 45 68 70 55

Suzuki, Isle Espagnac, 217 ave
République, Isle d'Espagnac   ☎ 05 45 69 09 69

Toyota, Espace Auto Charentais,
Les Montagnes, Champniers   ☎ 05 45 91 89 12

Vauxahll/Opel, Morgan's, 105 route
de Paris, Gond Pontouvre   ☎ 05 45 68 74 33

Chalais	Citroën, Chalais Auto, 3 route Bordeaux	☎ 05 45 98 16 75
	Fiat, Rabouté Serge, 71 route Bordeaux	☎ 05 45 98 24 42
	Ford, Garage Fortier, route Angoulême	☎ 05 45 98 10 71
	Lancia/Alfa Romeo, Rabouté Serge, 71 route Bordeaux	☎ 05 45 98 24 42
	Peugeot, Gadrat Blancheton, 61 route Barbezieux Also deals in Renault vehicles.	☎ 05 45 98 21 16
	Volkswagen, Garage Cornuault, Le Bourg, Montboyer	☎ 05 45 98 29 21
Cognac	Audi, Arcelin, ZI Merpins	☎ 05 45 82 44 33
	BMW/Mini, Albert Grammatico, rte Angoulême, Châteaubernard	☎ 05 45 32 50 93
	Citroën, Arnaud Meire, 75 avenue d'Angoulême	☎ 05 45 36 64 64
	Fiat/Alfa Romeo, J.F. Goutard, 32 avenue d'Angoulême, Châteaubernard	☎ 05 45 32 71 60
	Ford, Cellier Automobiles, rue Louis Blériot, Châteaubernard	☎ 05 45 82 00 88
	Hyundai, Fort, ZA Le Fief du Roy, Châteaubernard	☎ 05 45 35 01 80
	Land Rover, Fort, ZA Le Fief du Roy, Châteaubernard	☎ 05 45 35 01 80
	Mazda, Garage Deliry Alain, 185 rue de Crouin	☎ 05 45 82 42 95
	Mercedes, P. Launay, 21 avenue d'Angoulême, Châteaubernard	☎ 05 45 32 71 05
	Mitsubishi, Autos Saint Jacques, ZA boulevard de Javrezac	☎ 05 45 82 42 44

	Nissan, Garage Boiteau, avenue Montignac, Merpins	☎ 05 45 82 04 35
	Peugeot, Peugeot Cognac, 15 rue Anisserie, Châteaubernard	☎ 05 45 36 15 15
	Renault, GAMC, 242 ave Victor Hugo	☎ 05 45 35 86 86
	Saab, Erton's, 65 boulevard Emile Zola	☎ 05 45 82 54 46
	Seat, Docyan, 2 rue Artisanat	☎ 05 45 36 65 50
	Suzuki, Autos. St Jacques, ZA boulevard de Javrezac	☎ 05 45 82 42 44
	Toyota, Toys Motors, ZA, 3 rue Haute Sarrazine	☎ 05 45 35 06 06
	Vauxhall/Opel, Erton's, 65 boulevard Emile Zola	☎ 05 45 82 19 12
Confolens	Audi/Volkswagen, Centr'Auto Confolentais, route d'Angoulême, Ansac	☎ 05 45 84 02 08
	Citroën, Garage Roger Soulat, 12 avenue Général de Gaulle	☎ 05 45 84 00 27
	Peugeot, Espace Automobiles, ZE Croix St Georges	☎ 05 45 84 10 86
	Renault, Renault Confolens, 3 route de Limoges	☎ 05 45 84 07 00
Ruffec	Citroën, Vienne Sud Automobiles, 17 route d'Aigre	☎ 05 45 31 42 04
	Ford, Garage Musset, 56 avenue Célestin Sieur	☎ 05 45 31 06 31
	Peugeot, Pol Loussert, route de Bordeaux	☎ 05 45 30 35 30
	Renault, SARL Francois Caillaud, RN10 Villegats (RN10)	☎ 05 45 30 36 55
	Volkswagen, Garage Buisson, 39 avenue Célestin Sieur	☎ 05 45 31 01 39

Car Repairs & Service

Charroux   Cole et Fils, 1 rue St Antoine   ☎ 05 49 87 72 40
              British mechanic for service and repair of cars, car conversions
              from British to French, breakdown and recovery and 'man with
              a van' service.

Driving Lessons

Chef-Boutonne   Auto Ecole 'Virage', 57 Grand'
                Rue du Commerce   ☎ 05 49 07 66 69
                This driving school (which is just over the border, near Melle in
                Deux-Sèvres) gives refresher courses to foreigners and
                lessons to help adapt to driving on the right. They have both
                male and female driving instructors who speak English.

Tyre & Exhaust Centres

Angoulême   McPneus Chouteau, 91 route de Paris,
              Gond Pontouvre   ☎ 05 45 38 36 64

Chalais   Sauvaret Chalais Pneus, route de
              Bordeaux   ☎ 05 45 98 06 15

Cognac   Vulco, ZI Fief du Roy, Châteaubernard   ☎ 05 45 35 08 96
              (on the retail park east of Cognac)

Confolens   Arc en Ciel, rue Ouillette, ZI
              Croix St Georges   ☎ 05 45 84 07 36
              (on the industrial estate behind Weldom)

Ruffec   Vulco, 3 route Bordeaux   ☎ 05 45 30 05 88
              (on the south of the town towards the N10 southbound)

Pets

Dog Training

Cognac   Les Cani'Kazes de Cognac,
              45 rue Boussion   ☎ 05 45 82 24 36
              Dog training and agility training.

Mansle   Le Petit Page, Maine de Boixe   ☎ 05 45 20 35 83
              (tucked away to the right hand side of the south-bound Bison
              Futé rest area on the N10, just south of the town)

Soyaux   Centre Canin   ☎ 05 45 38 18 77
              (on the left as you leave Soyaux from Angoulême, just after the
              Crédit Agricole head office building)
              Caters for overweight dogs as well as dogs with physiological

problems and guard dogs. Obedience training and other courses are normally at the site but can be done at your home.

Farriers

General   Rémy Bacon, La Bourlie, Bouëx   ☎ 05 45 29 41 62

Jean-Christophe Danton, Gallée, Mosnac   ☎ 05 45 62 15 20

Horse Dentists

General   Christophe Gaillard   ☎ 06 11 63 37 61
Based just south of Poitiers, covering Vienne, Deux-Sèvres and travelling south as far as the northern Charente and Charente-Maritime.

Guy Chatignol   ☎ 05 59 65 14 96
Covers Charente, Charente-Maritime and Deux-Sèvres south.

Kennels & Catteries

The facilities listed below accept cats and dogs unless otherwise stated.

Angoulême   Animals' Cottage, Trellis, Jauldes   ☎ 05 45 69 74 25
(north-east of the town)

Chenil Logis de Champagnoux,
RD5 Mouthiers, route Blanzac, Pérignac   ☎ 05 45 64 14 50
(south of the town)

Mansle   Le Petit Page, Maine de Boixe   ☎ 05 45 20 35 83
(tucked away to the right hand side of the south-bound Bison Futé rest area on the N10, just south of the town)
Dogs only.

Pet Parlours

Angoulême   Toutou Chic, 29 avenue du Président
Wilson, Ruelle   ☎ 05 45 65 48 01
(south of the town)
Open Tuesdays to Saturdays by appointment.

Cognac   Cani Services, 132 avenue Victor Hugo   ☎ 05 45 35 34 06
(on the main road in from the south-east)

Confolens   Canimousse, 4 rue St Michel   ☎ 05 45 84 00 57

Ruffec   Le Cabotin, 16 rue République   ☎ 05 45 30 04 68
Open Tuesdays to Saturdays by appointment.

Riding Equipment

Angoulême   Galop – 16, route Paris, Champniers   ☎ 05 45 37 48 81
                 (on the N10 on the northern outskirts of the town)

Segonzac   Horse Wood, 2 rue Grande Champagne ☎ 05 45 83 48 59
                 💻 *www.horsewood.com*

SPA

Angoulême   Les Mesniers, Mornac   ☎ 05 45 65 76 99
                 (just east of the town)
                 Open from 3 to 6.30pm. Closed Wednesdays and Sundays.

Veterinary Clinics

Angoulême   Clinique Vétérinaire, 10bis boulevard
                 Winston Churchill   ☎ 05 45 95 54 20
                 This surgery has a vet who speaks English.

Chalais   Dr Linthout, route Barbezieux   ☎ 05 45 98 04 38

Cognac   Caillard et de Lamarre, 152 avenue
                 Victor Hugo   ☎ 05 45 35 27 90
                 (parking through the archway)

Confolens   Dr Festal, 9 boulevard Méaudre d'Assit ☎ 05 45 85 58 58

                 Dr Pipet, place du Docteur Defaut ☎ 05 45 85 30 88

Ruffec   Dr Régeon & Dr Hans, ZI de Ruffecois ☎ 05 45 31 31 33
                 (in a triangle of road between 3M builders' merchants and
                 Leclerc supermarket going out of the town towards La Faye).
                 These two vets work alternate weeks and, if you call the
                 number of the surgery that isn't open, your call will
                 automatically be diverted to the other.

Saintes   Dr Bétizaud, 5 avenue Saintonge   ☎ 05 46 92 08 81
                 Specialist horse vet.

Places To Visit

This section isn't intended to be a definitive guide to places to visit in
Charente but gives a wide range of ideas for the department. Prices and
opening hours were correct at the time of publication, but it's best to check
before travelling long distances.

Châteaux

Chalais	Château de Chalais, place de l'Hôtel de Ville	☎ 05 45 98 31 00

🖳 *www.chalais.free.fr*
With a Romanesque church and a 13th century cloister (restored in the 17th century), this château is the ancestral seat of the Talleyrand Périgord family. Open Wednesdays to Sundays 10am to 6pm from early June to the end of September.

La Rochefoucauld	Château La Rochefoucauld	☎ 05 45 62 07 42

A beautiful 'Loire' château but much closer, 15 minutes north-east of Angoulême. It has great history and there are talks given in both French and English that detail the history of the château. There are caves to explore and some beautiful rooms that you can wander around at your leisure. Open daily 10am to 7pm from Easter to October. From November to Easter it's open only on Sundays and public holidays with a tour starting at 2pm.

Villebois-Lavalette	Château de Villebois-Lavalette	☎ 05 45 64 71 58

This château has many features, including the original mediaeval fortress built in the eighth century. Open to the public in the summer.

Churches & Monuments

Aubeterre   Eglise Souterraine St Jean
This underground church is carved entirely out of a rock, the nave reaching 20m in height. Open every day of the year from 9.30am to noon and 2 to 6pm.

Doumérac	Monastère Orthodoxe de l'Icône de la Mère de Dieu de Korssoun	☎ 05 45 23 05 07

(near Grassac)
A distinctive building in a rural setting which is part of the Diocèse du Partiarcat of Moscow for France, Italy and Switzerland. Visits are possible Tuesdays to Sundays between 2 and 6pm. Ring the bell and then enter through the small door to the right of the building.

Nanteuil-en-Vallée	Abbaye de Nanteuil-en-Vallée	☎ 05 45 31 95 46

(just east of Ruffec)
Founded in 780, this historic monument is private but offers guided tours from 14th July to 31st August from 2.30 to 6.30pm. Tasting of a local spirit is available.

Museums & Galleries

Angoulême	ACAPA Artothèque 134 rue de Bordeaux,	☎ 05 45 92 34 10

Art gallery. Open all year from Tuesdays to Saturdays 2 to 6pm. Free entry.

Centre National de la Bande Dessinée
et de l'Image, 121 rue de Bordeaux ☎ 05 45 38 65 65
🖥 *www.cnbdi.fr*
This museum/gallery is the only one of its kind in France. It houses around 6,000 original drawings, tracing the history of the French cartoon from 1830 to the present day and includes work by comic artists from all over the world. Every year several exhibitions are mounted, the summer exhibitions designed to be of special interest to young visitors. July and August Mondays to Fridays 10am to 7pm, weekends 2 to 7pm (14th and 15th July only 2 to 7pm); rest of the year Tuesdays to Fridays 10am to 6pm, weekends and bank holidays 2 to 6pm (closed 1st January, 1st May and 25th December). Adults €5, children over six €2.50.

Fonds Régional d'Art Contemporain, Hôtel
Saint Simon, 15 rue de la Cloche-Verte ☎ 05 45 92 87 01
Temporary displays of modern art and a library of contemporary art. Open Tuesdays to Saturdays 10.30am to noon and 2 to 7pm. Free entry.

Musée de la Résistance et de La
Déportation, 34 rue de Genève ☎ 05 45 38 76 87
🖥 *www.museedelaresistance16.fr.fm*
(in the old quarter of Angoulême beside the Hôtel de Ville) Commemorates the second world war from the Germans' arrival in Charente, life under the occupation and the activity of the Resistance. Open July and August 9am to noon and 2 to 6pm Mondays to Saturdays, the rest of the year Mondays to Fridays 2 to 6pm. €2.50 entry.

Aubeterre-sur-Dronne Musée de la Poupée ☎ 05 45 98 02 71
Doll museum with over 950 exhibits. 1st June to 30th September daily 10.30am to 12.30pm and 3 to 7pm but closed Monday morning. Adults €2, children €1.

Cognac Musée de Cognac, 48 boulevard
Denfert-Rochereau ☎ 05 45 32 07 25
Amongst other collections this museum has a display of contemporary art, including those of Charentais artists. Open every day from 1st June to 30th September 10.30am to 12.30pm and 3 to 7pm. At other times of year closes at 5.30pm and is closed Monday mornings, Tuesdays and bank holidays. Adults €2.20.

Gensac-La-Pallue Nos Belles Motos ☎ 05 45 32 13 80
A collection of more than 150 motorcycles. April to September

every day except Thursdays 9am to noon and 2 to 7pm.
Adults €7, under 12s free.

Mosnac   Rêve Auto Jeunesse   ☎ 05 45 96 02 25
Motor Museum with over 200 unique vehicles dating from
between 1900 and 1960. Open every day in the school
holidays; by appointment at other times.

St Gervais   Musée de L'École Publique   ☎ 05 45 31 89 06
Museum of school life (if you want to be reminded!). Open on
the first Sunday of each month and every Sunday in July and
August, 2.30 to 6.30pm. Free entrance.

St Michel   Le Musée Du Papier, Moulin de Fleurac ☎ 05 45 91 50 69
🖳 *www.moulin-de-fleurac.com*
Since 1988 this museum has been installed in the old paper
works of Joseph Bardou, where paper is still made using 17th
century techniques. 1st April to 30th October Mondays to
Fridays 10am to noon and 2 to 7pm, weekends and bank
holidays 11am to noon and 3 to 7pm; 1st November to 31st
March Mondays to Fridays 2 to 6pm, weekends and bank
holidays 3 to 6pm. Adults €3.50, 5 to12-year-olds €2.50

Tusson   Association Archipelle, le Bourg   ☎ 05 45 30 32 67
(a few kilometres north-east of Aigre)
A workshop and museum of stained glass windows, with
exhibitions and introductory sessions. Open 10th July to 25th
August Tuesdays to Sundays 10am to 1pm and 2.30 to
6.30pm. €4.60 per hour for adults.

Parks, Gardens & Forests

General   Braconne Forest
(near Brie and Jauldes, west of La Rochefoucauld)
Enjoy a walk in this forest and take a look at la Grande Fosse –
the largest of the sheer vertical holes in the limestone rock that
are known as 'ink holes'. Ramblers' maps available at the
tourist office in la Rochefoucauld.

Parc Naturel Régional
Périgord-Limousin   ☎ 05 53 60 34 65
🖳 *www.perigord.tm.fr* – go to "Environment"
(between Angoulême, Limoges and Périgueux)
Regional park with plenty to be seen all year round:
scenery such as marshlands, peat bogs, lakes and chalk-
land meadows, and wildlife including otters, pond terrapin
and dippers. The park also hosts numerous fetes, including
mushroom and chestnut fairs, a brass band festival and
a turkey fair, and is headquarters of the French
Conker Federation.

| Cognac | Base Plein Air de Cognac, |
| | Allée Basse du Parc ☎ 05 45 82 46 24 |

Free playground with slides, aerial runways, trampoline, mini-golf, a volleyball pitch and, in season, pedalos and water bikes.

| Hiesse | Park Animalier de la Colline Enchantée, |
| | L'Age Vieille ☎ 05 45 89 65 45 |

(10km from Confolens)
Nature reserve with over 40 different kinds of animal, including porcupines, parrots, yak and wallabies. Picnic area and restaurant. July and August every day 10am to 8pm, April to June every day 2 to 6pm, September and October Sundays only, 2 to 6pm.

| Massignac | Aventure Parc, les Lacs de Haute |
| | Charente ☎ 05 45 24 07 43 |

This centre opened in 2003 and is designed for high rise adventure play. With Tarzan leaps, rope bridges, aerial ropeways, rope walls and more. There are four circuits with 63 games of increasing difficulty. Minimum age eight. Safety harnesses are provided, but sports shoes need to be worn. 15th June to 6th July and first two weekends in September 10am to 6pm, 7th July to 31st August 10am to 7pm. €19 entrance, €20 for a bungee jump. There's a mini-park for under eights, including large inflatables. €5.

Towns & Villages

Angoulême   The city is the international capital of cartoons and there are many wall paintings across the city, from carefully disguised walls of tower blocks to comic strips and thought-provoking paintings. A map is available at the tourist office marking their locations.

Aubeterre   On the southern border of Charente, this village is classified as one of France's prettiest and is built in the form of an amphitheatre on a chalky outcrop. There are several remarkable churches, narrow streets and ancient buildings. Down by the river Dronne are a playground, beach and snack bar while canoes can be hired in July and August for those wanting to explore further along stream. In July and August, the tourist office organises guided walking tours of the village lasting around 90 minutes, Tuesdays and Saturdays at 5pm, Thursdays at 9pm. The tour is in English every other Tuesday.

St Germain-de-   Leaflets are available in English from the tourist office in
Confolens   Confolens providing an itinerary for a detailed tour of

this village, which includes houses dating from the 13th century, and its château.

Vineyards

General | Les Etapes du Cognac, Maison des Viticulteurs, 25 rue Cagouillet ☎ 05 45 36 47 35
💻 *www.cognacetapes.com*
There are three signposted vineyard trails with over 100 stops, from vintners to restaurants and monuments. Details are available from tourist offices around Cognac and from Les Etapes du Cognac.

Angoulême | Caves Charlemagne, rue du Tropic ☎ 05 45 95 02 77
💻 *www.charlemagne.fr*
Producers of sparkling wine. Founded in 1921 and open all year Mondays to Fridays 10 am to noon and 2 to 5pm and Saturdays by appointment.

Cognac | Hennessy, Quai Richard Hennessy ☎ 05 45 35 72 68
💻 *www.hennessy.com*
After crossing the Charente by boat, visitors are shown into a cellar where the cognac is matured and shown the distillation process. Open every day: June to September 10am to 6pm; March to May and October to December 10am to 5pm (closed 1st May and 25th December).

Martell, 7 place Edouard Martell ☎ 05 45 36 33 33
💻 *www.martell.com*
Another famous brand of cognac. June to September, Mondays to Fridays 9.30 to 5pm, Saturdays and Sundays noon to 5pm; March, April, May and October tours Mondays to Thursdays at 9.30am, 11am, 2.30pm, 3.45pm and 5pm, Fridays at 9.30am and 11am. November to February by appointment only.

Domaine de Château Guynot, Tesson ☎ 05 46 91 93 71
💻 *www.château-guynot.com* (in English)
Producer of local apéritif, Pineau des Charentes. Open every day 10.30am to 12.30pm and 3 to 6.30pm.

Rémy Martin, Domaine de Merpins ☎ 05 45 35 76 66
💻 *www.remy.com*
You can tour the vineyards of this famous brand by train before descending to the cool cellars and finally sampling the products in the tasting area. Every day April to October (except 1st May): 1st April to 7th July, September and October, 10 to 11am and 1.30 to 4.30pm; 8th July to 31st August 10am to 5.30pm. Free entry for under 12s.

Jarnac | Courvoisier, 2 place du Château ☎ 05 45 35 56 16
💻 *www.courvoisier.com*

On the banks of the river Charente the Courvoisier building dominates the centre of Jarnac. The re-designed visitor centre offers displays, audio-visual shows and a shop. May to September 11am to 7pm.

St Sornin   Cave et Vignobles de St Sornin   ☎ 05 45 23 92 22
(just south-east of La Rochefoucauld)
The oldest vineyard in Charente, reputedly dating back to the middle ages. There is much to see here, including the vines and the bottling process. Open all year round Mondays to Saturdays 8am to noon and 2 to 6pm. €2 entry.

Verdille   Roland Vilneau, Le Breuil   ☎ 05 45 21 34 43
Wine producer.

Miscellaneous

General   Le Vélo-Rail   ☎ 05 45 71 16 64
Ansac, Confolens, Manot, Roumazières stations.
An extraordinary way to see the countryside, by cycling along a railway line on specially designed platforms, up to 18km if you feel up to it. Each 'platform' can take five, including two pedalling. €25 per cycle. 1st July to 31st August and weekends in June and September daily at 10am, 1.30pm and 5pm from Roumazières or Confolens. July and August 10am to 9pm; 1st October to 31st May and weekdays in June and September on request. Dogs welcome if on a lead. Optional combined trip rafting down the Vienne, returning by vélo-rail.

Route of Richard the Lionheart
This journey starts on the borders of Charente at Rochebrune, then crosses Vienne to Rochechouart and its 15th century fortress castle and ends in Arnac Pompadour. The route criss crosses the D901 taking in Châlus with its two châteaux and the site of Lionheart's death. Full details of the route are available from tourist offices and you will see 'Rte Richard Coeur-de-Lion' signs in the area.

Angoulême   Château de l'Oisellerie, La Couronne,   ☎ 05 45 67 31 76
Planetarium that hosts a variety of exhibitions, such as 'Le Château Hanté' (the haunted castle). Adults €4.60, students/children half price. Open Saturdays and Sundays during exhibitions and every day during the school holidays; shows at 3pm or 5pm.

Chassenon   Gallo Roman Baths   ☎ 05 45 89 32 21
Site of Roman thermal baths that have been recently discovered, including temples and a theatre. There are guided tours and a video to explain the site and how it was used. 1st June to 15th September 10am to noon and 2 to 7pm;16th September to 11th November 2 to 5.30pm.

Chazelles | Les Grottes du Quéroy | ☎ 05 45 70 38 14
(east of Angoulême)
Caves discovered in 1892. Tour lasts 45 minutes – sensible footwear recommended. Note that the temperature in the caves is 9°C! Miniature golf, a bar and restaurant nearby. April to mid-June and September to October Sundays 2 to 6pm. 15th to 30th June every day 2 to 6pm. July and August daily 11am to 7pm.

Trois-Palis | Chocolaterie Letuffe | ☎ 05 45 91 05 21
(west of Angoulême)
Tastings, video shows and workshop visits. Chocolate courses also available.

Villefagnan | Moulin des Pierres Blanches | ☎ 05 45 29 58 29
(10 minutes west of the N10 at Ruffec)
14th century windmill complete with sails. Guided tours from 1st July to 20th August every afternoon except Wednesdays.

Professional Services

Accountants

Angoulême | Cabinet d'Experts, Les Gibauds | ☎ 05 45 67 31 31
Has an English-speaking accountant.

Solicitors & Notaires

The following offices have an English-speaking *notaire*.

Angoulême | Cabinet Glaudet, 15 rue Beaulieu | ☎ 05 45 37 03 37

Ruffec | Cabinet Périllaud, 8 rue Raoul Hediart | ☎ 05 45 31 00 66
Both Laurent Périllaud and his assistant speak very good English.

Religion

Anglican Services In English

The Reverend Michael Hepper, 19 avenue René Baillargeon, Civray (☎ 05 49 97 04 21) will be pleased to give you details of any of the services listed below or to help in any way he can.

General | Holy Communion alternately at Brillac and Salles de Villefagnan parish churches
10.30am on first Wednesday of every month.

Grand Medieu | Holy communion in the parish church
10.30am on second Sunday of every month.

Cognac   Holy Communion in la Chapelle de l'Ecole de la
                Providence, rue de la Providence
                (follow the signs for the 'Hôpital' as far as the rue Montesquieu
                and turn right into rue de la Providence)
                10.30am on fourth Sunday of every month.

The Aquitaine Chaplaincy holds services in English in Bordeaux and publishes a monthly newsletter. Details from the Reverend Michael Selman, 1 Lotissement de la Caussade, Floirac (☎ 05 56 40 05 12).

Bordeaux   La Chapelle de l'Assomption, 370 boulevard Président
                Wilson
                (opposite the British Consulate)
                10.30am on Sundays.

Evangelical Churches

Angoulême   (Pastor) 47 boulevard Denfert Rochereau ☎ 05 45 95 69 45
Cognac   Bois Faucon, Sigogne   ☎ 05 45 32 61 60
                (north-east of the town)

Ruffec   Eglise Evangélique Vie et Lumière,
                16 rue du Chenais   ☎ 06 03 88 14 27

Protestant Churches

Angoulême   (Pastor) 224 rue Périgueux   ☎ 05 45 95 12 13

Jarnac   (Pastor) 7 rue Chabot   ☎ 05 45 81 01 33

Barbezieux   Eglise Réformée, 20 rue Trarieux   ☎ 05 45 78 10 92

Synagogues

La Rochelle   Maison Communautaire Israélite,
                40 cours Dames (in Charente-Maritime) ☎ 05 46 41 17 66

Restaurants

Angoulême   L'Alchimiste, 9 boulevard Berthelot   ☎ 05 45 68 79 72
                (near Galeries Lafayette)
                Open Mondays to Fridays for lunch and Thursdays to
                Saturdays for dinner. There's no set menu and main courses
                vary from €10 to €17.

                Buffalo Grill, RN10, Champniers   ☎ 05 45 68 35 63
                A reliable steak house-style restaurant that is part of a
                nationwide chain.

Chez Paul, 8 place Francis Louvel   ☎ 05 45 90 04 61
A restaurant/brasserie that's open until midnight every day. In
the summer there are tables outside on the square and in the
large shaded courtyard at the back. Set menus from €18 to
€23 and a mid-week lunchtime menu at €10.80.

L'Indochine, 27 rue de Genève   ☎ 05 45 94 82 30
(near the tourist office)
Chinese restaurant with take-away service, open noon to 2pm
and 7 to 10.30pm. Closed all day Mondays and Tuesday
lunchtimes. Set menus from €11.50 to €19.50.

Istanbul Restaurant, 19 rue Massillon   ☎ 05 45 95 05 73
A number of specialty dishes and traditional Turkish hospitality.
Closed Sundays.

Jardin de Kashmir, 17 rue Raymond
Audour   ☎ 05 45 95 03 03
Pakistani and Indian cuisine. Open Mondays to Saturdays until
11.30pm.

Napoli Centro, 13 rue Raymond Audour ☎ 05 45 94 01 51
Fish, pasta and meat dishes. Open Tuesdays to Fridays for
lunch and dinner, Monday and Saturday evenings only.

Le Palma, 4 Rampe d'Aguesseau   ☎ 05 45 95 22 89
(town centre)
A family restaurant that has been going for three generations.
Set menus from €13 to €29. Closed Saturday lunchtimes and
all day Sundays.

La Ruelle, 6 rue des Trois Notre-Dame   ☎ 05 45 95 15 19
(in the old quarter of the town to the side of the Hôtel de Ville)
A discreet restaurant with set menus from €21 to €41.

Soleil des Antilles, 19 rue Trois
Notre Dame   ☎ 05 45 94 70 15
Caribbean cuisine with live music typical of these islands every
Friday and Saturday. Closed Sundays and Mondays. Lunch
menu €9.50.

La Taverne de Maître Kantes,
12 place Hôtel de Ville   ☎ 05 45 95 41 14
(facing the Hôtel de Ville)
One of the few restaurants in Angoulême that serve food
continuously from noon until midnight. There are no set menus
and seafood is a speciality.

There are numerous brasseries in the old quarter of
Angoulême, some of which are open until the early hours
of the morning.

Aubeterre-sur-Dronne	**Hotel du Périgord** ☎ 05 45 98 50 46 Closed Sunday evenings and all day Mondays. Lunch menu €15.50, other set menus €25 to €36. No smoking in the restaurant, only in the lounge.
Chabanais	**La Croix Blanche, place la Croix Blanche,** ☎ 05 45 89 22 18 Two-star hotel/restaurant in the centre of Chabanais. Set menus at €17 and €20. English spoken.
	Le Vieux Moulin, route de Limoges, ☎ 05 45 84 24 97 (on the left just after Pinault, as you leave Chabanais in the direction of St Junien)
Chalais	**Bar du Marché, avenue de La Gare** ☎ 06 79 25 86 15 Snack meals such as duck and chips for €9. Open lunchtimes and evenings until 9.30pm. British owned.
	Champ Rose, Charmes d'Antan ☎ 05 45 60 20 75 (off the D674 north of the town) Set menus range from €15 to €52 per person; *à la carte* also available.
	Les Couleurs, 1 rue du Four Banal ☎ 05 45 98 07 63 (behind the 'lady drinking' fountain in the centre of town) Traditional and international cuisine.
	Relais du Château, Château de Chalais ☎ 05 45 98 23 58 Within the walls of the château, this restaurant has outside seating but more formal dining takes place inside. Open from Tuesday evenings to Sunday lunchtimes inclusive. Set menus from €16.50 to €28 as well as an *à la carte* menu.
	Le Tailleyrand, 18 place de Hôtel de Ville ☎ 05 45 98 15 77 (behind the Société Général bank) Lunchtime menu of €11. Closed Saturday lunchtime, Monday evenings, all day Tuesdays and annually in January. English spoken.
Cognac	**La Boîte A Sel, 68 avenue Victor Hugo** ☎ 05 45 32 07 68 An old grocery store transformed into a restaurant whilst maintaining the charm of times gone by. Set menus from €18 to €51. Closed Mondays.
	Le Domaine du Breuil, 104 rue Robert Daugas ☎ 05 45 35 32 06 A two-star restaurant with set menus from €17 to €29. English spoken.
	Le Cellier, rue du 14 juillet ☎ 05 45 82 25 46 Closed at weekends. Set menus from €14 to €25.

Château de l'Yeuse, 65 rue de Bellevue,
Châteaubernard   ☎ 05 45 36 82 60
🖥 *www.yeuse.fr*
(within the chateau on the eastern outskirts of the town).
Gourmet restaurant where local specialties are prepared with
originality. A mid-week menu of €23; evening menus go up to
€61. English spoken.

Le Coq d'Or, 33 place François I   ☎ 05 45 82 02 56
Open every day from noon till midnight. Set menus from €13 to €28.

Le Duguesclin, rue du 14 Juillet   ☎ 05 45 82 46 22
Pizzeria, crêperie and grill. Open lunchtimes and evenings
every day.

Le Hong Kong, 12 boulevard Denfert
Rochereau   ☎ 05 45 36 89 25
Chinese restaurant. Open Mondays to Saturdays noon to 2pm
and 7 to 11pm.

Hôtel d'Oléans, 25 rue Angoulême   ☎ 05 45 82 01 26
(on the pedestrian road running from Place François I)
Set menus from €17 to €28.

Le Manderin, 27 rue du Canton   ☎ 05 45 82 96 06
Chinese and Thai cuisine. Open every lunchtime and every
evening except Sundays.

Taj Mahal, 1 rue Plumejeau   ☎ 05 45 35 36 72
(from the Place François I in the town centre, go down between
Crédit Mutuel and Crédit Lyonnais and turn left after 20m)
Open every day noon to 2.30pm and 7 to 10.30pm.

Condac   Le Moulin De Condac   ☎ 05 45 31 04 97
(five minutes outside Ruffec)
A renovated 18th century mill on the banks of the Charente
with a terrace overlooking the river and a function room
upstairs. Italian food. Closed all day Mondays and Saturday
lunchtimes. Express menu €12 and set menus from €15.

Le Rejallant   ☎ 05 45 29 08 44
(on the banks of the river Charente)
A restaurant/bar with an outside terrace that serves a set menu
as well as *à la carte*. Open all day every day, including
breakfast-time.

Confolens   Auberge de la Tour,   ☎ 05 45 84 15 27
St Germain-de-Confolens
(just outside the town)

Dining room overlooks the river. €10 lunchtime menu Tuesdays
to Fridays. Other set menus €16 to €23 and *à la carte*.

Chez Flo, 9 place de la Fontorse   ☎ 05 45 84 08 29
(tucked away in the old quarter, on the other side of the river
from the main town by the old bridge)
Open noon to 2pm and 7 to 10pm Mondays to Saturdays,
Sundays 1 to 10pm. €8 lunch menu and €20 evening menu.

Emeraude, 20 rue Emile Roux   ☎ 05 45 84 12 77
Restaurant overlooking the river, with lunch menus from €8.50
and other set menus from €14.50 to €20 plus *à la carte*.

Mère Michelet, 19 allée de Blossac   ☎ 05 45 84 04 11
A traditional restaurant on the banks of the Vienne with set
menus from €10.50 to €20.

La Rochefoucauld La Vieille Auberge, 1 rue de Vitrac,   ☎ 05 45 62 02 72
Inside a three-star hotel. Open every day of the year.

Luxé   L'Auberge du Cheval Blanc, Luxé Gare ☎ 05 45 22 23 62
(opposite the railway station in Luxé, west of Mansle)
Closed Sunday and Tuesday evenings, all day Mondays and
throughout February. Menu of the day for €12.50 and other set
menus from €22 to €34.

Mansle   La Marmite, rue Watlinghton   ☎ 05 45 22 20 48
Traditional cuisine with a terrace on the banks of the river
Charente.

Montmoreau   Plaisir d'Automne, 1 rue St Denys   ☎ 05 45 60 39 40
(just behind the church)
Open noon to 2pm and 7.30 to 9pm. Set menus from €14 to
€29.

Nanteuil-en-   Auberge le St Jean, place St Jean Baptiste ☎ 05 45 89 11 79
Vallée   (opposite the church)
Open noon to 2pm and 7.15 to 9.30pm. Closed Sunday
evenings and all day Mondays. From November to March also
closed Saturday lunchtimes. Set menus from €13 and *à la
carte* menu available.

Ruffec   Le Côte de Boeuf, route Civray   ☎ 05 45 31 05 49
Traditional cuisine. Closed Mondays at 3pm and all day
Tuesdays. Set menus from €8.40 to €21.

Délices d'Asie, 20 rue Docteur Roux   ☎ 05 45 84 14 11
Specialises in Asian food. Open Tuesdays to Sundays till 9pm.
Take-away available all day.

La Mijotière, La Chèvrerie   ☎ 05 45 31 15 76
(signposted off the D26 north-west out of Ruffec)
Thai cuisine, including take-away service. Open noon to 1am
Tuesdays to Sundays. British owned.

La Toque Blanche, rue Général Leclerc   ☎ 05 45 30 30 30
(on the old N10 that runs through the centre of town)
A recently re-opened hotel and restaurant. Open every day
lunchtimes and evenings. Menu of the day is €11.30, with
further set menus from €15 to €29. English spoken.

Whisky Galore, rue Jean Jaurès   ☎ 05 45 29 07 12
Pasta and pizza restaurant with set menus from €15 to €20.
Take-away available.

St Fort-sur-le-Né Le Moulin de Cierzac, route de Cognac ☎ 05 45 83 01 32
Set in an 18th century mill with a shady park where you can
relax after your meal. Set menus starting at €13.
St Groux Les Trois Saules, le Bourg   ☎ 05 45 20 31 40
(just outside Mansle)
A country house atmosphere at this restaurant that has set
menus from €10 to €26 and a 'menu rapide' for €8.

Verteuil-sur-   Dixieland Café, 46 rue des Halles   ☎ 05 45 31 40 35
Charente   (south of Ruffec)
French, Italian and 'Tex-Mex' cuisine, with a piano bar every
Tuesday evening. Open Tuesdays to Sundays noon to 2am in
summer and 4pm to 2am in winter.

Rubbish & Recycling

Metal Collection

Cognac   Dimitri Chadutaud, 5 route
              Champagnères   ☎ 05 45 35 93 44
              (east of the town)

Confolens   Christian Nivelle, chez Pezeau,
              Roumazières Loubert   ☎ 05 45 71 73 22
              (south of the town)

La Rochefoucauld Guy Cluzeau, chez Salot, Rivières   ☎ 05 45 63 54 45
              (near the town)
              Old fridges, car shells, cookers, etc.

Shopping

When available, the opening hours of various shops have been included but are liable to change and so it's advisable to check before travelling long distances to any specific shop.

Alcohol

Angoulême   Cave de St Cybard, 111 rue Saintes   ☎ 05 45 95 92 43
(in the north of the town, past the paper museum)
Tuesdays to Saturdays.

Chalais   Cave le Vignoble, 34 place
Hôtel de Ville   ☎ 05 45 98 29 48
(near the tourist office)
Mondays and Wednesdays to Saturdays 9am to 12.30pm, and 3 to 7.30pm, Sundays 9.30am to 12.30pm.

Cognac   Saveurs des Cépages, 41 rue Bellefonds ☎ 05 45 36 21 82
Tuesdays to Saturdays, closing at 7.30pm.

Ruffec   Le Pressoir, 3 boulevard Duportal   ☎ 05 45 30 05 10
(on the right hand side going towards Intermarché from the traffic lights)

Architectural Antiques

Chail   Les Vielles Pierres du Mellois, Les Cerizat ☎ 05 49 29 31 23
(on the D948 from Melle to Sauzé-Vaussais)
Specialises in the sale of old building materials – mainly stone, but there's a large selection of reclaimed timbers in the far corner as you enter from the back.

British Groceries

Angoulême   Aux Iles Britanniques, 1 rue d'Arcole   ☎ 05 45 37 58 70
(near the Hôtel de Ville in the centre of the town)
Tuesdays to Saturdays 9.30am to 7pm.

Chalais   Le Petit Atelier, avenue de la Gare   ☎ 05 45 98 07 84
✉ *lepetitatlier@tiscali.fr*
(opposite Intermarché)
Sells English groceries and books. Summer: open Mondays and Wednesdays to Saturdays 9.15am to noon and 2.30 to 6pm. Winter: open Mondays, Fridays and Saturdays 9am to noon and 2.30 to 6pm, Wednesdays and Thursdays 9am to noon.

Ruffec   The Cockle Shell, 1 rue de la République   ☎ 05 45 85 93 55
(near the Hôtel de Ville)
Sells English groceries. It's possible to place orders for items not in stock. Mondays to Saturdays 9am to 6pm.

Building Materials

Angoulême	Pinault, route de Périgueux, Soyaux (south-east of the town)	☎ 05 45 95 06 21
	Point P, La Croix Blanche, Champniers (north of the town)	☎ 05 45 22 90 30
Chalais	Pinault, route Barbezieux	☎ 05 45 98 04 21
Cognac	Point P, avenue d'Angoulême, Châteaubernard 💻 www.pointp.fr	☎ 05 45 36 55 55
Confolens	Melin Matériaux, Le Mas Félix	☎ 05 45 84 04 99
Ruffec	3MMM Matériaux, route d'Aigre 💻 www.3mmm-materiaux.com (on the outskirts of the town past Leclerc)	☎ 05 45 30 35 79

Camping & Caravanning

Angoulême	Evasion 16, route Périgueux Repairs and service as well as caravan sales.	☎ 05 45 38 04 96

Chemists'

Chemists' are listed in the yellow pages under *Pharmacies* and should display a sign indicating which is the duty chemist outside normal opening hours; or you can dial 17 for this information.

Department Stores

Angoulême	Galeries Lafayette, 10 rue Périgueux 💻 www.galerieslafayette.com (near the bottom of the pedestrian shopping area below the Hôtel de Ville)	☎ 05 45 92 43 00

DIY

Angoulême	Mr. Bricolage, Les Montagnes, Champniers (in the north of the town) Mondays to Saturdays 9am to noon and 2 to 7pm.	☎ 05 45 97 86 86
	Castorama, 560 rue Bordeaux (south-east of the town)	☎ 05 45 91 38 28
Cognac	Bricomarché, 18 avenue Saintes	☎ 05 45 36 04 04

Mr Bricolage, Le Fief du Roy,
Châteaubernard   ☎ 05 45 35 06 66

Confolens   Bricomarché, avenue 8 Mai 1945   ☎ 05 45 84 43 84
(beside Intermarché)
Mondays to Saturdays 9.15am to 12.15pm and 2.15 to 7pm.

Ruffec   Mr. Bricolage, 55 route d'Aigre   ☎ 05 45 31 14 29
(next door to Leclerc supermarket)
Mondays to Saturdays 9am to 12.30pm and 2 to 7pm.

Fabrics

Angoulême   GP Decors, ZA Les Montagnes,
Champniers   ☎ 05 45 38 04 18
(on the retail park north of the town)

Chalais   Levalet, 6bis rue Barbezieux   ☎ 05 45 79 02 32

Cognac   Tissus Bonnet, 6 place Armes   ☎ 05 45 82 05 95
(in the town centre near the covered market)
Sells wool and dress and upholstery fabrics. Tuesdays to
Saturdays 9.30am to 12.15pm and 2.15 to 7pm

Confolens   Mercerie, 14 rue Marquis Foch   ☎ 05 45 84 16 23
Sewing and embroidery shop. Tuesdays to Saturdays 9.15am
to noon and 2 to 6.45pm.

Ruffec   Décor Tissus Ambiance Bébé,
38 rue de l'Hôpital   ☎ 05 45 31 03 80
(on the same road as Crédit Agricole)
Tuesdays to Saturdays.

Frozen Food

Angoulême   Picard Surgelés, 420 rue Bordeaux   ☎ 05 45 24 55 51

Picard Surgelés, 296 route Paris,
Gond-Pontouvre   ☎ 05 45 22 28 36
(on the north side of the town)

Thiriet Glaces, Les Montagnes,
Champniers   ☎ 05 45 69 36 84

Cognac   Picard Surgelés, 149 avenue Victor Hugo ☎ 05 45 81 37 24

Garden Centres

Angoulême   Jardiland, Les Montagnes, Champniers ☎ 05 45 69 38 29
(next to Géant to the north of the town, on the road off the N10

leading towards Limoges)
Part of a nationwide chain this large garden centre is open
Mondays to Saturdays 9.30am to noon and 2 to 7pm. Sundays
10am to noon and 2 to 7pm.

Chalais   Gamm Vert, route de Libourne   ☎ 05 45 98 24 23
                 Nationwide chain. Mondays to Saturdays 8.30am to noon and
                 2.30 to 7pm.

Cognac   Le Fief Fleuri, rue L. Bréguet,
                 Châteaubernard   ☎ 05 45 35 03 41
                 (off the ring road to the south of the town)
                 A large garden centre with a pet section including fish and birds
                 for sale. Mondays 2 to 7pm, Tuesdays to Saturdays 9.15am to
                 noon and 2 to 7pm, Sundays and bank holidays 10am to noon
                 and 2.30 to 6.30pm. Closed Sundays in July and August.

Confolens   Didier Devaine, avenue Général
                 de Gaulle   ☎ 05 45 84 03 98
                 (on the outskirts of town in the direction of Limoges.

Ruffec   Jardinière de la Garenne, 4 route
                 d'Aigre   ☎ 05 45 31 37 85
                 (at the bottom of the hill near the Leclerc supermarket)
                 Mondays to Fridays 9am to 12.30pm and 2 to 6.30pm,
                 Saturdays until 7pm.

Kitchens & Bathrooms

Angoulême   Hyper Cuisines AGC, Les Montagnes,
                 Champniers   ☎ 05 45 37 66 86

Ruffec   3MMM Matériaux, route d'Aigre   ☎ 05 45 30 35 79
                 🖳 *www.3mmm-materiaux.com*
                 This store has a specialist bathroom department.

Markets

Aigre   Thursday, Saturday and Sunday markets and a fair on the third
                 Wednesday of the month.

Angoulême   Centre
                 Large purpose-built covered food market every morning. In the
                 summer (especially on Saturdays) you may find many extra
                 stalls, which overflow to the parking area outside.

                 Place du Minage
                 Organic market the second and fourth Wednesdays of each
                 month from 4 to 8pm.

                 Marché Victor Hugo
                 Tuesdays to Sundays.

Gond-Pontouvre area
(on the north side of the town)
Thursday mornings in avenue Jean Sebire, Sunday mornings
in avenue Kennedy.

place Victor Hugo
(in the east of the town on the road to Soyaux)
Partially covered market on Tuesdays to Sundays.

place du Champ de Mars
(behind Galeries Lafayette in the centre)
Fair on 2nd and 15th of every month.

Aubeterre	Market every Sunday morning.
Barbezieux	Fair on the first Tuesday of each month and a market every Tuesday, Friday and Saturday.
Chalais	Monday morning market with a fair the first and third Monday of the month.
Cognac	Fair on the second Saturday of each month and a large market in the Halles, Place d'Armes, Tuesdays to Sundays until 1.30pm.
Confolens	Fair on 12th of each month and a market on Wednesday and Saturday mornings.
Jarnac	The indoor market is open every day except Monday and there's a fair on the first Saturday of the month.
La Rochefoucauld	Wednesday and Saturday market and a fair on 10th of each month (on 9th if 10th is a Sunday).
Mansle	Markets Tuesdays and Fridays and a fair on 25th of each month.
Rouillac	Large fair and market on 27th of each month, which closes off the whole town.
Ruffec	Market on Wednesdays and Saturdays and a fair on 13th and 28th of each month.
Villefagnan	Tuesday and Friday morning market.

Music

Angoulême	Thévenet Music, 13 rue d'Aguesseau ☎ 05 45 95 33 82 A large shop with everything from sheet music and drum

spares to keyboards and percussion instruments.
Tuesdays to Saturdays 9.30am to 12.15pm and 2.15 to 7pm.

Organic Food

Angoulême   Flory Santé, 225 avenue Général de
Gaulle, Soyaux   ☎ 05 45 92 13 92
Mondays 2 to 7pm, Tuesdays 9am to 7pm, Wednesdays to
Saturdays 9am to 12.30pm and 2 to 7pm.

Bio-coop, 69 route de Paris,
Gond Pontouvre   ☎ 05 45 69 10 00
(on the north side of the town)
A large shop with organic meat, fruit, vegetables, groceries,
bread and even pet food.
Tuesdays to Saturdays 9.30am to 12.30pm and 3 to 7pm.

Cognac   Bio-coop, 8 rue du Poitou,
Châteaubernard   ☎ 05 45 82 14 42
(behind Assedic)
Tuesdays to Saturdays 9.30am to 1pm and 3 to 7pm.

Ruffec   C'est la Nature qui a Raison, rue
Docteur Roux   ☎ 05 45 30 71 82
(opposite Société Général)
Tuesdays to Saturdays 9.45am to 12.30pm and 3 to 7pm.

La Rochefoucauld Bio Lavande, 37 rue des Halles   ☎ 05 45 70 34 79
Many organic products including bread. Tuesdays to Saturdays
9am to 1pm and 3 to 7pm (Saturdays to 6pm).

Post Offices

Post offices are listed in the yellow pages under *Courrier, colis*. There are
no post offices in the department that are open late or on Sundays.

Retail Parks

Angoulême   Les Montagnes
(on the N10 north of Angoulême)
Includes Géant hypermarket and many other stores, including:
● Atlas – furniture, beds, kitchens and interiors;
● Connexion – electrical store;
● Decathlon – sports store;
● Fly – furniture and household accessories;
● Jardiland – large garden centre, also open Sundays;
● Monsieur Meuble – furniture;
● Zooland – pet shop;
● A whole area dedicated to car dealerships.

Cognac   Châteaubernard
              (on the outskirts of the town)
              Shops include:
              ● BUT – general furniture and household accessories;
              ● Connexion – electrical store;
              ● Feu Vert – tyre and exhaust centre;
              ● Gémo – clothes and shoes;
              ● Joué Club – toy shop;
              ● Intersport – sports shop;
              ● Monsieur Meuble – furniture store;
              ● Mr Bricolage – DIY;
              ● Pinault – building materials.

Second-Hand Goods

Angoulême   Salle des Ventes de Paris,
              110 route de Paris, Gond Pontouvre   ☎ 05 45 69 00 07
              Open every day.

Chalais   Chalais Brocante, 65 rue de Barbezieux ☎ 05 45 98 05 45
              (on the outskirts of the town)
              Open Fridays, Saturdays, Sundays and bank holidays.

Cognac   Cognac Troc Dépôt Vente, impasse
              Barret, avenue P. Firion Martell   ☎ 05 45 35 39 96
              Toys, furniture, lights and bicycles.

Confolens   La Bonne Etoile, route d'Ansac   ☎ 05 45 84 05 95
              (on the edge of town on the road to St Claud)

Ruffec   Antiquités André Masseloux,
              La Leigne, Condac   ☎ 05 45 31 32 11
              (just east of the town)

Sports Goods

Angoulême   Décathlon, Les Montagnes, Champniers ☎ 05 45 37 54 64
              🖳 www.decathlon.fr
              (to the right of Jardiland)
              Sports superstore.

              Décathlon, avenue Itzehoé, La Couronne ☎ 05 45 67 70 70
              🖳 www.decathlon.fr
              (in the retail park south-west of the city)
              Sports superstore.

Cognac   Super Sport, ZI du Fief du Roy,
              Châteaubernard   ☎ 05 45 36 18 88
              (on the retail park south-east of the town)

Confolens   Marno Sports, 15 rue Emile Roux   ☎ 05 45 84 15 02
                  Tuesdays to Saturdays 9am to noon and 2.30 to 7pm.

Ruffec   Intersport, chemin des Meuniers   ☎ 05 45 31 59 82
                  (behind Leclerc)

Supermarkets & Hypermarkets

Angoulême   Auchan, route Bordeaux, La Couronne ☎ 05 45 24 45 24
                  (just off the N10 as you approach Angoulême from the south)
                  There's a business card machine, photo booth, café and
                  brasserie, chemist's and many shops within this hypermarket
                  complex.
                  Mondays to Saturdays 8.30am to 10pm.

                  Carrefour, avenue Général de Gaulle,
                  Soyaux   ☎ 05 45 37 02 02
                  (south-east of Angoulême)
                  Inside the foyer of this store there is a newsagent's that sells
                  English magazines as well as English papers, a butcher's,
                  photographer's, Crédit Agricole cash machine, key and heel
                  bar, dry cleaner's, chemist's, a photo booth and photocopier as
                  well as a business card machine and various clothes stores.
                  Mondays to Saturdays 9am to 8.30pm, Fridays 9am to 9pm.

                  Géant, Champniers   ☎ 05 45 22 44 00
                  (from the north of Angoulême follow directions to Limoges)
                  There are both France Télécom and SFR stores in the centre,
                  as well as restaurants, clothes shops and hairdressers.
                  Open until 10pm.

Cognac   Auchan, rue Anisserie, Châteaubernard ☎ 05 45 35 66 66
                  In the foyer is a large cosmetics/toiletries store, pet shop with fish
                  and birds, jeweller's, dry cleaner's, key and heel bar, gift wrapping
                  service, 'flunch' restaurant, photocopier, photo booth and
                  business card machine.
                  Mondays to Saturdays 8.30am to 10pm.

Swimming Pool Equipment

Angoulême   Zyke, RN10, Les Grandes Chaumes   ☎ 05 45 37 43 43
                  🖳 *www.zyke.fr*
                  (on the left as you approach Angoulême from the north, just
                  after the Bordeaux/Limoges slip road)
                  This store has a large display of above-ground and in-ground
                  pools, Jacuzzis, saunas and accessories. A design and build
                  service is offered.
                  Open Mondays to Fridays 9am to noon and 2 to 6.45pm,
                  Saturdays 9am to noon and 2 to 6pm.

Sports

The following is just a selection of the activities available, the large towns having a wide range of sports facilities. Full details are available from tourist offices or *mairies*.

Aerial Sports

Parachuting

Angoulême	Section Parachutisme du SC Angoulême	☎ 05 45 92 08 69
Cognac	Parachutisme Sportif Cognaçais, 53 rue d'Angoulême	☎ 05 45 81 90 53

Training and jumps carried out at the aerodromes at Royan and Bergerac from March to November. Tandem jumps possible for over 15s with a medical certificate.

Archery

Angoulême	Arc Club Angoumoisin	☎ 05 45 61 37 41
	Terrain de Tir à l'Arc, Plaine de Jeux des Trois Chênes	☎ 05 45 91 82 42
Cognac	Première Compagnie d'Archers de Cognac	☎ 05 45 32 34 15

Outdoor from April to September at Jardin d'Arc, rue du Dominant, Châteaubernard. Indoor training at Gymnase P. Lucuquiaud.

Confolens	Archers Confolentais	☎ 05 45 85 31 40

Archery for both leisure and competition from eight years old.

Ruffec	Association du Ruffécois, ZI de la Gare	☎ 05 45 31 39 63

Badminton

Angoulême	Foyer des Jeunes, avenue du Général de Gaulle, Gond Pontouvre	☎ 05 45 68 18 78

Monday, Thursday and Friday evenings.

Chalais	Salle Omnisports	☎ 06 88 30 39 14

Monday evenings.

Cognac	Association Cognac Badminton, Gymnase Beaulieu, rue du Port	☎ 05 45 96 59 32

Sessions all week.

Canoeing & Kayaking

Angoulême   Foyer des Jeunes, avenue du Général
                 de Gaulle, Gond Pontouvre   ☎ 05 45 68 18 78
                 Wednesdays and Saturdays 2 to 4.30pm.

Cognac   Cognac Canoë Club, Base Plain Air
                 de Cognac, Allée Basse du Parc   ☎ 05 45 82 44 51
                 Training all year on the river or in the pools.

Confolens   Club Canoë, 16 rue du Moulin   ☎ 06 89 56 34 11

Ruffec   Rejallant, Condac   ☎ 05 45 30 31 38
                 (just south of the town)
                 Half-day and mini-descents available as well as hiring by the
                 hour. €13 for half-day descent. Open every day: June and
                 September 2 to 6pm; July and August 9 to 6pm.

Clay Pigeon Shooting

Cognac   Société de Tir aux Pigeons, Stand
                 du Bois d'Ouliat   ☎ 05 45 32 03 62

Climbing

Angoulême   CSCS La Couronne, 1 allée des
                 Sports, La Couronne   ☎ 05 45 67 17 00
                 Tuesdays 6 to 8pm for 7 to 11-year-olds.

                 Foyer des Jeunes, avenue du Général
                 de Gaulle, Gond Pontouvre   ☎ 05 45 68 18 78
                 Mondays and Fridays for over ten-year-olds.

                 Halle des Sports, rue de La Croix Lanauve
                 Artificial wall.

Ruffec   Association l'ARAIGNEE, Mairie de
                 Les Adjots   ☎ 05 45 29 59 89
                 Climbing on artificial walls and natural sites. Training and
                 safety equipment provided.

Cycling

Angoulême   Angoulême Vélo Club, Le Bourg,
                 Villejoubert   ☎ 05 45 22 72 46

                 Vélodrome, impasse du Vélodrome,
                 route de Bordeaux   ☎ 05 45 91 89 87

| Cognac | Cyclotourisme Club, 1 rue du Port | ☎ 05 45 82 79 96 |

Rides depart from Place François I on Sunday mornings at 8 or 8.30am depending on the time of year.

| Confolens | Vélo Passion | ☎ 05 45 84 05 13 |

Rides leave place de l'Hôtel de Ville every Sunday morning for circuits from 30 to 100km.

| Ruffec | Cycle Touriste du Nord Charente | ☎ 05 45 31 64 94 |

Fencing

| Angoulême | Salle d'Escrime Taillefer, rue Abbé Rousselot | ☎ 05 45 92 63 46 |

Fishing

General | Fédération de La Charente pour La Pêche et la Protection du Milieu Aquatique, 60 rue du Bourlion, Gond Pontouvre | ☎ 05 45 69 33 91

Fishing permits and details of all locations for fishing in the department.

If there's a lake locally, permits will be for sale in a nearby *tabac* or at the *mairie*.

Football

Football clubs can be found even in small villages; the local *mairie* is the best place to find details.

Golf

Angoulême | Golf de l'Hirondelle, Chemin de l'Hirondelle | ☎ 05 45 61 16 94

18 holes, par 70, 5,365m. Recently re-designed, this course is gently sloping and wooded. Open all year but closed Tuesdays in the low season. Lessons for adults and children, covered driving range, buggy hire and club house with bar and restaurant. Green fees €25–35.

Aubeterre | Golf d'Aubeterre, Pillac, St Séverin | ☎ 05 45 98 55 13

(south of Angoulême on the boundary between Charente and Dordogne) 9 holes, par 31, 1,728m. Although a short course, it has numerous bunkers and other hazards and is suitable for players of all levels. Open all year. Green fee €20 (€11 for juniors). Snack bar.

Montbron | Golf de la Prèze, Ecuras-Rouzède | ☎ 05 45 23 24 74
🖳 *www.golfdelapreze.com*

(east of Angoulême)
Two 9 hole courses, a driving range and putting green. One course is 3,164m, par 36, with fast greens and is a technically demanding course of international standard. Open every day all year. Driving range, pitch and put, buggy hire, lessons and a clubhouse with bar. Green fees for 18 holes €26–€33.

St Brice   Golf Du Cognac, La Maurie   ☎ 05 45 32 18 17
                    💻 *www.golfducognac.asso.fr*
                    (on the banks of the river Charente)
                    18 holes, par 72, 6,142m. A gentle sloping course dotted with water hazards as it passes through vineyards and woodland. Open all year from 8am to 8pm May to September and 9am to 6pm October to April, closed Tuesdays in low season. Pro shop, golf carts, driving range, lessons and a clubhouse with three restaurants. Green fees €28–€40.

Horse Riding

Angoulême   Ecurie des Eaux Claires, Pierre Dure,
                    Puymoyen   ☎ 05 45 61 35 52
                    (on the south side of the town)
                    Lessons and outings.

Chalais   Les Ecuries de la Dronne, Chez
                    Chevreuil, Laprad-Aubeterre   ☎ 05 45 78 27 76
                    Lessons and outings.

Cognac   Les Ecuries de Boussac, Cherves
                    Richmont   ☎ 05 45 83 15 10
                    (on the north-west outskirts of Cognac)

Confolens   Centre Equestre de Jallais,
                    Domaine de Jallais   ☎ 05 45 84 13 45
                    Open every day from 9am to 8pm. All ages from five years old.

Ruffec   route d'Aigre, Villefagnan   ☎ 05 45 31 64 58
                    (ten minutes west of Ruffec)

Ice Skating

Angoulême   Centre Nautique Patinoire, rue des
                    Mesniers   ☎ 05 45 39 93 99
                    (in the same complex as Nautilis water park – see page 139)
                    Opened in February 2003. Has a 40m rink and a smaller area.

Jetskiing

Angoulême   Saint-Yrieix-sur-Charente   ☎ 05 45 92 75 67

Martial Arts

Angoulême   CSCS Rives de Charente, 5 quai
                 du Halage   ☎ 05 45 93 11 14
                 From five-year-olds to adults.

Chalais   Amicale Laïque de Chalais, Collège
                 de Chalais, 34 route Angoulême   ☎ 05 45 98 11 85
                 Classes Saturday for four-year-olds to adults.

Cognac   Judo Club Cognac, 122 rue de Marignan ☎ 05 45 82 40 04
                 Groups for all ages.

Confolens   Judo Club Confolentais, Salle du Judo,
                 rue du Moulin   ☎ 05 45 84 09 99
                 Classes Tuesdays, Wednesdays and Fridays.

Ruffec   Judo Club Ruffécois   ☎ 05 45 31 22 90

Motorcycle Riding

Angoulême   Motor's Club Angoumoisin   ☎ 05 45 70 31 57
                 Trial, motocross and road bikes.

Chalais   Centre de Loisirs de Brossac,
                 C.LA. Moto   ☎ 06 17 30 85 60
                 (between Barbezieux and Chalais in southern Charente)
                 Miles of paths through the countryside. Quads and similar
                 vehicles for two people. Children's quads and mini-motorbikes
                 also available, but only for use on the enclosed area.

Potholing

Angoulême   Association Spéléologique Charentais ☎ 05 45 92 57 09

Ruffec   Association l'Araignée, Mairie
                 des Adjots   ☎ 05 45 29 59 89
                 Training courses and safety equipment provided.

Rafting

Confolens   Charente-Limousine Nautique   ☎ 05 45 84 43 70
                 Trips on the Vienne.

Rowing

Angoulême   CSCS Rives de Charente, 5 quai du
                 Halage   ☎ 05 45 95 88 01
                 Adults and children, Wednesdays and Saturdays.

Cognac	Cognac Yacht Rowing Club, 27 rue Jean Bart	☎ 05 45 82 02 66

💻 *www.aviron-cognac.com*
The club is open every day with groups for all ages.

Sailing

Angoulême	Club de Voile, Plan d'Eau de la Grande Prairie, Saint Yrieix	☎ 05 45 68 42 46

💻 *www.fcol16.org*
Sailing and windsurfing lessons and courses available. Week-long courses for children in the school holidays.

Scuba Diving

Angoulême	Groupe Exploration Sous-Marine Angoulême	☎ 05 45 91 21 93
Cognac	ACERS, 1 rue du Port	☎ 05 45 82 07 73

Diving, marine biology, underwater photography and trips for teenagers and adults.

Ruffec	Le Masque et La Palme	☎ 05 45 31 33 94

(based at the indoor pool)
Weekly training.

Shooting

Angoulême	Stand de Tir des Trois Chênes, allée de La Poudrerie	☎ 05 45 91 82 42
Cognac	Société de Tir de Cognac, Stand du Dominant, Châteaubernard	☎ 05 45 82 74 58

Open Tuesdays, Wednesdays and at weekends.

Ruffec	Association Ruffécoise, ZI de la Gare	☎ 05 45 31 39 63

(signposted from near the station)

Snooker, Pool & Billiards

Some bars listed under **Bars & Nightlife** on page 86 also have billiards, pool or snooker tables.

Angoulême	Billard Club Angoumoisin, 84 rue Montauzier	☎ 05 45 91 31 96

French billiards.

	Le Six Pockets, boulevard Pasteur	☎ 05 45 38 76 96

(opposite the covered market)
Snooker.

| Cognac | Sixteen Pool, 177 avenue Victor Hugo ☎ 05 45 32 07 97 |
| | Pool and darts, table football, games machines and take-away pizzas. Mondays to Fridays 11am to 1am, Saturdays 3pm to 1am, Sundays 3 to 7pm. |

Confolens	Billard Club Confolentais, Cafétéria,
	3 avenue de Général de Gaulle ☎ 05 45 84 19 38
	Snooker. Training and recreational playing for over 16s.

Swimming

Chalais	5 allée Stade, Montmoreau ☎ 05 45 60 37 88
	(north of Chalais)
	An outdoor pool open only in the summer months.

| Cognac | Piscine Parc François I ☎ 05 45 35 29 70 |
| | An indoor pool open all year with an active swimming club. An outdoor pool on the same site is open only in the summer. |

Confolens	Stade Gary Pailler, route d'Angoulême ☎ 05 45 84 01 97
	(on the west side of Confolens)
	Outdoor pool.

Ruffec	place du Champ de Foire ☎ 05 45 31 07 28
	(near the hospital)
	Indoor and outdoor pools.

St Yrieix	Nautilis, 17 rue du Mesniers ☎ 05 45 95 50 00
	(next to the Plan d'Eau de La Grande Prairie west of Angoulême, signposted from the N10)
	A modern water park with a 50m pool and leisure pools with chutes and water cannons, etc. There's a restaurant, drinks bar, gym, sauna, relaxation pool and Jacuzzi. For the summer there's a 'lazy river' wave machine and water slides.

Tennis

Angoulême	Tennis Club Municipal Angoulême ☎ 05 45 78 08 28
	Tennis de La Grande Garenne, rue Pierre Aumaître ☎ 05 45 91 83 90
	Tennis Léonide Lacrois, rue Fontchaudière ☎ 05 45 95 26 52
	Tennis du Petit Frequet, rue du Pont de Vinson ☎ 05 45 92 45 43

| Chalais | Complexe Sportif ☎ 05 45 98 27 52 |
| | Courts can be hired hourly from €8 – enquire at the Centre |

	Social de Chalais. The complex also has an active tennis club for all abilities.	
Cognac	1 chemin du Brandat, St Brice	☎ 05 45 35 16 15
	The tennis club is open every day from 8am and 9.30pm in summer, 10.30pm in winter.	
Confolens	Public courts, avenue de la Libération	☎ 05 45 85 44 31
	(in the south of the town, by the river Vienne) Tennis courses available for all including short tennis for children.	
Ruffec	Tennis Club de Ruffec, route d'Aigre	☎ 05 45 31 36 44
	Family and individual membership. No lessons during the summer months.	

Waterpolo

Angoulême	Sporting Club d'Angoulême	☎ 05 45 22 98 66

Waterskiing

Angoulême	CAM's Motonautisme et Ski Nautique, Quai du Halage	☎ 05 45 92 76 22
	Centre open every day June to October, noon to 8pm.	

Tourist Offices

Angoulême	Comité Départemental du Tourisme de la Charente, place Bouillaud	☎ 05 45 69 79 09
	🖳 *www.lacharente.com*	
	Place des Halles, Angoulême	☎ 05 45 95 16 84
	🖳 *www.mairie-angouleme.fr* (by the indoor market) Mondays to Fridays 9.30am to 6pm, Saturdays 10am to noon and 2 to 5pm.	
Chalais	38 place de l'Hôtel de Ville	☎ 05 45 98 02 71
	Monday to Saturday 9am to noon and 2.30 to 6pm, Saturday 5pm.	
Cognac	16 rue 14 juillet	☎ 05 45 82 10 71
	🖳 *www.ville-cognac.fr* Winter: Mondays to Saturdays 10am to 5pm. July and August: Mondays to Saturdays 9am to 7pm, Sundays 10am to 4pm. May, June and September: Mondays to Saturdays 9.30am to 5.30pm.	

| Confolens | place des Marronniers | ☎ 05 45 84 00 77 |

Confolens   place des Marronniers   ☎ 05 45 84 00 77
             🖥 *www.tourisme-confolens.com*
             (near the market hall)
             Mondays to Saturdays 10am to noon and 2 to 5pm (July and
             August 7pm).

Ruffec   place du Marché   ☎ 05 45 31 05 42
             ✉ *ruffec@fnotsi.net*
             Mondays to Saturdays 9am to12.30pm and 2 to 6pm.

Tradesmen

Architects & Project Managers

General   Adams Gautier Poitou-Charentes   ☎ 05 49 64 42 96
             🖥 *www.adamsgautier.com*
             This is a British/French team that are experienced architects
             and also organise surveys, arrange building permits and carry
             out project management, renovation, landscaping and pool
             installation.

             Louis Albagnac, Le Bourg, St Fraigne   ☎ 05 45 96 56 08
             This French architect speaks English.

             Eric Archaimbault   ☎ 06 77 13 41 41
             ✉ *archaimbaulteric@wanadoo.fr*
             A bi-lingual project manager using only registered French
             tradesmen and covering the whole region of Poitou-Charentes.

Builders

General   Poitou Charente Renovations,
             La Bayette de Bioussac   ☎ 05 45 85 46 78
             ✉ *huckstepp.lee@wanadoo.fr*
             This British-run company covers the area from Confolens in
             northern Charente to Sauzé-Vaussais in the south-west corner
             of Deux-Sèvres and into the south of Vienne. It works with a
             team of French registered British tradesman including
             electricians, plumbers and roofers.

             Sarl Rema Services, St Pardoux   ☎ 05 53 60 76 20
             ✉ *remaservices@voila.fr*
             Although based just south of Charente, this company has
             English-speaking staff and undertakes building, roofing,
             electrics, plumbing and heating in the department.

Angoulême   Lapeyre Pierre, 167 rue Capitaine Fayre ☎ 05 45 69 02 67
             🖥 *www.lapeyre-pierre.com*
             General building firm undertaking stone work, renovation,
             carpentry and roofing.

	Léonard Rénovation, 60 rue Capitaine Fayre Building and renovation work.	☎ 05 45 61 82 00
Chalais	Martin Janick, 50 route Angoulême New building, renovation work and roofing.	☎ 05 45 98 07 18
Cognac	VBR Constructive, 142 rue Aristide Briand (near the library) New building, renovation and pool installation.	☎ 05 45 32 46 80
Confolens	Jean-Pierre Lagrange, 3 rue Buttes	☎ 05 45 84 09 32
Ruffec	STB, ZI Nord General builders.	☎ 05 45 31 08 22

Carpenters

Many carpentry firms that make windows and doors also work in aluminium.

Angoulême	Michel Dupuis, Les Chaumes de Crages, Z.E. Ma Campagne 🖳 *www.michel-dupuis.fr* General carpentry, conservatories, windows, wood and aluminium.	☎ 05 45 61 57 14
Chalais	Mas & Fils, Le Bourg, Montboyer 🖳 *www.mas-et-fils.com* Office and workshop in the centre of Montboyer.	☎ 05 45 98 15 28
	Alun Jones, Yviers English-speaking carpenter.	☎ 05 45 98 11 42
Cognac	L. Naud & Fils, 20 place R. Schumann Roofing and general carpentry.	☎ 05 45 82 06 84
Confolens	L.M. Clauduraud, Lessac Doors and windows, parquet floors and stairs.	☎ 05 45 84 08 67
Ruffec	Menuiserie 2000, 17 place Aristide Briand (showroom/office in the centre of town) Doors, shutters, security grilles, etc. English spoken.	☎ 05 45 85 57 30

Chimney Sweeps

Angoulême	Nettoyage Angoulême Services, 20 rue Gaudichaud	☎ 05 45 39 29 76
Chalais	Eric Carron, 23 ave. de l'Angoumois, Montmoreau	☎ 05 45 60 27 74
Cognac	Gérard Milliéroux, 2 rue Gilbert	☎ 05 45 32 32 68
Confolens	Techni-Net, le Bourg, Mazières	☎ 05 45 71 77 72
Ruffec	Stordeur, 35 rue Temple, Villefagnan	☎ 05 45 31 61 17

Electricians & Plumbers

Angoulême   Brunet, ZI des Agriers, rue des
Bosquets   ☎ 05 45 65 29 75
💻 *www.brunet-groupe.fr*
Installation, maintenance and repair of plumbing, heating and
electrical systems.

Ets. Jollet, ZI Agriers, rue du
Port Thureau   ☎ 05 45 91 31 91
General electrical firm, 24-hour emergency call out.

Chalais   Eric Carron, 23 ave de
l'Angoumois, Montmoreau   ☎ 05 45 60 27 74
Heating and plumbing.

Bernard Raison, 2 rue Emile Roux,
Chalais   ☎ 05 45 98 08 85

Cognac   C Viseaux & Fils, 143–145 rue de Boutiers ☎ 05 45 82 22 31
Electrics, plumbing and heating.

Confolens   J.D. Thromas, 13 rue Emile Roux   ☎ 05 45 84 13 97
General electrics.

Confolens   Ayrault, 6 Antoine Babaud, Lacroze   ☎ 05 45 84 01 11

Ruffec   Simon Kershaw, Le Bourg,
Beaulieu-sur-Sonnette   ☎ 05 45 89 38 02
This Briton deals with plumbing and heating, and bathroom and
kitchen installations.

C. Mazan, 8 rue de l'Hôpital   ☎ 05 45 31 29 02
Plumbing, heating and roofing.

	Michelet, 29bis route de Montjean	☎ 05 45 31 31 38

General electrics.

Villefagnan   Stordeur, 35 rue Temple   ☎ 05 45 31 61 17
An all-round company undertaking plumbing, roofing, heating and electrics and sweeping chimneys.

Painters & Decorators

General   Adam Blackaby   ☎ 05 45 98 07 25
A British tradesman based in southern Charente, who also undertakes property maintenance and gardening.

Plastering & Rendering

Chalais   Ross Newman, le Bourg, Bazac   ☎ 05 45 78 52 12
This French registered British plasterer also organises other English-speaking artisans.

Translators & Teachers

French Teachers & Courses

Angoulême   L'Association VECSI,
10 rue Ludovic Trarieux   ☎ 05 45 95 73 57
Group and individual courses can be arranged.

Chalais   Approches, Aubeterre   ☎ 05 45 98 13 78
This is an inter-cultural association that provides French lessons for foreigners. Accommodation can be found with either French or British families if a residential course is required.

Cognac   APEJ, 72 rue de Pons   ☎ 05 45 35 38 91

Confolens   Central Social Culturel du Confolentais ☎ 05 45 84 00 43

Château d'Assit, 2 rue St Michel   ☎ 05 45 84 00 43
(the large building next to the gendarmerie)
Courses specifically for English-speakers to learn French.

Ruffec   Sarah Rouche, Villiers le Roux   ☎ 05 45 31 30 39
✉ sarahrouche@wanadoo.fr

Horizons, Montjean Mairie
(north of Ruffec)   ☎ 05 45 31 29 90
Conversational French.

Translators

Angoulême	Keith Elliott, 20 rue St Gelais	☎ 05 45 92 34 34
	A Briton who is a court-approved translator.	
Barbezieux	Nadine Giraud, 28 bis rue Trarieux	☎ 05 45 78 16 73
Ruffec	Patricia Audebrand, 4 bis rue de l'Hôpital	☎ 05 45 65 54 89
	✉ *audebrand.patricia@wanadoo.fr*	
	All translation work carried out including quotes and liaison with tradesmen.	

Utilities

Electricity & Gas

Électricité de France/Gaz de France (EDF/GDF) is one company for the whole of France but operates its gas and electricity divisions separately. The numbers below are for general information; emergency numbers can be found on page 56.

General	GDF Région Centre Ouest, 35 rue Brigade Rac, Angoulême	☎ 05 45 24 24 24
	EDF Services Val de Charente	☎ 08 10 16 16 11

EDF local offices are listed below (there are no direct telephone numbers for these offices; you must dial one of the above numbers).

Angoulême	10 avenue Général de Gaulle
Barbezieux	1 rue Henri Fauconnier
Cognac	rue Balzac
Confolens	9 rue Merlie
Ruffec	rue du Docteur Maurice Tutard

Heating Oil

Angoulême	Auchan, La Couronne	☎ 05 45 67 21 21
Chalais	Garage Cornuault, le Bourg, Montboyer	☎ 05 45 98 29 21

Cognac	Avia, 44 boulevard Chatenay	☎ 05 45 35 26 26
Confolens	Société Charente Limousine Distribution, Chez Courteneuve, St Claud	☎ 05 45 71 30 74
Ruffec	SDPP Pourageuad Vallade, ZI Nord Quotes given for heating costs.	☎ 05 45 31 63 06

Water

The main water supply companies are listed below. If you aren't covered by one of these, your *mairie* will have details of your water supplier.

CISE	Combe à Baudet, Barbezieux	☎ 05 45 78 04 75
Générale des Eaux	15 rue Jean Bart, Cognac	☎ 08 11 90 29 02
SAUR	1 rue des Chasseurs, ZE de Puymoyen, Angoulême	☎ 05 45 61 16 17
SEMEA	2 rue Colonel Bernard Leley, Angoulême	☎ 05 45 37 37 37
SIAEP	7 rue Récollets, Confolens	☎ 05 45 29 54 80

Wood

| Cognac | Marcel Gauthier et Fils, Champ du Château Les Métairies (east of the town) | ☎ 05 45 81 16 69 |
| Confolens | SOS Bois de Chauffage, rue François Deguercy, Brigueil (south-east of the town) | ☎ 05 45 89 12 02 |

La Rochelle

3

Charente-Maritime

This chapter provides details of facilities and services in the department of Charente-Maritime (17). General information about each subject can be found in **Chapter 1**. All entries are arranged alphabetically by town, except where a service applies over a wide area, in which case it's listed at the beginning of the relevant section under 'General'. A map of Charente-Maritime is shown below.

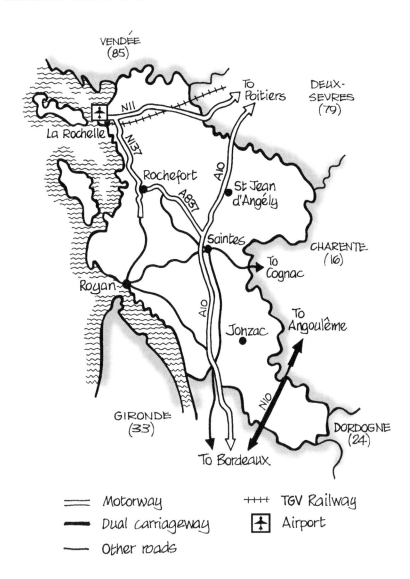

═══ Motorway	┼┼┼┼ TGV Railway
━━ Dual carriageway	✈ Airport
─── Other roads	

Accommodation

Camping

Jonzac	Les Castors, route de Montendre	☎ 05 46 48 25 65

Three-star campsite open March to October inclusive.

La Rochelle   There are many campsites in La Rochelle and the immediate area. Details of the two municipal campsites are given below. For information about all campsites in La Rochelle you can visit 🖥 *www.larochelle-info.fr* or contact the tourist office on ☎ 05 46 41 14 68.

Camping Port Neuf, boulevard
Aristide Rondeau   ☎ 05 46 43 81 20

Camping du Soleil, avenue Marillac   ☎ 05 46 44 42 53

Rochefort   Camping Le Bateau, rue des Pêcheurs
d'Islande   ☎ 05 46 99 41 00
Open all year round and has an outdoor pool.

Royan   Camping Municipal La Triloterie, 44ter
avenue Aliénor d'Aquitaine   ☎ 05 46 05 26 91

Camping Clairfontaine, 18 rue Colonel
Lachaud   ☎ 05 46 39 08 11
🖥 *www.camping-clairefontaine.com*

Camping Les Coquelicots,
7 rue Coquelicots   ☎ 05 46 38 23 21
🖥 *www.campingcoquelicots.com*

St Jean d'Angély Camping Municipal, quai de Bernouët ☎ 05 46 32 26 16
(alongside the river and the Atlantys water park)
A three-star site with many activities.

Saintes   Camping Au Fil de L'Eau,
6 rue de Courbiac   ☎ 05 46 93 08 00
(in the north of the town alongside the river).
The site has a swimming pool.

Châteaux

Saintes   La Rotonde, 2 rue Monconseil   ☎ 05 46 74 74 44
🖥 *www.larotonde.fr.st*
One of the most prestigious examples of a 19th century
bourgeois residence in the Saintes area. Overlooking the river

Charente it is one of the most spacious buildings in the town with large rooms, marble fireplaces and huge mirrors, running off a vast central corridor. Four double rooms with en-suite and one suite for four people. English spoken, open all year, double rooms €84, suite €153.

St Simon-de-Pellouaille   Château de Pellouaille, la Tillade   ☎ 05 46 90 00 20
(south of Saintes)
This château offers painting courses, horse riding and bicycle hire (on request). There are three bedrooms with en-suite facilities; dinner in the château is possible if booked. English is spoken and the château is open all year round. Rooms €75 to €110, evening meal €31.

Gîtes And Bed & Breakfast

La Rochelle   1, Perspective de l'Océan   ☎ 05 46 50 63 63
💻 *www.itea2.com/GDF/17*
Gîtes de France listed. Bookings can be made by phone or via the internet.

💻 *www.larochelle-info.com*
This information website for La Rochelle has a comprehensive list of accommodation available in the area.

Bars & Nightlife

There are two small brochures called *Vie Sorties Mag* and *Sortir* that are published regularly giving comprehensive details of fairs, concerts, nightlife and anything else happening in the Charente-Maritime area. Available free from tourist offices, libraries and you may also find it delivered to your home.

General   Orchestre Charente Océan   ☎ 05 46 92 34 72
This orchestra performs in auditoriums in Cognac, Saintes and Rochefort throughout the year.

Jonzac   Les Antilles, avenue Jean Moulin   ☎ 05 46 48 12 11
💻 *www.haute-saintonge.com*
This complex has a small stage area and holds cabaret and theme evenings.

Le Canotier, rue des Carmes   ☎ 05 46 48 45 57
Bar with theme evenings, concerts and karaoke.

Casino de Jonzac, avenue Jean Moulin,
Les Antilles   ☎ 05 46 48 16 16
Open Mondays, Tuesdays, Fridays, Saturdays and Sundays 8pm to 2am, Saturdays until 3am. Identification is required for entry. Games room, black jack and roulette. There's a cocktail

bar every evening from 8pm and a restaurant from Fridays to Tuesdays 7.30 to10.30pm. Frequent theme evenings, dinner dances and a tea dance with an orchestra the first Sunday of each month from 3pm.

Le Coq d'Or, 18 place du Château   ☎ 05 46 48 00 06
This bar/brasserie has pool, video games and table football.

Landes   Au Café des Jours Heureux   ☎ 05 46 59 91 51
(between Surgères and St Jean d'Angély)
This concert bar has metal, punk, funk and French singers performing on a regular basis.

La Rochelle   Bowling des Minimes, rue Trinquette   ☎ 05 46 45 40 40
Also has snooker tables.

Casino Barrière, Esplanade du Mail   ☎ 05 46 34 12 75
Bar, restaurant, machines, roulette and black jack.

L'Harmattan, 28 rue Bletterie   ☎ 05 46 41 12 81
🖳 *www.harmattan-bar.com*
Music bar and cocktails, open every day, happy hour 7 to 8pm, 11pm to midnight.

Le Petit Train de Saint-Trojan, la Gare,
rue Camille Samson   ☎ 05 46 76 01 26
🖳 *www.le-ptit-train.com*
Night time train rides through the forest, sand dunes and past the beaches of Ile d'Oléron, restaurant at the station. Various dates throughout the summer, departing at 8.30pm and 9pm.

L'Oxford and Club Papagayo,
Plage de la Concurrence   ☎ 05 46 41 51 81
Open every night except Tuesdays, two different clubs/discos.

Le Phare Café, 13 quai Valin   ☎ 05 46 42 18 48
DJ every Friday evening.

CAP 82, 82 avenue E. Grasset   ☎ 05 46 52 16 75
This concert bar has karaoke Sundays from 9.30pm as well as blues and jazz evenings. Open Tuesdays to Sundays 6.30pm to 2am.

Jules & Jim, rue Rambaud   ☎ 05 46 67 00 55
(behind Verdun Commissariat)
Club, café and concert bar with shows and various acts.

Luna Park, route de Dirée, les Mathes   ☎ 05 46 22 30 66
Theme park with rides and various amusements, for adults and children. Open every evening from 8pm.

Along the seafront of La Rochelle there are numerous restaurants (one with live shows), cafes and bars, all with outside seating, including a cocktail bar where the drinks are served in a variety of unusual receptacles. Meanwhile in the streets there are side shows, magicians and numerous acts to entertain. **Note that during the summer the old port of La Rochelle is closed to traffic in the evenings.**

Rochefort

Casino Fouras, place Bugeau, Fouras   ☎ 05 46 84 63 16
Venue with cinema, restaurant, bar, cabaret, disco and games machines. Open10am until dawn.

Le Comptoir des Îles, 72 rue Républiques ☎ 05 46 99 08 32
Karaoke.

L'Extravangance Club, 51 rue du
Docteur Peltier   ☎ 05 46 88 45 72
(just across from the tourist office)
Open Tuesdays to Saturdays, 5pm to 2am, Sundays 9pm to 2am.

Fair Play, avenue Wilson   ☎ 05 46 99 64 99
Snooker tables and games rooms.

Le Galway, 46 rue du Docteur Peltier   ☎ 05 46 99 88 85
Irish pub across from the tourist office hosting a variety of live acts.

Guinguette 2000, 2 rue de la Mauratière ☎ 05 46 87 05 06
Disco.

Le Mini Golf Tropica, Le Cadoret,
direction of Fouras   ☎ 05 46 84 07 07
Two 18-hole courses of crazy golf, tropical/discovery themes. From mid-May there's night time golf until midnight. In the summer season it is open every day from 2pm to 2am.

La Rhumerie, place Colbert   ☎ 05 46 99 08 32
A pub with snooker tables, and a karaoke on Tuesdays to Saturdays with over 1,000 songs.

Salle Roger Rondeaux, Espace Gazin,
Fouras   ☎ 05 46 84 03 31
Concert venue that hosts dance evenings, concerts, orchestras and other shows.

Royan

Casino Barrière, Plage de Pontaillac   ☎ 05 46 39 03 31
Casino on the beach open every day until 3am, the Atlantic

café has more than 20 cocktails, quiet areas and somewhere to eat. Live music Saturdays from 10pm. The casino has 175 machines, roulette, stud poker and black jack. Identification required for access to the casino.

Au Bureau, 49 boulevard Aristide Briand ☎ 05 46 05 08 76
Bar/brasserie that is open all year from 10am to 2am, food served continuously from noon to 1.30am.

Pont 10, Le Port de Royan   ☎ 05 46 39 01 10
(down by the marina)
This music café is for the over 20's, open all year.

Le Kouba, La Corniche, St Georges
de Didonne   ☎ 05 46 06 08 78
(on the beach at Saint Georges)
Bar and disco.

Le Domaine, route de Breuillet   ☎ 05 46 22 60 60
Four bars, two clubs and a restaurant.

St Jean d'Angély La Salsa, 4 place du Marché   ☎ 05 46 59 00 53
Concerts and live entertainment.
Bar de l'Hôtel de Ville, 10 place de
Hôtel de Ville   ☎ 05 46 32 00 73
Arcade games and table football.

Ellis Park, 10 rue Gambetta   ☎ 05 46 09 93 49
This bar/pub is open Mondays to Fridays 9am to midnight, Fridays and Saturdays 9am to 2am and Sundays 10am to 9pm. There's outside seating in the pedestrian square.

St Savinien Le Morgan, Le Mung   ☎ 05 46 90 57 31
(north of Saintes)
Three different clubs, open Friday and Saturday evenings. Tea dances held Thursdays 2 to 7pm.

Stage de Percussions et Danses
Afro-Cubaines   ☎ 05 46 90 20 92
African, Salsa, percussion, lessons, courses, concerts and evening entertainment.

Saintes Le Manoir, route de Bordeaux   ☎ 05 46 93 20 78
This nightclub is open every evening.

Saintes Bowling, 12 rue des Rochers   ☎ 05 46 95 04 04
🖳 *www.saintesbowling.com*
Ten lanes for bowling, French billiards, pool and snooker tables, bar, mini golf and table football. Open every day all

year. Sundays to Thursdays 2pm to 2am, Fridays, Saturdays and bank holidays 2pm to 3am.

Saintes Vegas, route de Royan   ☎ 05 46 97 00 00
🖳 *www.saintes-vegas.com*
A club that has eight different areas and holds discos, dinner dances, themed evenings and has a restaurant. There's a dinner dance on the first and third Saturday of every month.

Business Services

Computer Services

Jonzac	Multimédia Boutique, 30 rue Sadi Carnot	☎ 05 46 48 04 75

Sale and maintenance of computers.

La Rochelle   Abaque Informatique, 29 rue Moulin
Benoit, Lagord   ☎ 05 46 67 16 76
All computer needs catered for.

Rochefort   Cyber J, 127bis rue Thiers   ☎ 05 46 99 81 25
Repairs, spares and internet access. Tuesdays to Saturdays 10am to 7pm.

Royan   Cedimatel, 6 rue Paul Doumer   ☎ 05 46 05 91 13
Open Monday afternoons through to Saturday afternoons.

St Jean d'Angély SOS Micro, 31 rue Pascal Bourcy   ☎ 05 46 32 02 87
Open Tuesdays to Saturdays 10 to noon, 3 to 7pm.

Saintes   Micro, rue Alsace Lorraine   ☎ 05 46 93 51 75
Some English is spoken. Open Tuesdays to Saturdays 10 to 12.30pm, 2.30 to 7pm.

Employment Agencies

(see page 50)

Communications

Fixed Telephones

General   France Télécom: Dial 1014 or go to
🖳 *www.francetelecom.fr*
Local shops are listed below.

Rochefort   53 avenue Charles de Gaulle

La Rochelle	rue Moulin de Vendôme, Lagord (outskirts)
	31 rue Saint Yonn (town centre)
Royan	8bis boulevard de la République
Saintes	28 rue Gautier

Internet Access

Jonzac	Jonz@c Médi@ Pole, 83 rue Sadi Carnot ☎ 05 46 04 79 18
	(tucked away in the corner of the courtyard)
	Open Mondays to Fridays 2 to 7pm. Training on Wednesday
	mornings arranged by appointment.
La Rochelle	La Poste, 6 rue de l'Hôtel de Ville ☎ 05 46 30 41 30
	Mondays to Fridays 8.30am to 6.30pm, Saturdays 8.30am to
	12.30pm.
Rochefort	Cyber J, 127bis rue Thiers ☎ 05 46 99 81 25
	(near the bus station)
	Tuesdays to Saturdays 10am to 7pm.
Royan	Cyber Atlantys de Royan, Salle Le Chay
	Palais des Congrès ☎ 05 46 23 47 97
	(situated at the far end of avenue Gambetta, looks like a large
	office building)
	Nine computers with ADSL lines. Mondays, Wednesdays and
	Saturdays 9.30am to 6pm, Tuesdays and Fridays 9.30am to
	8pm, Thursdays 9.30am to 12.30pm, 2 to 6pm.
St Jean d'Angély	SOS Micro, 31 rue Pascal Bourcy ☎ 05 46 32 02 87
	Open Tuesdays to Saturdays 10 to noon, 3 to 7pm
	Fridays late session, 8pm to midnight. €5 for 1 hour.
Saintes	Tourist Office, 62 cours National ☎ 05 46 74 23 82
	Open Mondays to Saturdays 9.30 to12.30, 2.15 to 6pm.
	To use the internet you just need a phone card.

Mobile Telephones

All France Telecom stores sell mobile phones.

Jonzac	Odyssée Telecom, 9 rue Sadi-Carnot ☎ 05 46 49 37 59
	Open Tuesdays to Saturdays.
	Central Phone, 44 rue de Four ☎ 05 46 04 19 21
	Open Tuesdays to Saturdays.
La Rochelle	Bouygues Telecom, 38 rue Chaudrier ☎ 05 46 51 19 53

	Espace SFR, avenue Michel Crépeau	☎ 05 46 30 07 30
Rochefort	Espace SFR, 80 rue de la République	☎ 05 46 88 09 09
	ATP, 18 avenue La Fayette	☎ 05 46 82 19 82
Royan	Espace SFR, 5 cours Europe	☎ 05 46 05 90 00
	Indiana Phone, cours Europe	☎ 05 46 06 15 08

St Jean d'Angély Central Phone, 9 rue Gambetta ☎ 05 46 59 27 27
Open from Tuesdays to Saturdays from 10am.

Saintes Espace SFR, 1 rue St Pierre ☎ 05 46 96 67 67
Open all day Mondays to Saturdays.

Mobistore, 24 rue Victor Hugo ☎ 05 46 96 21 21

Domestic Services

Baby Sitting & Crèches

Rochefort Office Municipal Jeunesse,
97 rue de La République ☎ 05 46 82 10 40

Crèche Municipale, 1 rue Champlain ☎ 05 46 99 06 90

Curtain Making

General Carol Weekes 'Les Petites Pommes',
Les Hâtes, Couture ☎ 05 45 90 88 36
✉ *dacawe@wanadoo.fr*
Curtains made to measure for addresses in Poitou-Charentes.

Equipment & Tool Hire

Asnières-la- Cemta Perdreau Location, RN150 ☎ 05 46 59 17 01
Giraud (near St Jean d'Angély)
Elevators, mini diggers, compressors etc.

Aulnay Sofral, ZA Ormeau (close to Intermarché) ☎ 05 46 33 31 84
High pressure cleaners to mini skips and compressors.

Rochefort Loca 17
16 avenue Armand Salle ☎ 05 46 99 75 09
A wide range of equipment from diggers to floor polishers.

Tonnay-Charente Locatoumat, Zac de la Croix Biron   ☎ 05 46 83 42 92
💻 *www.locatoumat.com*
Equipment for building, decorating and gardening.

Fancy Dress Hire

Rochefort   L'Art Lequin, 51 rue Gambetta   ☎ 05 46 87 22 55

Launderettes

La Rochelle   Lava Pratick, 20 Pépinière

Jonzac   Laverie Jonzacaise, 62 rue Sadi Carnot

Rochefort   Laveries & Cie
(one in avenue Charles de Gaulle and another in the far corner of the marina.)
Open seven days a week, 7am to 9.30pm,

Royan   Le Lavoir, place du Docteur Gantier
(opposite the station)

St Jean d'Angély   Laverie Angérienne, 65 avenue Général Leclerc

Saintes   Laveries et Cie, 46 terrace cours Reverseaux

Septic Tank Services

General   Jean-Claude Bernaud
St Mandé-sur-Brédoire   ☎ 05 46 33 15 71
All tank-related services are available including empting, cleaning and pipe blockages cleared.

Sanitra Fourrier, Les Petits Bonneveaux,
St Vivien   ☎ 05 46 56 24 51
Also has units in Châtelaillon, Jonzac, and Saujon.

Entertainment

Cinemas

Jonzac   Cinéma Familia, 1 rue Sadi Carnot   ☎ 05 46 48 14 45

La Rochelle   Cinéma CGR, avenue H. Becquerel   ☎ 08 92 68 04 45
💻 *www.cgrcinemas.com* 8 screens

Rochefort   Cinéma ABC, 104 rue Pierre Loti   ☎ 05 46 99 10 68

	Apollo, rue du Docteur Peltier	☎ 05 46 99 01 80
Royan	Cinéma Le Lido, 65 Front de Mer	☎ 05 46 05 24 10
	ABC, 49 Front de Mer	☎ 05 46 05 27 25
St Jean d'Angély	Cinéma Eden, boulevard Joseph Lair	☎ 05 46 32 02 26
Saintes	Cinéma Olympia 2000, 136 avenue Gambetta	☎ 05 46 97 21 21
	Cinéma Gallia, 67ter cours National	☎ 05 46 92 20 32

English Books

There's a selection of English books at all the libraries below.

	Mon	Tue	Wed	Thu	Fri	Sat
Jonzac 12 rue Verdun ☎ 05 46 48 26 64	closed	3.00–6.00	10.00–12.00 3.00–6.00	closed	10.00–12.00 3.00–6.00	10–12.00
La Rochelle Avenue Marillac, Les Minimes ☎ 05 46 45 71 71	1.00–7.00	1.00–7.00	10.00–12.00 1.00–6.00	closed	1.00–7.00	10–12.00 2.00–6.00
Rochefort La Corderie Royale ☎ 05 46 82 66 00	closed	1.30–8.00	10.00–12.00 1.30–6.00	closed	12.00–6.00	10–12.00 1.30–6.00
St Jean d'Angély Abbaye Royale ☎ 05 46 32 61 00	3.00–7.00	closed	9.30–5.00	closed	1.30–5.00	10–12.00
Saintes place de l'Echevinage ☎ 05 46 93 25 39	closed	1.30–6.00	10.00–5.00	1.30–6.00	1.30–6.00	10–12.00 2.30–6.00

Festivals

March/April	Châtelaillon Plage	☎ 05 46 56 26 97

Festival International de Cerfs-Volants
A festival of kite flying that takes place on the beach.

May	St Georges-de-Didonne	☎ 05 46 06 87 98

Musiques et Gastronomies du Monde. An annual festival which invites you to travel to the heart of sound and tastes of the planet. Amongst others there's Cuban, Caribbean and reggae music during this festival whilst food from all over the world can be discovered; including African, Thai, oriental and Latin American.

Late May/ early June	La Rochelle International yachting weeks.	☎ 05 46 41 14 68

July	Montguyon	☎ 05 46 04 10 60

Festival 'Mondiofolk'. Folklore festival bringing dance, singing and music from all over the world to fill the streets for five days, with Mexico, Argentina, Fiji and many other countries bringing their traditions and entertainment to Montguyon.

July	St Palais-sur-Mer	☎ 05 46 23 22 58

Festival Européen d'Art Pyrotechnique. A large extravaganza over the lake of St Palais sur Mer, with a competition between other European countries.

November	La Rochelle	

The last Sunday of November is the day of the La Rochelle marathon, which is the second-largest in France.

Theatres

Ile d'Oléron	Castel, 5 rue de la République, St Pierre d'Oléron	☎ 05 46 75 13 13

A show venue on the Ile d'Oléron, with concerts, theatrical productions, films and comedies.

Ile de Ré	'La Maline', avenue Mail, La Couarde sur Mer	☎ 05 46 29 93 53

💻 *www.ardc-la-maline.net*
(situated on the island west of La Rochelle)

La Rochelle	La Coursive, 4 rue St Jean du Pérot	☎ 05 46 51 54 00
	Théâtre de La Ville en Bois, 20 Quarter rue Albert I	☎ 05 46 41 64 81
	Théâtre de l'Utopie, 39 rue Thiers	☎ 05 46 41 71 33

Rochefort	La Coupe d'Or, 101 rue de la République	☎ 05 46 82 15 15

Theatrical and dance productions, music events and cabarets are all held here. A full brochure is available from the theatre or tourist office.

	Atelier d'Art Dramatique, 2 rue La Touche Tréville	☎ 05 46 87 58 45

St Jean d'Angély   Comédie de l'Eperon 'La Barrière'   ☎ 05 46 32 23 88
Theatrical productions and workshops for teenagers and
adults. Contact Mme Marie-José Fourchaud.

Saintes   Gallia Théâtre, 67bis cours National   ☎ 05 46 92 10 20
(in the centre of the town)
A newly-restored theatre.

Video & DVD Hire

Jonzac   Vidéo Loisirs, 22 rue Sadi Carnot   ☎ 05 46 49 42 50
(opposite the cinema)
Mondays to Saturdays 2.30 to 8pm.

La Rochelle   Choc Vidéo, 1 rue Voiliers   ☎ 05 46 50 54 00
Videos, DVDs and DVD players for hire.
Open Mondays to Saturdays 10am to 1pm, 3 to 9pm, Sundays
3 to 9pm, closed bank holidays.

Rochefort   Espace Vidéo, 100 rue République   ☎ 05 46 99 20 20
Also a 24 hour dispenser.

Royan   King 7 Vidéo, 102 boulevard de
Lattre de Tassigny   ☎ 05 46 06 69 93
Also a 24-hour video and DVD dispenser.

St Jean d'Angély Zoom Video, 29 boulevard Général Leclerc ☎ 05 46 32 26 73
Open Mondays to Saturdays, 3.30 to 8.30pm, from 4pm
Mondays.

Saintes   Ciné Vidéo, 48 cours National   ☎ 05 46 74 09 60
(on the right going up the hill towards the tourist office)
Open seven days a week and has a 24 hour dispenser.

Leisure Activities

This section isn't intended to be a definitive guide but gives a wide range
of ideas for the department. Prices and opening hours were correct at the
time of publication, but it's best to check before travelling long distances.

Art Classes

La Rochelle   Atelier Noël, Espace Art'Chipel,
Les Minimes   ☎ 05 46 44 59 60
Personalised courses and demonstrations available in all
techniques including oil painting, water colours and pastels.

Rochefort   Ecole-Atelier, 69bis rue Grimaux   ☎ 05 46 87 08 31
Drawing and painting classes.

Royan   L'Atelier, rue des Arts   ☎ 05 46 05 78 70
                    Courses all year in drawing, painting, modeling, engraving,
                    calligraphy and binding.

St Jean d'Angély   Atelier d'Arts, 48 avenue Général de Gaulle ☎ 05 46 32 06 86
                    Art, design, silk painting and more, adults and children. Contact
                    Mme Maryvonne Texier.

Saintes   Ecole de Dessin de Saintes, Maison des
                    Associations, 31 rue du Cormier   ☎ 05 46 98 65 33
                    Pastels, paints, sculptures and modelling.

Ballooning

Jonzac   Jonzac Aérodrome, route de Neulles   ☎ 05 46 48 06 47

Bike Hire

La Rochelle   Place de Verdun   ☎ 05 46 34 02 22
                    First two hours free, subsequent hours €1 per hour.

Royan   Royan Bicycles, Galerie Botton Royan   ☎ 05 46 06 08 18
                    Bikes and baby carriages available.

St Jean d'Angély   Kayak Club Angérien,
                    30 quai de Bernouët   ☎ 05 46 32 59 61
                    Mountain bikes for hire.

Boat & Train Rides

Ile d'Oléron   P'tit Train de St Trojan   ☎ 05 46 76 01 26
                    Train rides through the forest, sand dunes and past the
                    beaches of Ile d'Oléron, taking you to places inaccessible by
                    road.

La Rochelle   Vieux Port   ☎ 05 46 50 68 44
                    An excursion that includes a trip past Fort Boyard, for a whole
                    or half day, leaving from the old port of La Rochelle.

Royan   Petit Train Touristique de
                    La Côte de Beauté   ☎ 05 46 05 50 05
                    It leaves Royan from the promenade on the seafront in the
                    centre of town in the afternoons and evenings for rides lasting
                    from 40 minutes to an hour. €5 per person, free for under
                    three-year-olds.

Saintes   B.Palissy II   ☎ 05 46 74 23 82
                    💻 *www.ot-saintes.fr*
                    Aboard the B.Palissy II, various trips are available. The
                    shortest is two hours, departs at 4pm and costs €10. There's
                    also a gastronomic one which costs around €35.

Traditional Boat Trip   ☎ 05 46 74 23 82
🖳 *www.ot-saintes.fr*
Traditional wooden boats with a capacity for 40 people, trips
every day except Mondays. On Saturdays and Sundays you're
also offered a Charentais aperitif. Adults €4,50, children €2,50.

St Savinien   Saviboat, Ile de la Grenouillette   ☎ 05 46 90 14 67
Novelty boats to be captained by adults or children around the
lake and waterway in the park. Closed during the winter
months.

Bridge

Jonzac   Jonzac Bridge Club, 10 rue Paul Bert   ☎ 05 46 48 11 99
Regular tournaments Thursdays at 8.15pm and friendly
matches Fridays at 3.45pm. Beginners welcome Tuesdays at
8.15pm.

Rochefort   Bridge Rochefortais, 37 rue du
                   Docteur Pujos   ☎ 05 46 87 33 18

Royan   Bridge Club du Château de Mons,
                   36 rue Pierre du Gua   ☎ 05 46 05 96 23
Meetings everyday at 2.30pm, tournaments Mondays,
Thursdays and Saturdays 2.30pm, Tuesdays at 8.30pm. First
visit free.

St Jean d'Angély   Club de Bridge, 40 avenue Port Mahon ☎ 05 46 32 59 37
Meetings several times a week.

Saintes   Bridge Club de Saintes, 11 rue St Eutrope ☎ 05 46 93 78 21

Children's Activity Clubs

Jonzac   Centre Municipal de Loisirs,
                   avenue de Gaulle   ☎ 05 46 48 28 27
Activities organised for school holidays and Wednesdays.
Open from 7.30am-6.30pm.

La Rochelle   Centre de Loisirs, Base Nautique,
                   Esplanade St Jean d'Acre   ☎ 05 46 41 18 47
Children's activities organised all year round.

Royan   There are six children's holiday clubs along the beaches of
                   Royan, catering for 3 to 13-year-olds. They generally close for
                   lunch.

                   Les Dauphins, Plage de Pontaillac   ☎ 06 19 70 13 98

	ABC, Plage de Pontaillac	☎ 06 80 00 40 00
	Les Pingouins, Plage de la Grande Conche	☎ 06 61 23 44 33
	Les Guignols, Plage de Foncillon	☎ 06 81 04 97 98
	Les Tritons, Plage de la Grande Conche	☎ 06 16 56 36 55
	Les Hippocampes, Plage du Chay	☎ 06 61 17 65 49

Rochefort   Baby Gym, La Rochefortaise   ☎ 05 46 99 04 67

Centre de Loisirs 'Les Grenouilles'   ☎ 05 46 87 07 00
Activities organised throughout school holidays.

St Jean d'Angély Centre Aéré, 8 allée d'Aussy   ☎ 05 46 32 27 46
Activities organised for school holidays and Wednesdays. For
teenagers there are also summer camps. The office is open
Mondays, Tuesdays, Thursdays and Fridays 9am to 11am, 2 to
4.15pm

Evasion, 1 rue Lacoue   ☎ 05 46 32 33 46
Club for 6 to 16-year-olds. Summer mountain camps and
excursions. Contact Mr Jean-François Barussaud.

Circus Skills

Jonzac   Salle Jeanne d'Arc, St Genis   ☎ 06 83 36 08 34
(just east of Jonzac)
Both children and adults can learn artistic skills, co-ordination,
balance and games.

Rochefort   Ap'Art, 18 rue de la République   ☎ 05 46 87 58 45
Courses in circus skills.

Crazy Golf

La Rochelle   There are various crazy golf courses behind the beaches
on the coast south of La Rochelle.

Royan   Mini Golf du Parc   ☎ 05 46 06 61 02
(in the park to the east of the town)

Mini Golf du Pontaillac,
Square de La Trémoille   ☎ 05 46 39 25 29
(near the casino on the sea front)
Both the above have 18 holes and are open from 10am to
midnight in season.

St Jean d'Angély There's a course in the park.
(alongside Atlantys water park)

Dancing

Jonzac   Ecole des Arts de la Haute Saintonge   ☎ 05 46 48 31 26
Ballet, contemporary, African and traditional, waltz, tango and
others.

La Rochelle   Académie de Danse, 27 rue Villeneuve   ☎ 05 46 41 07 13

Rochefort   Ecole de Danse, Port de Plaisance   ☎ 05 46 87 32 58
(near the marina)
Ballet and jazz.

                Swing Danse, 2 rue du 14 Juillet   ☎ 05 46 44 11 82
Rock, waltz, tango and salsa.

Royan   Les Ateliers de la Danse,
                39ter rue du Vivier   ☎ 05 46 38 53 60
(off boulevard Georges Clemenceau)
There are jazz, ballet and flamenco courses, as well as
traditional courses such as the waltz, tango etc.

St Jean d'Angély Danse Animation Création,
                67 avenue du Port   ☎ 05 46 32 03 66
Dance shows, rock and roll classes, keep fit, step and
aerobics. Contact Mme. Bernadette Leroux.

                Danse Arabesque, Gymnase du Col   ☎ 05 46 59 70 12
Adult gym and jazz classes.

Saintes   USS Danse et Fitness, 20bis Cours Genêt ☎ 05 46 91 14 92
Jazz, fitness and classical dance.

Flying

Jonzac   Aéroclub, route de Neulles   ☎ 05 46 48 06 47
Flying school, introduction and sightseeing flights.

La Rochelle   Aéro-Club de La Rochelle,
                Aérodrome de Laleu   ☎ 05 46 42 54 74
Contact Didier Baele.

                Aéro-Club Rochelais, Aéroport de
                La Rochelle   ☎ 05 46 42 54 42
Contact Patrick Chansigaud.

Rochefort   Aéro Club du Pays Rochefortais   ☎ 05 46 83 15 88
Aérodrome St Agnant.

Royan	PB Hélicoptères, Aérodrome de Royan-Médis	☎ 05 46 02 45 04

💻 *www.pbhelicopteres.com*
Flying school and tourist flights.

	Héli Atlantique, Aérodrome de Bois Fleury	☎ 05 46 47 03 33

Saintes	Aéro Club de Saintes, Aérodrome de Saintes, Thénac	☎ 05 46 93 08 97

Lessons and tourist trips. 30 minutes €54, 40 minutes €80 and 1 hour €110. The price is the total cost for three people going up. A minimum 40 minutes are needed if you want to go out over the coast.

St Pierre d'Oléron Atlantique Aviation

💻 *www.atlantique-aviation.com*
(Based on Ile d'Oléron)
Trial and sight seeing flights.

Gyms & Health Clubs

La Rochelle	Le Rochelois, 66 boulevard Winston Churchill	☎ 05 46 43 88 36

This gym is open seven days a week, including bank holidays, with various gym and step classes, a summer pool, tennis, sauna and weights.

Royan	Groupe Gym'club, 1bis rue du Phare du Chay	☎ 05 46 38 61 57

Conventional gym with weights, machines, sauna and classes. Open Mondays, Tuesdays, Thursdays and Fridays 9am to 8.30pm, Wednesdays 3 to 8.30pm, Saturdays 8.30 to noon. Payable per session, weekly or monthly.

St Jean d'Angély	Club Haltérophilie-Musculation, 58 route de Niort	☎ 05 46 32 02 76

Gym, fitness and weights. Men, women and juniors are all welcome. Contact Mr Philippe Giovannini.

Karting & Quad Bikes

Rochefort	L'Houmeau, route Ile de Ré	☎ 05 46 50 88 90

Royan	Karting du Fief de la Mer, 13 rue Arsonval	☎ 05 46 05 79 94

600 metre track for training or kart hire, karts suitable for seven-year-olds upwards. Open all year, out of season from 10am to 8pm, high season 9.30am to 1am.

St Jean d'Angély Angély Racing Kart,
Circuit de Polouaille   ☎ 06 85 20 47 99
Open every day from 4 to 8pm from 1st July to 30th
September, closed Tuesdays. Weekends and bank holidays 3
to 8pm; 1st March to 30th June and 1st October to 15th
December. Minimum age 12.

Saintes   Les Gonads, off RN137 Saintes to Pons. ☎ 05 46 93 76 86
270cc karts, open 10am to midnight in the summer, weekends
and bank holidays by reservation. Minimum age eight.

Lakes & Beaches

Châtelaillon-   Information line   ☎ 05 46 56 26 97
Plage   A 3km (2mi) long fine sandy beach with volleyball, football, a
beach club for children, shows and games. Nearby there's
tennis, clay pigeon shooting, crazy golf, a casino and *pétanque*.

Fouras   Situated on a peninsula facing Ile d'Aix and Fort Boyard
(north-east of Rochefort)
There are sandy beaches including the southern beach at Port
des Barques.

Ile d'Oléron   🖳 *www.marennes-oleron-tour.org*   ☎ 05 46 85 65 23
This island is the largest in Charente-Maritime with vast
beaches of fine sand and sheltered from the on-shore breezes
by the pine forests.

Ile de Ré   ☎ 05 46 09 00 55
Long beaches on every side of this island and alongside each
of the ten villages, ideal for families, it has kids' clubs, swings,
trampolines and games.

La Palmyre   ☎ 05 46 22 41 07
(just north-west of Royan along the coast)
This seaside resort is set in a vast forest with 30km of beach
and cycle paths looking out to the sea and Ile d'Oléron.
Children's beach clubs, water sports centre and numerous
surfing spots.

Royan   There are various beaches along the coastline by Royan,
with children's clubs, beach tents, sun beds and other
facilities all close to hand. There are also two naturist
beaches, la Côte Sauvage and la Grande Côte.

Grande Conche, boulevard Garner   ☎ 05 46 23 00 00
This is the largest beach of them all, with more than 2km of
fine sand with four other sandy beaches nearby. All of these
beaches have at least one kids club in July and August.

Music

Jonzac	Ecole des Arts de la Haute Saintonge	☎ 05 46 48 31 26

Full range of instruments taught, including orchestral.

La Rochelle   Ecole Nationale de Musique et de Danse,
15 rue des Fonderies   ☎ 05 46 41 07 37

Ballet Atlantique, 4 rue St Jean du Perot   ☎ 05 46 41 17 75

Rochefort   Gammon Frédéric, 94bis rue Thiers   ☎ 05 46 87 35 94
Introduction to music as well as piano and voice training.

Rock School, Office Municipal Jeunesse,
119 rue Pierre Loti   ☎ 05 46 82 10 41
Guitar, drums, didgeridoo, percussion.

Royan   Ecole de Musique, rue des Arts   ☎ 05 46 06 51 00
Open all year during term time.

St Jean d'Angély   École Municipale de Musique,
Abbaye Royale   ☎ 05 46 32 27 70
Mr Philippe Savored is the director.

Saintes   Ateliers Musician Saintais,
15 rue St Eutrope   ☎ 05 46 74 37 06
Lessons in all disciplines, from singing and guitar to percussion
and saxophone. Minimum age five.

Photography

St Jean d'Angély   32 avenue de Rochefort   ☎ 05 46 59 08 76
Contact Mr Jean Echard.

Saintes   Caméra Photo Club de Saintonge,
42 rue St Eutrope   ☎ 05 46 74 21 21
Lessons in photography and video techniques.

Scouts & Guides

Rochefort   Scouts de France   ☎ 05 46 99 35 38
Contact Mr Dutreix.

Social Clubs & Organisations

Contact Groups

St Jean d'Angély   AVF St Jean, 132 Faubourg Taillebourg   ☎ 05 46 33 13 05
This organisation is run by Mme Jacqueline Schitz and is
specifically to welcome new arrivals to St Jean d'Angély, of

whatever nationality. Provides linguistic help and organising culinary and sporting activities. Meetings every Thursdays 2 to 4pm. Closed during the summer.

Rotary Clubs

Rochefort	10 rue du Docteur Pujos	☎ 05 46 87 50 90
St Jean d'Angély	49 boulevard du 14 juillet President – Mr Philippe Rivet.	☎ 05 46 32 34 97

Town Twinning

Rochefort	Comité de Jumelage de Rochefort Rochefort is twinned with Burton in England.	☎ 05 46 99 69 42
	Comité de Jumelage – Tonnay Charente Tonnay Charente is twinned with Sandown in the Isle of Wight.	☎ 05 46 88 03 61
Saintes	Amitiés Saintes-Salisbury, 14bis chemin des Sables Saintes is twinned with Salisbury in England.	☎ 05 46 92 11 82

Stamp Collecting

Jonzac	Amicale Philatélique de Jonzac	☎ 05 46 48 49 29
Rochefort	Amicale Philatélique, 61 rue Chanzy Contact Mr Thevenin.	☎ 05 46 99 43 45
Royan	Club Philatélique de La Côte de Beauté, 61bis rue Paul Doumer, 1st floor, Salle Alphonse Daudet Meetings at 3pm on the first Friday of every month from September to June and on Sundays at 10am except the first Sunday of the month.	☎ 05 46 22 67 13
Saintes	Amicale Philatélique Saintaise, Maison des Associations, 31 rue du Cormier	☎ 05 46 93 23 09

Tree Climbing

If you like exploring tree tops, this is the activity for you. Age restrictions may apply.

Ile d'Oléron	Parc Aventure Forestier, Plage de Gatseau, This adventure park is based around nature with a 'professional' circuit for those searching for a thrill, through to circuits for beginners and a course suitable for children over	☎ 05 46 75 27 48

four. Rope ladders, aerial runways, and monkey bridges, within three hectares of managed forest. Open every day from 9am to 9pm. Safety equipment provided.

Vintage Cars

La Rochelle   Amicale Rochelaise de Véhicules
Anciens G. Bossis, 29 rue de Passy   ☎ 05 46 27 16 81

Walking & Rambling

Tourist offices have guide books or information sheets for walkers.

Jonzac   Jonzac Rando   ☎ 05 46 48 49 29
Organised by the tourist office.

Rochefort   Association des Randonneurs Pédestres,
19 rue Jean Jaurès   ☎ 05 46 87 69 56

Royan   Les Randonneurs du Pays Royannais   ☎ 05 46 38 54 77
A series of walks are organised each month, both mid-week and weekends.

Saintes   Saintonge Aunis Randonnées, 155 route
de la Chapelle-Chaniers   ☎ 05 46 98 03 06

Water Parks

Châtelaillon-   Centre Aquatique   ☎ 05 46 56 44 11
Plage/Angoulins   🖳 *www.centre-aquatique.com*
(five minutes south of La Rochelle)
Giant water slide, aqua aerobics, sauna, gym room and water babies. Adults €4.75, children €3.

Jonzac   Les Antilles, avenue Jean Moulin   ☎ 05 46 48 12 11
🖳 *www.haute-saintonge.com*
This is a 'West Indies' tourist complex that opened in August 2002 and has a 60m toboggan, fitness, health spa, lake with a wave pool, (summer only) restaurant, sandy beaches – all in a tropical temperature, sauna, gym and much more. For those not participating there's a high level café from where you can watch over the activities or a tropical pathway with seating along the way and a café/bar at the end. Open all year round, every day from 10am in the school holidays.

Les Mathes   La Pinède Water Park, La Fouasse   ☎ 05 46 22 45 13
Five giant water slides, covered pool, spa, Jacuzzi and river rapide. Open May to September.

Périgny   Parc Aquatique, Avenue Lumière   ☎ 05 46 45 70 20
Water park with pools, a park and games for all the family.

St Jean d'Angély   Atlantys, 40 Chemin des Ports   ☎ 05 46 59 21 50
An indoor water park, with a 54 metre toboggan, Jacuzzi, a
variety of different pools for all age groups, including a
competition standard pool for serious swimmers. Beauty
rooms, aqua-gym and steam rooms.

Yoga

Jonzac   13 rue du Docteur Laporte   ☎ 05 46 48 25 72

La Rochelle   Association Yoga, 9 rue de La Frégate,
                  Lagord   ☎ 05 46 00 36 98
Courses held throughout the week at different venues. First
session free.

Rochefort   Centre de Yoga Traditionnel,
                  97 rue Thiers   ☎ 05 46 99 97 64

Saintes   USSCC Yoga, Maison des Associations,
                  31 rue du Cormier   ☎ 05 46 96 30 30
A variety of classes and venues each week.

Medical Facilities & Services

Ambulances

In the event of a medical emergency dial 15.

La Rochelle   ☎ 05 46 27 25 19
Rochefort   ☎ 05 46 99 15 80
Royan   ☎ 05 46 05 51 18
St Jean d'Angély ☎ 05 46 59 05 21
Saintes   ☎ 05 46 74 34 73

Doctors

English-speakers may like to contact the following doctors.

Jonzac   Cabinet Médical, 10 boulevard
                  Denfert Rochereau   ☎ 05 46 48 14 58

La Rochelle   Cabinet Médical, 1 avenue Moscou   ☎ 05 46 42 59 42

Rochefort   Dr Bizière, 69 rue Jean Jaurès   ☎ 05 46 99 22 11

Royan   Cabinet Médical, 13 boulevard
                  Albert I   ☎ 05 46 05 10 72

| St Jean d'Angély | Philippe Reversac, 17 place Marché | ☎ 05 46 59 06 14 |
| Saintes | Maison Médicale St Palais, 2 avenue Aristide Briand | ☎ 05 46 74 14 99 |

Dentists

English-speakers might like to contact the following dentists.

La Rochelle	Anqélique Ardouin, 1 quater rue St François	☎ 05 46 41 41 20
Pons	Véronique Fontana, 30 rue Emile Combes (north-east of Jonzac)	☎ 05 46 91 30 89
Rochefort	Mr Brouquet-Laglaire, 57 rue Docteur Peltier	☎ 05 46 99 08 73
Royan	Cabinet Cénac, 3 rue Pasteur	☎ 05 46 05 15 21
St Jean d'Angély	Bernard Foucher, 22 rue Jacobins	☎ 05 46 32 08 49
Saintes	Plazanet & Ouankpo, 5 rue Berthonnière	☎ 05 46 93 17 60

Emergency Services

Fire Brigade

Dial 18.

Gendarmerie Nationale

Some of the smaller gendarmeries are being merged with others and the station then open limited hours, but the local number will always be put through to the station that is on duty.

Jonzac	16 boulevard René Gautret	☎ 05 46 48 04 55
La Rochelle	121 rue Gonthières	☎ 05 46 00 50 99
Rochefort	place Dupuy	☎ 05 46 87 38 10
Royan	93bis boulevard Georges Clemenceau	☎ 05 46 38 34 22
Saintes	17 rue de Chermignac	☎ 05 46 93 01 19
St Jean d'Angély	3 rue Dampierre	☎ 05 46 32 04 27

Health Authority

Local offices of the Caisse Régionale Assurance Maladie Centre Ouest (CRAMCO) are listed below:

La Rochelle	avenue Albert Einstein (main office)	☎ 05 46 07 41 67
Rochefort	rue des Tamaris	☎ 05 46 84 39 90
St Jean d'Angély	Hôtel de Ville, place Hôtel de Ville	☎ 05 46 72 32 46
Saintes	4 rue René Cassin	☎ 05 46 93 83 00

Hospitals

All the hospitals below have an emergency department.

Jonzac	Centre Hospitalier de Jonzac, 4 avenue Winston Churchill	☎ 05 46 48 75 75
La Rochelle	Centre Hospitalier de la Rochelle, rue du Dr Schweitzer	☎ 05 46 45 66 26
Rochefort	Hôpital Civil, 16 rue du Dr Peltier (emergencies entrance on rue Camille Pelletan)	☎ 05 46 82 20 20
Royan	Centre Hospitalier de Royan, 20 avenue Saint Sordelin à Vaux sur Mer	☎ 05 46 39 52 52
St Jean d'Angély	Hôpital Saint Louis, 18 avenue Port	☎ 05 46 59 50 50
Saintes	Centre Hospitalier de Saintes, place du 11 novembre	☎ 05 46 92 76 76

Motoring

Breakers' Yards

Aytré	Récup-Autos, route Surgères (just south of La Rochelle)	☎ 05 46 45 29 96
Jonzac	Jonzac Auto Pièces, Chez Marchand	☎ 05 46 48 18 73
Saintes	Casse de Saintonge, Moulin de Brandet, 33 rue Rétard	☎ 05 46 74 43 38

Car Dealers

Jonzac	Audi/VW, Garage Mazurier, 3 boulevard René Gautret	☎ 05 46 48 06 94
	Citroën, Garage Mallet, route Montendre	☎ 05 46 48 00 04
	Ford, Eternum Auto's, route Pons, St Martial de Vitaterne	☎ 05 46 48 73 86
	Peugeot, Garage Belot, place Champ de Foire	☎ 05 46 48 08 77
	Renault, Martin & Fils, route Pons	☎ 05 46 48 06 11
	Vauxhall/Opel, Garage Mérias, route Jonzac à St Genis	☎ 05 46 48 50 70
La Rochelle	Alfa Romeo, La Scala, 170 rue Emile Normandin	☎ 05 46 44 46 24
	Audi/VW, CAR, avenue Jean Moulin	☎ 05 46 44 30 47
	BMW, H. Cornierf, ZAC Beaulieu, Puilboreau	☎ 05 46 27 34 34
	Chrysler/Jeep Prestige Auto, avenue Jean Moulin	☎ 05 46 45 48 22
	Citroën, Bretonnier Agent, 8 rue Trompette	☎ 05 46 34 79 79
	Daewoo, Cap Auto, 21 avenue Avignon, Lagord	☎ 05 46 42 32 02
	Fiat/Lancia, La Scala, 170 avenue de Normandin	☎ 05 46 44 46 24
	Ford, Porte Dauphine Auto's, 2 avenue Porte Dauphine	☎ 05 46 67 76 29
	Honda, Cachet Giraud, 13 rue Gaspard Monge	☎ 05 46 34 34 00
	Hyundai, Royan Impérial, ZA Villeneuve Les Salines	☎ 05 46 50 61 60

	Jaguar, 2 avenue Commandant Charcot, Aytré	☎ 05 46 45 20 15
	Land Rover, LGA. ZAC Beaulieu Est, rue 18 Juin, Puilboreau	☎ 05 46 67 45 45
	Mazda, RCO, 28 avenue Commandant Lysiack, Aytré	☎ 05 46 07 06 07
	Mercedes-B, Savia, ZAC Beaulieu, rue 18 Juin, Puilboreau	☎ 05 46 67 54 22
	Nissan, Cassagnau, ZAC des Fourneaux, Angoulins s/Mer	☎ 05 46 27 99 27
	Peugeot, Chuillet Michel, 101 avenue Emile Normandin	☎ 05 46 44 20 35
	Renault, La Rochelle Auto, ZA Villeneuve Les Salines, Aytré	☎ 05 46 44 01 00
	Rover, LGA, ZAC Beaulieu Est, rue 18 Juin, Puilboreau	☎ 05 46 67 45 45
	SAAB, Village Auto, ZA Tasdon Lac	☎ 05 46 45 48 22
	Seat, Docyan, 9 rue Abbé Grégoire, ZA Villeneuve les Sal.	☎ 05 46 50 61 60
	Skoda, LGA, ZAC Beaulieu Est, rue 18 Juin, Puilboreau	☎ 05 46 67 45 45
	Toyota, Rémy Goudé Autos, ZAC de Villeneuve Les Salines	☎ 05 46 45 03 02
	Vauxhall/Opel, Euro Garage, rue Libération, Puilboreau	☎ 05 46 68 06 11
	Volvo, Cachet Giraud, 3 rue Gaspard Monge	☎ 05 46 31 11 11
Rochefort	Alfa/Lancia, La Scala Autos, 12 rue Villeneuve Montigny	☎ 05 46 99 88 88
	Audi / VW, CAR Conces, 70 avenue 11 novembre 1918	☎ 05 46 99 64 04

BMW/Mini, Espace Bienvenue,
route Rochelle, le Vergeroux ☎ 05 46 99 16 13

Citroën, 46–48 avenue Docteur Diéras ☎ 05 46 87 41 55

Fiat, La Scala Autos,
12 rue Villeneuve Montigny ☎ 05 46 99 88 88

Ford, Garage Zanker, 76 rue Gambetta ☎ 05 46 82 17 50

Mitsubishi, Bienvenue Sarl,
route Rochelle, Le Vergeroux ☎ 05 46 99 06 65

Peugeot, Lara, 28 avenue du
Pont Rouge, Tonnay Charente ☎ 05 46 99 02 76

Renault, Pyronnet, 22 avenue
Déportés et Fusillés ☎ 05 46 87 36 20

Seat, Docyan, 105 avenue
du 11 novembre ☎ 05 46 87 44 80

Suzuki, Garage Gabardos,
56 rue Belle Judith ☎ 05 46 99 84 84

Toyota, Pascal Aguillon,
1 avenue Pont Neuf, Tonnay Charente ☎ 05 46 87 84 87

Vauxhall/Opel, Auto Service,
17 avenue Pont Neuf, Tonnay Charente ☎ 05 46 99 92 82

Royan | Alfa/Lancia, La Scala, 54 avenue
Louis Bouchet ☎ 05 46 05 10 00

Audi/VW, Royan Auto, 340 route
Royan, Médis ☎ 05 46 05 70 89

BMW/Mini, Garage Bienvenue,
43 avenue Maryse Bastié ☎ 05 46 05 01 62

Chrysler/Jeep Royan Impérial Auto,
3 rue Marco Polo, Médis ☎ 05 46 06 76 05

Citroën, Ardon Royan, 24 boulevard
de Lattre de Tassigny ☎ 05 46 05 04 26

Fiat, La Scala, 54 avenue Louis Bouchet ☎ 05 46 05 10 00

Ford, Garage Zanker, 11 rue Notre Dame ☎ 05 46 05 69 87

Hyundai, Royan Impérial,
3 rue Marco Polo, Médis ☎ 05 46 06 76 05

Mazda, Tantin, 176 avenue Rochefort ☎ 05 46 02 16 15

Mercedes, Patrick Launay,
74 avenue Louis Bouchet ☎ 05 46 05 05 49

Nissan, Cassagnau, 44 avenue
Maréchal Leclerc ☎ 05 46 05 01 66

Peugeot, Richard Concess. Zone Cial
38 rue Lavoisier ☎ 05 46 05 03 55

Renault, Garage du Chay,
75 avenue de Pontaillac ☎ 05 46 38 48 88

Toyota, Toys Motors, 4 rue Lavoisier ☎ 05 46 05 98 98

Vauxhall/Opel, Barnes,
52 avenue Louis Bouchet ☎ 05 46 22 11 15

Saintes   Audi/VW, Voiville Auto,
avenue Saintonge ☎ 05 46 92 01 44

Alfa/Lancia, La Scala, 18–20
avenue Salvador Allendé ☎ 05 46 93 89 00

Citroën, Garage Ardon, route Bordeaux ☎ 05 46 93 88 01

Fiat, La Scala, 18–20 avenue
Salvador Allendé ☎ 05 46 93 89 00

Ford, Auto Palau, 13 rue Brandes ☎ 05 46 93 43 44

Hyundai, Fort, ZI Les Charriers ☎ 05 46 93 07 36

Nissan, Cassagnau,
15 rue Ormeau de Pied ☎ 05 46 74 61 61

Peugeot, Saca Guerry, route de Royan,
ZI de l'Ormeau de Pied ☎ 05 46 93 48 33

Renault, Saintonge Auto,
145 avenue Gambetta   ☎ 05 46 93 55 38

Rover, Fort, ZI Les Charriers   ☎ 05 46 93 07 36

Seat, Docyan Autos, 5 rue Echalas   ☎ 05 46 92 15 70

Toyota, Mondiomobile, rue de
l'Ormeau de Pied   ☎ 05 46 92 50 00

Vauxhall/Opel, Barn's,
ZI de l'Ormeau de Pied   ☎ 05 46 93 22 15

St Jean d'Angély Audi/VW, Drevet Autos,
19 fbg Taillebourg   ☎ 05 46 32 01 74

Citroën, Sagla, ZI La Sacristinerie   ☎ 05 46 32 44 44

Fiat, Garage St Jean,
11 avenue Port Mahon   ☎ 05 46 32 38 80

Mercedes, Savia, 5 rue Industrie,
ZI du Point du Jour   ☎ 05 46 59 03 03

Peugeot, Lara Autos, 27 avenue
du Point du Jour   ☎ 05 46 59 09 09

Renault, SAGA, route de Saintes   ☎ 05 46 32 40 22

Vauxhall/Opel, Garage Berthelot,
4 rue Charente-Maritime   ☎ 05 46 32 09 10

Driving Lessons

Chef-Boutonne   Auto Ecole 'Virage', 57 Grand' Rue
du Commerce   ☎ 05 49 07 66 69
This driving school gives refresher courses to foreigners and
lessons to help adapt to driving on the right. They have both
male and female driving instructors who speak English.

Tyre & Exhaust Centres

Jonzac   Pneus Service France, 23 rue Félix Faure ☎ 05 46 48 39 58

La Rochelle   Euromaster, 153 boulevard André Sautel ☎ 05 46 34 85 71

Rochefort   Vulco, ZAC Fraternité, Tonnay Charente ☎ 05 46 88 20 08

| Royan | Point S, 3 rue Petrus Rideau | ☎ 05 46 05 46 93 |

| St Jean d'Angély | Angély Centre Auto, 6 rue Charente-Maritime (on the Leclerc complex) | ☎ 05 46 25 05 42 |

| Saintes | Vulco, 8 rue Côte de Beauté (opposite the Ibis hotel) | ☎ 05 46 94 08 18 |

Pets

Dog Training

| Cabariot | Centre Initiation et Education (near Rochefort) | ☎ 05 46 83 32 23 |

| Echillais | Les Carrières Noires, route de Royan (near Rochefort aerodrome) Dog training for more than 19 years. | ☎ 05 46 83 35 66 |

| Semussac | Hotel Chiens Chats, route Bordeaux | ☎ 05 46 05 75 61 |

| Tonnay Charente | Dalle Philipe, Ile de la Mazarine | ☎ 05 46 99 22 48 |

Farriers

| St Georges-des-Coteaux | Michel Cathala, 5 impasse Bois des Freshneaux | ☎ 05 46 92 90 85 |

Horse Dentists

| General | Christophe Gaillard (based just south of Poitiers) Covers Vienne, Deux-Sèvres and travels as far as northern Charente and Charente-Maritime. | ☎ 06 11 63 37 61 |

| | Guy Chatignol Covers Charente, Charente-Maritime and southern parts of Deux-Sèvres. | ☎ 05 59 65 14 96 |

Kennels & Catteries

The facilities listed below accept cats and dogs unless otherwise stated.

| Rochefort | Canicat, 20 avenue La Fayette, Rochefort Cattery only. | ☎ 05 46 88 47 91 |

| Semmusac | Hotel Chiens Chats, route Bordeaux | ☎ 05 46 05 75 61 |

▲ French Ploughing Championships, Villefagnan

▲ Charentes house, Grosbout

▶ Chocolaterie, La Rochefoucauld

▼ Château Rochefoucauld, La Rochefoucauld

▲ Montmorillon

▲ Château de Saint Germai

◀ Indoor Market,
Niort

▼ Cathédrale St Pierre
Angoulême

▲ River Vienne, L'Isle Jourdain

▲ *Mural, Angoulême*

 ►

Hôtel de Ville,
Angoulême

▲ *River Gartempe, Montmorillon*

▲ *River Thouet, Thouers*

▲ *Windmill, Villefagnan*

◀ *Harbour, La Rochelle*

▼ *Nautilus Water Park, Angoulême*

Tonnay-Charente Dalle Philippe, Ile de la Mazarine   ☎ 05 46 99 22 48

Pet Parlours

Jonzac   Pil'Poil, 42 rue Sciafer   ☎ 05 46 70 65 95
Open Mondays to Saturdays, but closed on Wednesdays.

La Rochelle   Alidog, 10 rue Minage   ☎ 05 46 41 02 22

Lav'o Chien, 37 avenue Porte Royale   ☎ 06 19 86 78 77
This is a specially adapted service for you to wash and dry
your own dog, open seven days a week.

Rochefort   Le Petit Fauvre, 52 rue du Docteur Peltier ☎ 05 46 99 67 65
(opposite the main tourist office)

Royan   Toutouchien Matouchat,
69 boulevard Albert I   ☎ 05 46 05 54 52

St Jean d'Angély La Coupe Au Poil, 3a rue Petit Champ   ☎ 05 46 24 08 22

Saintes   Un Amour de Chien, 21 rue Desiles   ☎ 05 46 98 16 83
Tuesdays to Saturdays 9am to noon, 2 to 6pm.

Riding Equipment

Aytré   Mise en Selle
ZAC Belle Aire, rue Jules Verne   ☎ 05 46 44 77 37
🖳 *www.mise-en-selle.fr*
(just south of La Rochelle)

SPA

La Rochelle   rue Guignarderie, Lagord   ☎ 05 46 34 32 03
Open Mondays to Saturdays, closed bank holidays.

Saintes   route de Varzay   ☎ 05 46 93 47 65
Open every day 2.30 to 6.30pm.

Veterinary Clinics

Jonzac   Clinique Vétérinaire, 19 rue Garenne   ☎ 05 46 48 26 26

La Rochelle   Clinique Vétérinaire, 101 rue Gambetta ☎ 05 46 41 00 23

Rochefort   Clinique Vétérinaire, 48 rue Antoine
Chanzy   ☎ 05 46 87 22 22

Royan   Clinique Vétérinaire, 69 ave Pontaillac ☎ 05 46 23 87 02

St Jean d'Angély   Mr Labarrère,16 square Lussault   ☎ 05 46 32 03 53

Saintes   Les Arcades, rue Monconseil   ☎ 05 46 74 48 87
                  (just off Place Blair down by the river)
                  This surgery has several people who speak English.

Saintes   Dr Bétizaud, 5 avenue Saintonge   ☎ 05 46 92 08 81
                  A specialist horse vet.

Places To Visit

This section is not intended to be a definitive guide but gives a wide range of ideas for the department. Please note that when prices and opening hours have been quoted, they are as a guide only and it's best to check before travelling long distances.

Châteaux

Buzay   Château de Buzay   ☎ 05 46 56 63 21
                  Built around 1770 this château has impressive architecture,
                  perfectly preserved interior décor and formal gardens. Open
                  from 1st July to 30th September from 2.30 to 5.30pm, In May,
                  June and October the château is only open to groups by
                  appointment.

Jonzac   Château de Jonzac, place de Château   ☎ 05 46 48 49 29
                  A 16th century château with ramparts and a cloister, it is also
                  home to the tourist office. Guided tours are available on
                  Tuesdays at 3pm from the tourist office and there are tours in
                  English during July and August. Enquiries need to be made at
                  the tourist office for dates and times.

Marennes   Château de la Gataudière   ☎ 05 46 85 01 07
                  Privately owned and originally built in the 18th century. There's
                  a magnificent sculpted stone reception hall, a dining room with
                  wood paneling and a sitting room lined with brocade of the
                  period. There are also vaulted galleries in both stone and
                  marble. Guided visits are available every day from 10am to
                  noon, 2 to 6pm (in winter 5pm). Closed December to February
                  inclusive and Mondays from 1st October to 30th November and
                  from 10th March to 1st June.

Port d'Envaux   Château de Panloy   ☎ 05 46 91 73 23
                  Guided visits are available to see the château, the tapestries,
                  panelling and hunting gallery. Outside there's the pigeon loft,
                  the old laundry and some stables. Open every day from Easter
                  to November except Mondays. 10am to noon, 2 to 6.30pm.

St Jean d'Angély   Château de Beaufief, Mazeray   ☎ 05 46 32 35 93
An extravagant 18th century building situated in a park with a chapel. There's an art exhibition of both painters and sculptors. Open every day from Easter to 1st November.

St Porchcaire   Château de La Roche Courbon   ☎ 05 46 95 60 10
Formal French gardens with geometric lawns, ornamental ponds, terraced gardens with caves tucked away. The château was built as a fortified castle with four stately towers and a keep, transformed into an elegant home during the 17th century. It is open every day between 11th February and 9th January from 10am to noon, 2 to 6.30pm (5.30pm in winter) but closed on Thursdays from mid-September to mid-May and Sundays mornings in winter. The gardens are open every day, all year from 9am to 7pm (5.30pm winter).

Islands

Ile de Ré

The long beaches of fine sand and the outstanding climate make the island a favourite venue for those who enjoy sunshine and fresh air. It is also the ideal place for relaxation and sightseeing.

Fruit and vegetable markets are held in all the villages during the summer months, with local produce given pride of place. Sailing and water sports clubs teach young and old windsurfing, sand yachting, fun boarding, sea canoeing, surfing and kite-surfing. Horse riding is available along the beaches and cycling is popular with more than 90km of cycle tracks through vineyards, salt marshes and forests.

There's plenty of sightseeing to be done with the harbour, abbey, museums and guided tours of the villages.

There's a toll bridge to the north of La Rochelle that connects the island to the mainland, a bus service operates on this route..

Ile d'Oléron

Brightly coloured boats go back and forth, laden with oysters, then there are the fine sandy beaches that are ideal for children, sports and water games, backed by vast pine and oak forests.

There's a bird sanctuary and wildlife park, a nature reserve and folk museum. Various boat trips are available, full day, half day or shorter ones. There are vast beaches on all sides (children's' beach clubs on most of them) and numerous cycle tracks leading to the beaches or linking villages via the forest to vineyards or marshes.

There are markets every morning in the summer season, a folktale festival late July, a jazz festival the first fortnight in August and throughout the summer numerous fetes and festivities based on oysters, musical events and concerts in all the island's villages.

The island is linked to the mainland by a 3km viaduct (no toll charge) or you can cross by bus from Rochefort, La Rochelle and Saintes.

Ile d'Aix

This island is totally reserved for pedestrians and cyclists and is accessible from Fouras. It is possible to walk around the island in less than 3 hours, alternatively you could take a carriage ride.

There's an African museum with hunting trophies and African weapons and 'objets d'art', as well as the Emperor's House. On the west coast and part of the east coast there are some fine sandy beaches and to the north-east some little creeks, ideal for those seeking a quiet spot in which to relax. Twenty-five minute crossing from Pointe de la Fumée in Fouras.

Museums & Galleries

La Gua
La Poche de Royan, route de Marennes ☎ 05 46 22 89 90
A historical museum situated 15km north-east of Royan, a complete inventory of the second world war with vehicles, photographs, notices and documents dedicated to one of the last places of German occupation on the Atlantic coast in 1944/1945. Open all year, 10am to noon, 2 to 6.30pm, It does not close for lunch during July and August.

La Rochelle
Maritime Museum, place B. Moitessier ☎ 05 46 28 03 00
Rush headlong into the wind tunnel, go on board a fishing boat, visit the weather ship and stroll along the former quays, plus see a variety of different exhibits and shows. Open from 1st April to September 10am to 6.30pm (7.30pm during July and August), October and February 4 to 6.30pm, closed November to January inclusive. Adults €7.60, 4 to 16-year-olds €5.30.

Musée du Flacon à Parfum,
33 rue du Temple ☎ 05 46 41 32 40
An impressive collection of around 1,000 bottles, miniatures and samples, labels and powder boxes. Open all year Mondays 2.30 to 7pm, Tuesdays to Saturdays 10am to noon, 2 to 7pm, July and August open Sundays and bank holidays 3 to 6pm. Adults €4.30, children €3.80.

Musée des Automates & Musée des
Modèles Réduits, rue de la
Désirée, La Ville en Bois ☎ 05 46 41 64 51

Here you enter the world of mechanical models, presented in fairy tale settings. At the museum of Réduits (miniature models) there are plenty of things to see: automobiles, navigation history and railroads; vast model railway systems and a sound a light show with a naval theme. The automation museum has 300 moving characters with both antique and contemporary automations. Prices depend on whether you are seeing one museum or both. The prices are as follows: one museum, adults €6,50 and children €4; both museums, adults €10 and children €5,50.

Rochefort	Musée des Commerces d'Autrefois,	
	12 rue Lesson	☎ 05 46 83 91 50

This museum has preserved the memories of small shops from the start of the 20th century, including a café, a hat maker and grocer. The shops are completely reconstructed and display their products, posters and every day objects. Open 10 to noon and 2 to 7pm out of season, closed Sundays mornings and all day Tuesdays. 1st July to 31st August 10am to 8pm every day.

Royan   Musée de Royan, Hôtel de Ville,
            80 avenue de Pontaillac   ☎ 05 46 38 85 96

Collections include documents of local history, regional paintings with both permanent and temporary displays. Free entrance and open all year Tuesdays to Fridays 2 to 6pm and Saturdays 3 to 6pm in July and August.

Saintes   Musée de l'Echevinage,
            3 place Echevinage   ☎ 05 46 93 52 39

An art museum in the pedestrian streets of Saintes. Tuesdays to Saturdays 10am to 12.30pm, 1.30 to 5pm, Sundays 1.30 to 5pm. Free entry Sunday and Wednesday afternoons. Closed 1st November to 25th December and 1st January to 1st May.

Parks, Gardens & Forests

General   La Forêt d'Aulnay
            (east of Aulnay)

Although a lot of damage was caused during the storms in 1998 this is still an impressive forest and great area for walking and exploring.

Rochefort   Conservatoire du Bégonia
            1 rue Charles Plumier   ☎ 05 46 99 08 26

Greenhouses containing more than 1,500 species of begonia, making this the largest collection in the world. Tours given Tuesdays to Saturdays every hour from 2pm to 5pm, last tour is at 4pm November to 1st February, closed bank holidays.

Royan   Les Jardins du Monde, 5 avenue des
            Fleurs de La Paix   ☎ 05 46 38 00 99

💻 *www.jardins-du-monde.com*
A flower and leisure park with a tropical greenhouse, orchid exhibition, collection of bonsai, themed gardens and landscapes around a lake such as a Japanese garden, bamboo maze and children's play area. Open July and August 10am to 8pm every day, September to June 10am to 6pm, closed Tuesdays.

Saint André-de-Lidon   Parc Botanique, Domaine du Chaillaud ☎ 05 46 90 08 10
💻 *www.deau.com*
A unique world of fragrance and colour, with 600 species of trees, shrubs, perennials, roses and a 19th century greenhouse. There's a free guided tour of the estate as well as tastings of regional products. Open daily all year round 9am to 7pm. Picnic area.

Zoos & Wildlife Parks

Cadeuil   Le Village des Oiseaux   ☎ 05 46 94 43 49
(near the junction of the D728 and D733)
An ornithological park with three hectares. Open Easter to 15th June 2 to 7pm, 16th June to 8th September 10am to 7pm and 9th September to 30th October 2 to 6pm.

Ile de Ré   Réserve de Lilleau des Niges   ☎ 05 46 29 50 74
This bird sanctuary enables you to see the thousands of birds during migration and the winter months. There's a cycle track and footpaths which provide good views.

La Rochelle   Le Nouvel Aquarium, Bassin des Grands Yachts   ☎ 05 46 34 00 00
💻 *www.aquarium-larochelle.com*
An amazing aquarium with sharks through to tiny multi coloured fish. Open every day of the year, October to March 10am to 8pm, April to June and September 9am to 8pm, July and August 9am to 11pm. Adults €12, under 18's €9. To see everything takes around two and half hours.

Le Palmyre   Zoo de la Palmyre, 6 avenue Royan   ☎ 05 46 22 46 06
💻 *www.zoo-palmyre.fr*
The largest private zoo in France, situated in the heart of a 14 hectare forest, with lions, tigers, zebras, rhinos, elephants, crocodiles, pythons and tortoises. Open every day all year 9am to 7pm (6pm October to March). Adults €12, 3 to 12-year-olds €8. An average visit takes around four hours. Snack bars, sandwiches and a *crêperie* can be found inside the park.

Meux   Zoo de Meux   ☎ 05 46 48 30 34
(between Jonzac and Barbezieux)
This zoo has over 350 animals from lamas to deers, parrots to

bison. Open from 10am to 8pm April to October and during school holidays.

St Clément-des-Baleines | L'Arche de Noé | ☎ 05 46 29 23 23
On the western tip of Ile de Ré this zoo and flower garden has a superb collection of birds, turtles, butterflies and insects from all over the world and has a show of parrots in free flight. Open Easter to the end of the November school holidays.

Miscellaneous

Churches of interest are signposted from main roads and motorways and can be easily identified, e.g. *Eglise XIVème Siècle* = 14th century church.

General | Châteaubranch Aventure,
Château de la Gataudière | ☎ 05 46 85 01 07
💻 *www.gataudiere.com*
In the grounds of the château at Marennes there's a tree-top park with monkey bridges, rope swings and full safety equipment. Open every weekend March to June, September to November 10am to 4pm, all school and bank holidays 9am to 4pm, July and August 9am to 5pm.

Aulnay | Eglise Romane Saint Pierre | ☎ 05 46 33 14 44
This church dates from the 12th century and is a true masterpiece of Poitevin Romanesque art. It is in an exceptional state of preservation. The church towers above a ground of strange tombstones and there's a 15th century Hosainnière Cross. The south doorway is the gem of the church, which stands out by its four archivolts decorated with a bestiary, figures of the Apocalypse, the Apostles and the Prophets.

Brouage | Place Forte De Brouage | ☎ 05 46 85 77 77
The centre of European military architecture in the heart of the Halle au Vivres. An exhibition of the workrooms recreated from the plans. You can discover the secrets of the art of defence and enjoy the trails that will transform the visit into an adventure.

Châtelaillon-Plage | Hippodrome de Royan,
avenue Hippodrome | ☎ 05 46 56 16 19
Horse racing and trotting held here, with meetings from April to August. There's also a restaurant (☎ 05 46 22 56 56). Leaflets with full calendar of events available from local tourist offices.

Gémozac | Labyrinths, Cravans | ☎ 08 25 30 49 34
💻 *www.labyrinthus.com*
An amazing selection of mazes made up from hedges, wood, water and maize, along with dancers, actors and musicians

hidden behind hedges or down dead-end paths. A typical forest village, craftsman workshops and an exhibition on the Indian culture. Open 10.30am to 7.30pm from 7th July to 2nd September.

Ile d'Oléron	Parc Aventure Forestier, Plage de Gatseau	☎ 05 46 75 27 48

This adventure park is based around nature with a 'professional' circuit for those searching for a thrill, through to circuits for beginners and even for little adventurers of aged four and above. Rope ladders, aerial runways, and monkey bridges, within three hectares of managed forest. Open every day from 9am to 9pm, full security equipment provided.

Jonzac	Le Moulin du Cluzelet	☎ 05 46 58 49 29

(off rue du Cluzelet)
This restored and working flour mill is open Tuesdays to Sundays from mid-May to mid-October from 10.30am to noon, 2.30 to 6.30pm.

Heurtebise Leisure Park   ☎ 05 46 48 14 07
Open spaces, picnic area, restaurant, climbing wall, archery, pedalos, swimming (life guards in the summer), play area for children and skate ramp.

Station Thermale, Domaine d'Heurtebise ☎ 05 46 48 59 59
The spa water was discovered in 1979 and allows for the treatment of rheumatic and respiratory illness. It is a modern spa built in an ancient stone quarry and is open from February to December. This spa benefits from the latest technology in architecture that makes this unique in Europe for its site and design.

La Palmyre	Youpi-Land, Le Port	☎ 05 46 22 30 60

A park of games for young children, bouncy castles, train rides, trampolines etc. Open every day from April to September.

La Rochelle	☎ 05 46 41 14 68

Daily guided tours during July and August (except Sundays and bank holidays). They leave from the tourist office at 10.30am for a walk around the town or at 2.30pm by carriage. Booking needed for the afternoon tour.

La Tremblade	Tour of the Oyster Beds, Harbour	☎ 05 46 36 90 41

At low tide you can have a guided tour across the basin and its' oyster beds. When the waters have risen there's a tour of the oyster harbour and refining tanks.

Meschers	Les Grottes de Régulus et des Fontaines	☎ 05 46 02 55 36

💻 *www.meschers.com*
Guided visits to discover the history and legends of these

troglodyte caves. There's also a panoramic view over the estuary. Open from Easter to 1st November.

Pons   **Le Château des Enigmes**   ☎ 05 46 91 09 19
A day out to amuse the whole family. A journey of 23 games that cross the park and the château. A château full of clues and you are entertained while you take an exceptional journey to the heart of history. Parking is free, there's a shop and a restaurant or you can take a picnic. Open every day from Easter to November from 10am.

Rochefort   **The Hermione**   ☎ 05 46 84 30 30
🖥 *www.ville-rochefort.fr or* 🖥 *www.hermione.com*
The Hermione was a frigate built in Rochefort that sailed to the US in 1780 and was later shipwrecked in 1793. A full scale replica of this vessel is being built in the dry docks at Rochefort and visits can be made every day, with information available in English. Under 10's free.

St Martial-sur-Né **Elevage d'Oies Foie Gras Manicot**   ☎ 05 46 49 52 72
🖥 *www.manicot.fr*
Visit this *foie gras* farm to see the birds, their breeding methods and taste the product. Visit the farm June to September 10am to noon, 2.30 to 6.30pm, sales 9am to 7pm, closed Sundays and bank holidays.

Saintes   **Gallo-Roman Amphitheatre**
(west of the town centre near the park)
Built in the early part of the 1st century it could hold more than 15,000 spectators.

                L'Abbaye aux Dames   ☎ 05 46 97 48 48
An abbey with roman art from the 12th century, including a shop specialising in literature and music. Open every day 10 to 12.30, 2 to 7pm.

Tesson   **Domaine de Château Guynot**   ☎ 05 46 91 93 71
🖥 *www.chateau-guynot.com*
Visit spirit storerooms, a distillery, a cooling house, an 18th century arched cellar and a beautiful park and kiwi plantation. Open to the public 10.30am to 12.30pm, 3 to 6.30pm seven days a week for a guided tour and free tasting of the regional drink, Pineau.

Professional Services

Accountants

The following offices have an English speaking accountant.

| Saintes | Cabinet Apparailly, 30 rue Gautier | ☎ 05 46 74 02 55 |

| | KPMG Entreprises, 9 rue Ormeau de Pied | ☎ 05 46 74 29 91 |

Solicitors & Notaires

The following office has an English-speaking *notaire*.

| Saintes | Société Civile Notariale, 4 rue Bois d'Amour | ☎ 05 46 74 36 86 |

Religion

Anglican Services In English

There are no anglican services in English in Charente-Maritime. Those living in the east or the south of the department can find English-language services in neighbouring Charente and Gironde (see page 118).

Evangelical Churches

| Matha | Eglise Evangélique Libre, 26 rue Cognac (south-east of St Jean d'Angély) | ☎ 05 46 58 50 47 |

| La Rochelle | Eglise Evangélique de Pentecôte, 9 rue Raisin | ☎ 05 46 00 07 19 |

| Royan | Eglise Evangélique, 99 boulevard Georges Clemenceau | ☎ 05 46 22 90 69 |

| Saintes | Eglise Protestante Evangélique de Saintes, 11 rue Colonel de Faucher | ☎ 05 46 93 79 86 |

Protestant Churches

| La Rochelle | Eglise Réformée, 2 rue Brave Rondeau | ☎ 05 46 41 14 20 |

| Rochefort | Eglise Protestante Evangélique, 30 Quéreux Laiterie | ☎ 05 46 99 63 79 |

| | Eglise Réformée, 22 rue Casse aux Prêtres | ☎ 05 46 99 04 71 |

| Royan | Eglise Protestante Baptist Alliance, rue Coquelicots, St Georges de Didonne | ☎ 05 46 06 04 85 |

| Saintes | Eglise Réformée de France, 3bis cours Reverseaux | ☎ 05 46 92 15 52 |

Synagogues

La Rochelle   Maison Communautaire Israélite,
40 cours Dames   ☎ 05 46 41 17 66

Restaurants

Aulnay   Le Colombier, place Aristide Briand   ☎ 05 46 33 31 42
Set menus for €10 and €16, Tuesday to Saturday lunchtimes
and an *à la carte* menu with many seasonal dishes.

Boutenac   Relais de Touvent, rue Saintonge   ☎ 05 46 94 13 06
A three-star restaurant with set menus from €14 to €33, closed
Sundays evening and all day Mondays.

Courcoury   L'Amaryllis, place de l'Eglise   ☎ 05 46 74 09 91
(just south of Saintes)
Lunchtime menu €11.50 Mondays to Fridays, other menus
from €18 to €22. Closed Tuesday evenings and Wednesdays.
Traditional and seasonal cuisine.

Epargnes   Le Presbytère, le Bourg   ☎ 05 46 90 73 27
South of Cozes this restaurant is tucked away at the side of the
church through large gates. Menus from €15 to €34, closed
Tuesdays evening and all day Wednesdays.

Gémozac   La Caravelle, 25 rue Carnot   ☎ 05 46 94 20 70
There's a bar, the restaurant is in a separate room. Traditional
cuisine. Generous portions. €10 lunchtime menu, closed
Tuesdays.

Jazennes   Le Roze, 115 rue Foy   ☎ 05 46 94 55 90
(between Gémozac and Pons)
A popular local restaurant in an old Charentaise house, with
good quality food and a salad bar.

Jonzac   Chez Marie, rue St Gervais   ☎ 05 46 48 99 71
Open for lunch Tuesdays to Sundays and evenings Mondays
to Saturdays with set menus from €8 to €19.

Restaurant Le Club, 8 place Eglise   ☎ 05 46 48 02 27
Traditional cuisine, specialising in fish and grilled meats.
Lunchtimes only with a set menu of €9.

Le Grill du Château, 14 rue J. Sclafer   ☎ 05 46 48 47 14
(tucked away at the bottom of the hill)
This restaurant only has an *à la carte* menu and is closed all
day Sundays and Monday evenings. Main courses range from
€7.50 to €13.

Restaurant de la Seugne, 3 place
Fillaudeau, Marcouze, Mosnac   ☎ 05 46 48 50 56
💻 *www.valdeseugne.com*
This restaurant is in a three-star hotel on the edge of Mosnac,
on the D134 to St Georges. Lunch menu €15, other menus
start at €19 per person up to €59 per person, as well as *à la
carte*. Open every evening 15th June to 15th September, rest
of the year closed all day Tuesdays and Wednesday
lunchtimes.

La Rochelle   Along the *quai* of the old port there are numerous
restaurants with outside seating overlooking the port.

Chez Serge, 46 cours des Dames   ☎ 05 46 50 25 25
A gastronomic restaurant on the port with fish a speciality.
Lunch menu for €26 with other set menus rising to €70.

Kashmir, 7 rue des Cloutiers   ☎ 05 46 34 88 45
Indian restaurant open seven days a week, lunch and evening.

La Boucherie, Les Minimes   ☎ 05 46 30 48 30
(near the marina with parking at the CGR cinema at rue Henri
Becquerel)
This restaurant specialises in meat dishes. Menus range from
€8.40 to €25.

Les Comédiens, 15 rue de la Chaîne   ☎ 05 46 50 51 98
(at the far end of the port)
Varied menu with entertainment Saturday evenings and
Sunday lunchtimes. Shows with singers at the weekends.

La Grande Rive, 26 quai Duperré   ☎ 05 46 41 44 53
(by the old port)
There are menus ranging from €12 to €21, open lunchtimes
and evenings seven days a week.

Le Ketch, rue du Lazaret   ☎ 05 46 45 17 17
(by the large marina)
Serving traditional cuisine this restaurant is open every day in
the summer, closed Wednesdays out of season. €10 express
lunch menu and other menus ranging from €13 to €20.

L'Océanide, quai Louis Prunier   ☎ 05 46 50 61 50
A traditional restaurant with a €10 lunch menu and evening
menus up to €22.

L'Orangerie, 26 rue Admyrault   ☎ 05 46 41 08 31
💻 *www.restaurantlorangerie.com*
(in a small road between the cathedral and the old port)
A restaurant of fine French cuisine. Lunchtime menus are €10

and €15 with evening menus going up to €32 plus *à la carte* menu. Closed January.

Le Tire-Bouchon, 16 rue du Cordouan   ☎ 05 46 41 68 00
(just below le Jardin des Plantes)
This restaurant has a €9.50 lunchtime menu and evening menus starting at €13 rising to around €30. Closed Wednesday evenings.

Mortagne   Café de la Rive, 42 rue du Port   ☎ 05 46 90 50 86
(tucked away in the corner of the marina)
Menus €12 to €19, *à la carte* and children's menus. Open seven days a week for lunch and dinner. The low beamed ceilings and fire are very welcoming.

Restaurant du Port, rue du Port   ☎ 05 46 90 50 32
Outdoor seating by the edge of the marina in the summer, regional cuisine available. Closed Tuesdays to Thursdays.

Pons   The Auberge Pontoise,
23 avenue Gambetta   ☎ 05 46 94 00 99
Good food and service with lunchtime menus from €11.50 to €29 and evening menus from €17 to €29. Children's menu available, oysters in Pineau a speciality. Open all week except Sunday evenings.

Café du Donjon, place de la République   ☎ 05 46 94 64 04
(overlooks the Donjon and Hôtel de Ville)
Set lunchtime menu for €10. Breakfast and snacks are also available.

Hôtel de Bordeaux, 1 avenue Gambetta   ☎ 05 46 91 31 12
Two-star hotel restaurant in the centre of Pons with menus from €15.

Rochefort   There are many restaurants and brasseries around the pedestrian square of Place Colbert with outdoor seating in the summer.

Corderie Royale, rue Jean
Baptiste Audebert   ☎ 05 46 00 35 35
A three-star hotel and restaurant. Closed January.

Escapade Restaurant, 7 rue Autrusseau,
St Georges de Didonne   ☎ 05 46 06 24 24
Open April to October with set menus from €15.

Hôtel des Remparts, 43 avenue
Camille Pelletan   ☎ 05 46 87 12 44
Newly opened restaurant with menus around €13 to €24.

Le Bouchon de Paris,
127bis avenue de La Fayette   ☎ 05 46 88 05 01
This brasserie is open seven days a week with an €11
lunchtime menu.

Le Club House, 21 avenue La Fayette   ☎ 05 46 87 35 59
This brasserie has a wide selection of salads, meat and pasta
dishes.

Le Gabier, Bassin de Bourgainville   ☎ 05 46 87 56 24
Overlooking the marina this brasserie has tables indoors and
outdoors. Lunch and dinner menus ranging from €10 to €24
with fish a speciality. Closed Sundays.

Le Galion, 38 rue Toufaire   ☎ 05 46 87 03 77
(on the corner by the entrance to La Corderie)
Traditional and regional cuisine including seafood and frogs
legs (*cuisses de grenouille*). Menus ranging from €18 to
€27.50, menu of the day €10. Closed all day Mondays and out
of season closed Sundays evening.

La Marina, Quai Tahiti   ☎ 05 46 88 43 89
A restaurant with a panoramic view over the marina and menus
from €11 to €32.50.

Le Marrakech, 67 rue Toufaire   ☎ 05 46 99 10 69
Moroccan cuisine, closed Tuesdays.

La Palmier, 32 rue Lesson   ☎ 05 46 99 66 22
Tunisian and Moroccan cuisine, open Tuesdays to Sundays.

La Pirate, 15 rue Lesson   ☎ 05 46 87 16 27
An intimate restaurant with a lunch menu of €9.50 and other
menus from €17 to €23. Closed Saturday lunchtimes and
Sundays.

Le Rose Biff, 12 avenue La Fayette   ☎ 05 46 99 78 83
This restaurant specialises in beef with lunchtime menus of
around €10 and other menus from €16 to €29. Closed
Sundays and Mondays.

Le Royal, 28 rue Edouard Grimaux   ☎ 05 46 99 71 84
Chinese and Thai cuisine, menus from €9 to €19.80. Closed
Mondays.

Royan   There are many restaurants, cafes and bistros on the seafront,
both set back on 'Front de Mer' and down by the quai right by
the marina. In the summer they have outdoor, shaded dining,
some are open all year round.

Grand Soleil, 21 boulevard
Georges Clémenceau   ☎ 05 46 05 13 07
Restaurant specialising in cheese and meat fondues but they
need to be booked a day in advance with prices ranging from
€11 to €16 per person. Other menus available.

Le Bambou, 100 boulevard de
Lattre de Tassigny   ☎ 05 46 02 15 30
Vietnamese cuisine. Takeaways available.
Closed Mondays out of season.

L'Escale de Bougainville,
Quai de Louisiane   ☎ 05 46 99 54 99
(by the marina)
This restaurant has set menus from €16 to €37.

Le Marrakech, 40 avenue Paris   ☎ 05 46 38 03 03
Indian restaurant that is open every day. Take-aways available.

Le Pavé Bleu, 52bis Front de Mer   ☎ 05 46 05 14 59
This restaurant provides menus in English and specialises in
Limousin beef. Set menus from €13.50 to €28.

Le Portique, 7 Front de Mer   ☎ 05 46 05 01 78
(a distinctive green curved restaurant)
A steak house style brasserie but with seafood and *choucroute*
(meat and bean) dishes.

La Siesta, 140 avenue Gambetta   ☎ 05 46 38 36 53
A wide variety of cuisine with Indian, Mexican, Asian and Italian
menus and lots of seafood. Set menus ranging from €11 to
€20. With dining on two levels, the first floor gives a wonderful
elevated view over the marina.

Restaurant Le France, 2 rue Gambetta   ☎ 05 46 05 17 41
Traditional cuisine with set menus from €23 to €38 plus *à la
carte*. Closed all day Mondays and Sunday evenings.

St Fort-sur-le-Né Le Moulin de Cierzac, route de Cognac ☎ 05 45 83 01 32
Just on the border with Charente this restaurant is in an 18th
century mill. Set menus from €15 at lunchtime and evenings
€25 to €42. Closed all day Mondays and in January.

St Jean d'Angély L'Ancre Marine, 12 place Marché   ☎ 05 46 59 26 63
(opposite the indoor market)
This *crêperie* is closed Wednesday evenings and Sundays.

Bar de l'Hôtel de Ville, 10 place
de Hôtel de Ville   ☎ 05 46 32 00 73
Snacks available all day.

Hôtel de la Place, place Hôtel de Ville   ☎ 05 46 32 69 11
💻 *www.hoteldelaplace.net*
(set back in the corner of the square)
Menus from €12 to €38, open every day

Le Bistrot Gourmand, rue Gambetta   ☎ 05 46 32 28 28
(in the square opposite the tourist office)
Outdoor seating available.

La Salsa, 4 place du Marché   ☎ 05 46 59 00 53
(just below the covered market)
Offers sandwiches, salads, steak frites, Tuesdays to Saturdays
8.30am to 12.30am. The bar is open until 2am. Hosts concerts
and shows in the summer.

Le Scorlion, Abbaye Royale   ☎ 05 46 32 52 61
(in the same courtyard as the library, tucked behind the tourist
office) Tuesdays to Fridays there's a €15 menu of the day and
there are also €26 and €36 menus plus *à la carte*.

Les Jacobins, 26 rue des Jacobins   ☎ 05 46 32 54 89
Restaurant and pizzeria. Seating indoors (air-conditioned) or
outdoors in the courtyard. Traditional menu €16.80, Saveurs
menu €21 and quick lunchtime menu €10.50. With pizza
takeaways there's a 15% discount.

New Asia, rue des Jacobins   ☎ 05 46 26 21 36
Oriental cuisine. Lunchtime menu €9, express menu €10 and
other menus ranging from €12 to €18. Takeaways available.

St Léger   Le Rustica, le Bourg   ☎ 05 46 96 91 75
(between Pons and Saintes)
This restaurant has good quality regional cuisine with menus
ranging from €13 to €35. Closed Sunday evenings and
Mondays.

Saintes   Le Bistrot Galant, rue St Michel   ☎ 05 46 93 08 51
Set menus €22.50 and €30.50 with a 'bistro' menu of €15.10
plus *à la carte*. Closed Sundays and Mondays, open Sunday
lunchtimes in the summer.

Chez Tartrine, 10 place Blair   ☎ 05 46 74 16 38
There are no set menus displayed at this restaurant but main
courses range from €12.50 to €16.

Le Cioulette, 32 rue de Pérat   ☎ 05 46 74 07 36
Gourmet food with menus from €16, closed Saturday
lunchtimes and all day Sundays.

Le Jardin du Rempart, 36 rue du
Rempart, rue Piétonne   ☎ 05 46 93 37 66
(in the pedestrian streets off the main thoroughfare in the
centre of Saintes)
Restaurant and grill including seafood.

Le Mandarin, rue Alsace Lorraine   ☎ 05 46 93 57 24
Menus from €8.80 to €18.80. Open seven days a week,
lunchtimes and evenings. They also sell Asian groceries.

Le Petit Marrakech, rue de la Comedie   ☎ 05 46 91 43 84
Moroccan cuisine, including takeaways, closed Sundays.

Le Tilleul, avenue Gambetta   ☎ 05 46 74 23 01
(on the other side of the river to the main city centre)
Outdoor seating under the shade of a huge tree, set menus of
€9 and €19, with several seafood dishes.

Raj Mahal, 9 rue Victor Hugo   ☎ 05 46 93 49 48
(up a side street from the river)
Indian restaurant. Open every day.

Relais du Bois Saint Georges Parc
Atlantique, Cours Genet   ☎ 05 46 93 50 99
A bistro and a gastronomic restaurant combined. Menus €18,
€23 and €36. Open seven days a week.

Rubbish & Recycling

Metal Collection

La Rochelle	Le Floch C Ets, rue Gustave Ferie, Périgny	☎ 05 46 44 30 00
Royan	Ecocollecte, 8 rue Aristide Maillot, St Sulpice de Royan (just north of Royan)	☎ 06 61 99 54 07
Surgères	Thierry Callac, ZI Ouest	☎ 05 46 07 15 42

Shopping

Alcohol

Jonzac	Caves Christophe, 14 rue de Verdin (just down from the indoor market)	☎ 05 46 48 28 28

| La Rochelle | La Cave, 83bis boulevard André Sautel ☎ 05 46 67 16 45 |

Rochefort | Les Relais de Vignes, 33 avenue du
Colonel Fuller ☎ 05 46 87 60 73
(opposite the Champion supermarket)
Tuesdays to Saturdays 9am to 12.30pm, 3 to 7pm.

Royan | Le Pressoir, 71 boulevard de La
République ☎ 05 46 05 26 87
(set back off avenue Gambetta)
Open mornings, Tuesdays to Sundays.

St Jean d'Angély   Au Panier Gourmand, rue Gambetta   ☎ 05 46 33 34 82

Saintes | Cave Saintongeaise, 15 avenue
Salvador Allende ☎ 05 46 74 60 31

Architectural Antiques

Chail | Les Vielles Pierres du Mellois,
Les Cerizat ☎ 05 49 29 31 23
On the D948 Melle to Sauzé-Vaussais road this business
specialises in the sale of old building materials. Although
mainly stone, there's a large selection of reclaimed timbers in
the far corner as you enter from the back.

British Groceries

Saintes | La Perfide Albion, rue Arc de Triomphe ☎ 05 46 94 24 98
(on the east of the river, on a small road running parallel to
avenue Gambetta)
Open Tuesdays to Saturdays 9.30am to 12.30pm, 2 to 7pm.

Building Materials

Jonzac | Tout Faire, 23 rue 19 Mars 1962 ☎ 05 46 48 08 47

La Rochelle | Thébault Paul, 58bis avenue
Edmond Grasset ☎ 05 46 34 87 88

Rochefort | Point P, 10 avenue 11 novembre ☎ 05 46 87 20 44
🖳 *www.pointp.fr*

Royan | Docks des Matériaux de Construction,
53 boulevard Georges Clemenceau ☎ 05 46 05 02 20

Saintes | Point P, Domaine de Terrefort,
route Haute de Cognac ☎ 05 46 93 61 66

Camping & Caravanning

Rochefort   COCV, Le Vergeoux Nord   ☎ 05 46 99 02 64
                   (on the N137, exit 31)
                   There's a permanent display of caravans and they also carry
                   out repairs and services.

Chemists'

Chemists' are listed in the yellow pages under *Pharmacies* and should
display a sign indicating which is the duty chemist outside normal opening
hours; or you can dial 17 for this information.

Department Stores

La Rochelle   Galeries Lafayette, 31 rue Palais   ☎ 05 46 41 27 33
                   (near the old port in the centre of town)

Saintes   Nouvelles Galeries, Cours National   ☎ 05 46 93 47 22
                   Situated on the corner by the bridge at the bottom of the hill. A
                   fairly large department store. Open Mondays to Saturdays
                   9.30am to 7.30pm.

DIY

Jonzac   Bricomarché, 3bis avenue Faidherbe   ☎ 05 46 48 29 33
                   Open Mondays to Saturdays 9am to 12.15pm, 2.30 to 7pm.

La Rochelle   Obi, rue Libération, Puilboreau   ☎ 05 46 68 05 66
                   (on the retail park on the eastern outskirts)

Rochefort   Bricomarché, Le Brillouet   ☎ 05 46 87 60 09

Royan   Mr Bricolage, 2 rue Antoine de Lavoisier ☎ 05 46 05 06 28
                   Open 9am to noon, 2 to 7pm Mondays to Saturdays.

St Jean d'Angély Super Catena, 41 rue France III   ☎ 05 46 32 46 03
                   Open Mondays to Fridays 9.15am to 12.15pm, 2.15 to 7pm.
                   Saturdays 9am to 12.30pm, 2 to 7pm.

Saintes   Mr. Bricolage, 8 boulevard Recouvrance ☎ 05 46 93 17 14
                   (near Leclerc on the outskirts of Saintes)

Fabrics

Jonzac   Le Champ, Centre Commercial Leclerc ☎ 05 46 48 51 66
                   (in the Leclerc complex)

La Rochelle   Atlant, 148 avenue Cimetière   ☎ 05 46 27 09 13
                   Open Mondays 2 to 7pm, Tuesdays to Saturdays 10am to
                   noon, 2 to 7pm.

| Rochefort | Tisseco, ZAC Villeneuve Montigny
(in the retail park opposite Intermarché) | ☎ 05 46 99 09 44 |

| Royan | Royan Mousses Coutures,
rue Antoine de Lavoisier | ☎ 05 46 05 20 22 |

| St Jean d'Angély | Décoral, 114 rue France III
(opposite Gamm Vert on the Leclerc complex)
Furnishing fabric, household linens, rugs and carpets. | ☎ 05 46 32 52 74 |

| Saintes | Tissus Bonnet, 9 avenue Gambetta
Fabric and haberdashery. | ☎ 05 46 74 05 88 |

Frozen Food

| La Rochelle | Picard Surgelés, 1 boulevard Joffre | ☎ 05 46 43 44 21 |

| Royan | Picard Surgelés 54 rue Pierre Loti | ☎ 05 46 23 17 98 |

| Saintes | Thiriet Glaces, 7 avenue Saintonge | ☎ 05 46 92 00 62 |

Garden Centres

| Jonzac | Espace Emeraude, boulevard Baie St Paul ☎ 05 46 86 40 00
Mondays to Saturdays 8.30 to noon, 2 to 6.30pm |

| La Rochelle | Jardinerie Turffaut Cybèle,
6 rue 11 Novembre, Puilboreau
(on the south side of town)
Mondays to Saturdays 9.30 to 12.30pm, 2 to 7pm. | ☎ 05 46 68 11 18 |

| Rochefort | Art Vert, 1 rue Charles Plumier
(opposite the begonia gardens) | ☎ 05 46 82 15 20 |

| Royan | Art Verte, 119 avenue de Rochefort | ☎ 05 46 38 39 08 |

| St Jean d'Angély | Gamm Vert, 91 rue France III
(near Leclerc, in the same commercial area)
Mondays to Saturdays 9am to noon, 2 to 7pm. | ☎ 05 46 32 13 39 |

| Saintes | Jardiland, Près de la Caserne
des Pompiers | ☎ 05 46 90 30 30 |

Kitchens & Bathrooms

| La Rochelle | Lapeyre la Maison, RN137, avenue
Fourneaux, Angoulins-sur-Mer | ☎ 08 25 82 51 17 |

Saintes   Charantaise d'Ameublement,
                   16 rue Fougères   ☎ 05 46 93 24 23
                   (close to Leclerc, east of Saintes)
                   Italian and French designs direct from the factory. Open
                   Mondays 10.30am to 8pm, Tuesdays to Fridays 10am to 8pm,
                   Saturdays 2 to 7pm.

Markets

Fouras   There's a market every day, all year round, at rue de La Halle
                   until 2pm. From June to September, there's also an evening
                   market from 4 to 7pm.

Gémozac   Market Friday mornings.

Ile d'Aix   There are markets in the morning on Mondays, Wednesdays
                   and Saturdays in June and all day every day from July to
                   September.

Ile d'Oléron   Every morning during the summer. Evening market every
                   evening in Boyardville and Mondays at Le Grand Village-Plage
                   during high season.

Jonzac   Tuesdays and Fridays is market day with a fair on the second
                   Friday of the month.

Pons   There's a market Wednesdays and Saturdays and the fair is
                   the first Saturday of each month and the second Sunday of
                   December.

La Rochelle   Tuesdays at Tasdon; Wednesdays at Villeneuve les Salines;
                   Wednesdays and Saturdays in the centre of the town;
                   Thursdays at Port Neuf; Fridays at Mireuil and Sundays at La
                   Pallice.

Rochefort   Three markets a week, on Tuesdays, Thursdays and
                   Saturdays, with a fair on the second Thursday of every month.

Royan   There's a large indoor market in Royan every day and there's a
                   fair on Wednesdays and Sundays.

Saintes   Tuesdays and Fridays at Cours Reversaux; Wednesdays and
                   Saturdays at Saint Pierre; Thursdays and Sundays at Saint
                   Palais and there's a fair on the first Monday of each month.

St Jean d'Angély   Markets every Saturday and Wednesday morning. There's a
                   big fair on 23rd and 24th June, and the monthly fair is on the
                   third Saturday of each month except in June.

Tonnay-Charente   The market is on Sunday mornings.

Music

Saintes	Blanchard Musique, avenue Gambetta	☎ 05 46 93 62 41

A large shop with a wide selection of instruments. Open Tuesdays to Saturdays 9.30am to 12.15pm, 2.15 to 7pm.

Organic Food

Jonzac	Les Caves du Château, 20 rue James Scalfer	☎ 05 46 48 43 50

This wine store stocks some organic foods.
At the Thursday market in Jonzac there's also an organic stall.

Rochefort	Bio-Monde, 3 impasse Fichemore	☎ 05 46 99 03 46

🖳 *www.biomonde .fr*
(in the right hand corner of the Champion car park, which can be found by going straight across the 'sluice gates' roundabout as you approach Rochefort from the south-east) Mondays 3 to 7.30pm, Tuesdays to Saturdays 9 to 7.30pm.

Royan	Centre Diététique, place Charles de Gaulle	☎ 05 46 05 77 07

Open afternoons, Mondays to Saturdays.

St Jean d'Angély	Bio St Jean, rue Grosse Horloges	☎ 05 46 32 49 41

Tuesdays to Saturdays 9am to 12.30pm, 3 to 7pm. July and August closed for lunch until 3.30pm.

Retail Parks

La Rochelle   Puilboreau
(on the east side of La Rochelle)
Commercial centre includes:
- BUT – furniture and accessories;
- Carrefour – hypermarket;
- Conforama – furniture, household appliances and accessories;
- Darty – household electrical, hi-fi, etc;
- Décathlon – sports store;
- Fly – furniture;
- Monsieur Meuble – furniture store.

Royan   (on the outskirts of Royan)
Retail park including:
- Casa – gift and home accessories;
- Conforama – furniture and household electrical;
- Connexion – electrical;
- Fly – furniture;
- Leclerc – hypermarket;
- Mr Bricolage – DIY store;

- Mr Meubles – furniture;
- Super Sport – sports goods;
- A whole area dedicated to car dealerships, including Mercedes and Fiat.

Saintes

(on the outskirts of Saintes, on route de Royan)

Retail park includes:

- Casa – household goods, from table mats to deck chairs. (A good shop for rummaging around);
- Jardinière – garden centre;
- JouetLand – toy shop;
- Leclerc – hypermarket;
- Mr Brico – DIY store;
- Sesame – furniture and household goods;
- Super Sport – sports goods.

Second-Hand Goods

Jonzac	C&F Poulard, 24 avenue M. Chauvin	☎ 05 46 48 26 83
	Troc Chic, 14 place du Champ de Foire	☎ 05 46 48 52 66
La Rochelle	Allo Brocante, 280 avenue Jean Guiton	☎ 05 46 67 92 45
	Antiquomane, 125 boulevard André Sautel	☎ 05 46 34 16 70
Rochefort	Kivendtou, 38 rue Wilson (near the railway station) Open Tuesdays to Fridays 2.30 to 6pm, weekends 3 to 6.30pm.	☎ 05 46 99 81 53
	Brocante de La Charente, 29 avenue de la Libération	☎ 05 46 99 06 14
Royan	Domaine de la Brandelle, chemin Brandelle, St Georges de Didonne	☎ 05 46 06 33 33
	Débarras, 26 rue Arago, ZI Royan 2	☎ 05 46 05 53 32
St Jean d'Angély	Carrefour du Meuble, 1 avenue de Gaulle	☎ 05 46 32 57 02
Saintes	Bourse aux Affaires, 5 petite rue Pont Amillion	☎ 05 46 93 27 37
	La Trocante, 44 avenue Jules Dufaure	☎ 05 46 35 18 22

Sports Goods

Jonzac   Multisports, 2 avenue Gambetta   ☎ 05 46 48 02 81

La Rochelle   Décathlon, ZAC de Beaulieu,
                   Puilboreau   ☎ 05 46 68 00 00
                   💻 *www.decathlon.fr*

Rochefort   Décathlon, ZAC des Pêcheurs d'Islande ☎ 05 46 82 89 81
                   Open Mondays to Saturdays 9.30am to 7.30pm.

Royan   Super Sport, ZAC de Belmont, Médis   ☎ 05 46 06 98 90
                   (on the retail park going east out of Royan)

St Jean d'Angély Intersport, route de la Rochelle   ☎ 05 46 59 28 35
                   (in front of Intermarché)
                   Large sports shop.

Supermarkets & Hypermarkets

La Rochelle   Carrefour, RN137, Angoulins-sur-Mer   ☎ 05 46 56 50 00
                   (north-east of Angoulins-sur-Mer, just off the N137)
                   Mondays to Saturdays 9am to 9pm (Fridays to 10pm).

                   Carrefour, rue 14 Juillet, Puilboreau   ☎ 05 46 68 03 22
                   (to the east of La Rochelle by the main intersection of the N137
                   ring road around the town and the N11 east)
                   Mondays to Saturdays 9am to 9pm.

                   Leclerc, 124 boulevard André Sautel   ☎ 05 46 34 18 67
                   Mondays to Saturdays 9am to 7.30pm (Fridays 8pm).

Rochefort   Leclerc, 66 avenue 11 novembre   ☎ 05 46 82 12 80
                   (on the south side of the town centre, but still within the loop of
                   the Charente river)
                   Mondays to Saturdays 9am to 7.30pm (Fridays to 8pm).

Royan   Leclerc, 2 route Antoine de Lavoisier   ☎ 05 46 05 11 89
                   Mondays to Saturdays 9am to 7.30pm (Fridays 8pm).
                   This hypermarket is part of a large shopping complex,
                   complete with café seating overlooking the atrium area. There
                   are clothes shops, restaurants, travel agent's, dry cleaner's,
                   hairdresser's and a crèche.

Saintes   Carrefour, 80 cours Marechal Leclerc   ☎ 05 46 93 32 70
                   Mondays to Saturdays 9am to 8pm (9pm on Fridays). This
                   shopping centre has a newsagent's that sells British papers
                   and other stores. There's also a business card machine, photo
                   booth, cash machine and a photocopier.

Leclerc, rue Champagne St Georges   ☎ 05 46 93 26 96
(on route de Royan)
Open 9am to 8pm Mondays to Saturdays (9pm Fridays).
Within the complex there are a post office, café, brasserie/
crêperie, newsagent's, photographer's, cash machine, TV and
electrical store, dry cleaner's, heel and key bar and a florist.

Swimming Pool Equipment

Royan   Charente Piscines, 34 rue Chata,
                 St Georges de Didonne   ☎ 05 46 05 49 57
                 Installation, design, maintenance and renovation.

Saintes   Aqua Creations, rue Pierre
                 et Marie Curie   ☎ 05 46 74 11 51
                 💻 *www.aquacreations.fr*
                 Ready to use pools, kits and above ground pools available, as well
                 as maintenance, products and accessories, spas and saunas.

Sports

This is just a selection of the activities available, the large towns having a
wide range; full details are available from the tourist office or the *mairie*.

Aerial Sports

Royan   Aérodrome de Royan-Médis   ☎ 05 46 05 55 20
                 💻 *www.europhenix17.fr*
                 The regional centre for parachute training.

Archery

Rochefort   SAR Tir à l'Arc, Polygone et Jardins,
                 avenue de Torrelavega   ☎ 05 46 83 14 89

St Jean d'Angély Les Archers d'Angély, 26 rue du Bourg,
                 La Fayolle, St Denis du Pin   ☎ 05 46 32 26 30
                 President Mr Gérard Maissant.
Saintes   Archers Saintais, Maison des
                 Associations   ☎ 05 46 93 16 85

Badminton

Jonzac   Held at the Gymnase Municipal   ☎ 05 46 48 49 29

La Rochelle   Badminton Rochelais,
                 Gymnase de Beauregard   ☎ 05 46 41 02 81
                 Contact Claude Bourmaud.

Rochefort   Rochefort Club, 3 rue Amiral Lartigue   ☎ 05 46 99 67 65

Saintes   Badminton Saintais, 79 rue
                   du Docteur Jean   ☎ 05 46 92 54 65

Canoeing & Kayaking

La Rochelle   Neway, 7 place Bernard Moitessier   ☎ 05 46 45 14 90
                   Canoe hire and courses available.

                   Société des Régates Rochelaises,
                   Avenue Capitainerie   ☎ 05 46 44 62 44
                   Canoe hire and courses available.

Rochefort   Canoë-Kayak du Pays Rochefortais,
                   Port Neuf   ☎ 05 46 88 40 80
                   Including sea kayaking.

St Jean d'Angély   Kayak Club Angérien,
                   30 quai de Bernouët   ☎ 05 46 32 59 61
                   This club is open in July and August from 9.30am to 7.30pm,
                   except Mondays. The rest of the year; Tuesdays 5 to 7pm,
                   Wednesdays 2 to 6pm, Saturdays 2 to 6pm and by
                   arrangement at other times. Canoes and kayaks are available
                   for hire and there are trips along the river.

Saintes   Centre Nautique, Saintes   ☎ 05 46 84 61 66
                   Canoeing/kayaking on the Charente river.

Clay Pigeon Shooting

Rochefort   Le Pigeon d'Argile, Tonnay Charente   ☎ 05 46 99 90 52

Saintes   La Martinière, St Georges des Coteaux   ☎ 05 46 92 96 91
                   (a few kilometres west of Saintes)

Fencing

Saintes   Cercle d'Escrime Saintais, Salle
                   d'Arme, 1bis passage Ancienne-Caserne   ☎ 05 46 92 01 02
                   (behind l'Abbayes aux Dames)
                   Meetings are held on Wednesday and Friday evenings from
                   6pm.

Fishing

Annual fishing permits can be bought locally from fishing tackle shops and
tabacs close to fishing lakes. They will also have maps of local fishing sites
and rivers.

Football

Football clubs can be found even in small villages. Contact your *mairie* to obtain details of a local club.

Golf

Ile d'Oléron	Golf d'Oléron, La Vieille Perrotine	☎ 05 46 47 11 59

A links course on the edge of the ocean with views over Ile d'Aix and Fort Boyard. Nine holes, 2,908m, par 36. Booking necessary. Open all year, green fees ranging from €23 to €26, lessons available, driving range, practice putting greens, pro-shop and club house.

Marsilly	Golf de la Prée, route de Nieul-sur-Mer	☎ 05 46 01 24 42

(ten minutes north of La Rochelle)
An 18 hole seaside course, 5,931m, par 72. There are five holes against the wind, many bunkers and water hazards, it is similar to the Scottish links course. Open all year. Green fees for 18 holes €32 to €45. Lessons, driving range, six hole beginners' course, buggy hire, pro-shop and club house with restaurant.

Royan	Golf de Royan, St Palais-sur-Mer	☎ 05 46 23 16 24

(in the heart of a forest only 1km from the sea)
18 holes, 5,970m, par 71 with most holes played through pine lined fairways. Open all year, lessons, driving range, pro-shop, buggy hire and club house with both a quick and gourmet restaurant. Green fees €28 to €47.

Saintes	Golf de Saintonge, Fontcouverte	☎ 05 46 74 27 61

Just a few miles north of Saintes, this is an 18 hole course, 4,790m, par 68. Open all year, green fees ranging from €23 to €35.50 with special rates for couples and young players. Lessons, driving range, buggy hire, pro-shop and club house with restaurant.

Horse Riding

Jonzac	Les Ecuries du Val de Seugne,
Base de Loisirs l'Heurtebise	☎ 05 46 04 58 08

Individual, group lessons and riding out.

La Rochelle	Société Hippique d'Aunis,
Ferme St Mathurin, La Jarne	☎ 05 46 44 32 34

Open all year.

Rochefort	Centre Equestre du Liron, Breuil Magné	☎ 05 46 84 45 86

Royan	Société Hippique de Royan Côte de
Beauté, Le Maine Gaudin,

St Palais-sur-Mer   ☎ 05 46 23 11 44
🖥 *www.centreequestreroyan.levillage.org*
Rides available on the beach and in the forest. Open all year.

St Jean d'Angély   Jean-Pierre Meneau, 3 cité   ☎ 05 46 59 02 74
Point du Jour

Saintes   Sud Ouest Western Riding, 2 route
Chez Thoreau, Fontcouverte   ☎ 05 46 74 18 67
(just north of Saintes)
Lessons available.

Ice Skating

Royan   During the winter months Royan has an ice rink on the
beach, open until the end of February.

Jetskiing

Royan   Gap Océan, Port de Royan, Ponton 4   ☎ 05 46 05 24 25
Jet skis for hire, with or without licence.

Jet Océan, De Talmont, La Palmyre   ☎ 05 46 49 16 03
Three seater jet skis for hire.

Martial Arts

La Rochelle   ALPR Judo, Thierry Blaisot   ☎ 05 46 44 56 06

Rochefort   Judo Club Rochefortais, Polygone,
avenue de Torrelavega   ☎ 05 46 87 37 94

Royan   Ecole de Judo/Ju Jitsu, gymnase des
Chaumes, Echillais   ☎ 06 15 91 14 08

Saintes   Judo, cours Genêt, Salle Patricia-Mottier   ☎ 05 46 92 69 86
Contact Mme Savarit.

Motorcycle Riding

Jonzac   Moto Club Jonzacais   ☎ 05 46 48 49 29

Rochefort   Moto Club du Pays Rochefortais   ☎ 05 46 85 46 10
Contact Mr Grand.

Potholing

Saintes   Spéléo Club Saintais, 11 rue Pont
des Monards   ☎ 05 46 93 43 47

Roller Skating

Jonzac	There's a small skate park at the Base de Loisirs l'Heurtebise.

Rochefort   Roller Club, gymnase de La
              Vieille Forme   ☎ 05 46 99 01 02

              Stade Rouge, Skate Park Tonnacquois   ☎ 05 46 88 74 12
              (behind rue Emile Zola)

Saintes   Hockey in Line, Gymnase route
              de Rochefort   ☎ 05 46 74 66 11
              Roller hockey.

              There's also a skate park on avenue de Tombouctou, close
              to the Collège Edgar Quinet.

Rowing

La Rochelle   Club d'Aviron de Mer, Les Minimes   ☎ 05 46 41 63 39
              Contact Véronique Guillard.

Saintes   Club d'Aviron Saintais, 6 rue de Courbiac   ☎ 05 46 74 01 66
              (beside the swimming pool in the north of the town)
              Open to 10 to 70-year-olds.

Sailing

Rochefort   Club Nautique Rochefortais, rue des
              Pêcheurs d'Islande   ☎ 05 46 87 34 61

              Ecole de Voile, rue Tabarly, Fouras   ☎ 05 46 84 61 66

Royan   Océan Voile, Le Cécilia, Port de Royan,
              Ponton 5   ☎ 05 46 06 35 53
              A 13m (42ft) sailing yacht available all year for introductory
              sessions and courses. Weekend or week cruises available on
              request.

Scuba Diving

Rochefort   Club Rochefortais des Sports sous-Marins,
              15 rue de la Ferronnerie   ☎ 05 46 83 13 99

Royan   Roc Plongée, Esplanade du Port   ☎ 05 46 38 37 18
              Sea diving possible from June to September. Instruction and
              courses.

St Jean d'Angély   52 rue du Manoir   ☎ 05 46 32 11 20
Both river and sea dives. Beginners welcome. Instruction
available for examinations. Contact Mr Jean-Pierre Charles.

Saintes   ASPTT Sports Sous-Marins,
                   Centre Sportif de la Boisnarderie   ☎ 05 46 93 16 02

Shooting

Jonzac   Société de Tir, Domaine de Chailleret   ☎ 05 46 48 49 73

La Rochelle   Atlantic Tir Club, avenue Porte Royale   ☎ 05 46 50 52 94

Rochefort   Tir Sportif Rochefortais, Polygone,
                   avenue de Torrelavega   ☎ 05 46 82 08 89

St Jean d'Angély   Club de Tir Angérien, Gymnase du Coi   ☎ 05 46 32 43 33
Indoor and outdoor ranges.

Saintes   Société Saintaise de Tir, Les Perches,
                   ZI des Charriers   ☎ 05 46 97 87 95

Snooker, Pool & Billiards

Some bars listed under **Bars & Nightlife** on page 152 also have billiards,
pool or snooker tables.

Rochefort   Le Roller, 48 rue de la République   ☎ 05 46 99 22 22
Snooker.

Royan   Espace Billard Océan, 3 rue
                   Jeanne d'Arc   ☎ 05 46 38 41 44
French billiards, snooker and pool. Bar, games and a giant
television. Open seven days a week from 3.30pm to 2am.

St Jean d'Angély   Billard Club Angérien, Salle Brossard,
                   11 place de la Biscuiterie   ☎ 05 46 59 00 66
French billiards and pool. Both leisure and competition playing.
Contact Mr Rolland Rousseau.

Squash

Royan   Espace Squash, 18 rue Henry Dunant   ☎ 05 46 06 77 77
Seven courts, bar, rest area and shops.

Surfing

Royan   Surf Club du Pays Royannais,
                   Plage de Pontaillac, 13 allées des Fleurs   ☎ 06 81 95 10 17
Group or individual courses available.

Swimming

Jonzac	Les Antilles, avenue Jean Moulin	☎ 05 46 48 12 11

💻 *www.haute-saintonge.com*
This water complex has an indoor pool.

La Rochelle Piscine Palmilud, avenue Louis Lumière,
Périgny   ☎ 05 46 45 70 20
(on the eastern outskirts of La Rochelle)
This is a water park which also has a conventional swimming
pool.

Rochefort rue Charles Maher   ☎ 05 46 99 02 22
Indoor pool, open all year.

Royan 1 boulevard Clémenceau   ☎ 05 46 05 67 70
25m indoor pool. Open all year, opening hours change
depending on school holidays and term times. Lessons and
aqua aerobics available.

Piscine de Foncillon, boulevard
Germaine de La Falaise   ☎ 05 46 39 93 21
Outdoor seawater pool by the beach. Open from 31st May to
mid-September.

St Jean d'Angély Atlantys   ☎ 05 46 59 21 50
This water complex is open all year round.

Saintes rue de Courbiac   ☎ 05 46 93 26 80
Outdoor pool. Open from the end of June to the beginning of
September.

Piscine Louis Starzinsky   ☎ 05 46 93 76 20
Indoor pool.

5 cours Charles de Gaulle   ☎ 05 46 93 11 51
Swimming club. Indoor pool.

Tennis

Many communes have their own tennis courts (of varying quality). Keys
and payment usually via the *mairie*.

Jonzac La Pouyade, boulevard Baie St Paul   ☎ 05 46 48 08 58

La Rochelle Tennis Club Rochelais, 42 avenue
Aristide Briand   ☎ 05 46 34 12 51

	Stade Bouffenie, avenue Pierre de Coubertin	☎ 05 46 43 45 15
Rochefort	Tennis Centre, avenue de Torrelavega	☎ 05 46 87 18 55
	Tennis Club, 1 rue de La Casse aux Prêtres	☎ 05 46 99 29 10
Royan	Le Garden Tennis, 4 allée des Rochers	☎ 05 46 38 45 77

Open all year 9am to 7.30pm, July and August 8am to 8pm. Courts booked by the hour.

| St Jean d'Angély | Tennis Club Angérien, Centre Georges Neuville, Faubourg St Eutrope | ☎ 05 46 32 49 83 |

Adult and junior sections. Free courses for new club members.

| Saintes | USSCC Tennis, Stade Yvon-Chevalier | ☎ 05 46 93 77 44 |

Watersports

| Royan | Station Nautique du Pays Royannais, Palais des Congrès | ☎ 05 46 23 47 47 |

Activities for children from the age of four. Windsurfing, catamaran, surfing, body boarding, speed sailing. Equipment hire and courses from two to five days.

Tourist Offices

Châtelaillon-	5 avenue de Strasbourg, Plage ▣ *www.chatelaillon-plage.fr*	☎ 05 46 56 26 97
Ile d'Oléron	route de Viaduc, Bourcefranc ▣ *www.marennes-oleron-tour.org*	☎ 05 46 85 65 23
Ile de Ré	5bis rue de la Blanche, Le Bois Plage en Ré	☎ 05 46 09 00 55
Jonzac	25 place Château ▣ *www.jonzac.fr*	☎ 05 46 48 49 29

Open November to March Mondays to Saturdays 9.30am to noon, 2.30 to 6pm. April to June 9.30am to 12.30pm, 2 to 6pm, July and August until 7pm, Sundays 10am to 12.30pm, 3 to 6.30pm.

| La Rochelle | Comité Départmental du Tourisme, Maison de la Charente-Maritime, 85 boulevard de la République | ☎ 05 46 31 71 71 |

place Petite Sirène   ☎ 05 46 41 14 68
💻 *www.larochelle-info.com &*
💻 *www.larochelle-tourisme.com*
Out of season Mondays to Saturdays 9am to 6pm, Sundays 10am to 1pm. July and August 9am to 8pm Mondays to Fridays and Sundays 9am to 5pm.

Rochefort   avenue Sadi Carnot   ☎ 05 46 99 08 60
💻 *www.ville-rochefort.fr* or 💻 *www.tourisme.fr/rochefort*
(near the large car park in the north-west of the town centre)
Open Mondays to Saturdays 9.30am to 12.30pm, 2 to 6pm (during the summer opening hours are longer and it doesn't close for lunch).

There's another tourist office by la Corderie but it's open only in the summer and limited hours.

Royan   Rond-Point de la Poste   ☎ 05 46 05 04 71
💻 *www.royan-tourisme.com*
September to May, Mondays to Saturdays 9am to 12.30pm, 2 to 6pm, Sundays and bank holidays 10am to 12.30pm. June and August Mondays to Saturdays 9am to 7.30pm, Sundays 10am to 1pm, 3 to 6pm.

St Jean d'Angély   8 rue Grosse Horloge   ☎ 05 46 32 04 72
💻 *www.angely.net*
Open Mondays to Fridays 9.15 to 12.15pm, 1.30 to 6pm, Saturdays 9.30am to 12.30pm, 3 to 5pm. July and August until 7pm Mondays to Saturdays, Sundays 10.30am to 12.30pm.

Saintes   62 cours national   ☎ 05 46 74 23 82
💻 *www.ville-saintes.fr* or 💻 *www.ot-saintes.fr*
Open Mondays to Saturdays 9.30am to 12.30pm, 2.15 to 6pm.

Tradesmen

Architects & Project Managers

General   Adams Gautier Poitou-Charentes   ☎ 05 49 64 42 96
💻 *www.adamsgautier.com*
This is a British/French team that are experienced architects and also organise surveys, building permits and carry out project management; new, renovations, landscaping and pools.

Eric Archaimbault   ☎ 06 77 13 41 41
💻 *archaimbaulteric@wanadoo.fr*
A bi-lingual project manager using only registered French tradesmen and covers the whole region of Poitou-Charentes.

St Fraigne   Mr Louis Albagnac, Le Bourg   ☎ 05 45 96 56 08
                    This French architect speaks English.

Builders

General   R. Englefield   ☎ 05 46 33 22 58
                    A British builder, based in Charente-Maritime.

Aulnay   Quincaillerie Générale, 12 route de
                    Poitiers   ☎ 05 46 33 10 42
                    (through a gate on the right just before you reach Intermarché
                    on the main road)
                    Artisans who can undertake plumbing, electrics, small building
                    jobs, wood flooring, ceilings and partitioning. Open 9am to
                    noon, 2 to 6pm. Tool hire available.

Jonzac   Alan Herpin, 20 place Marché   ☎ 05 46 04 78 05
                    New and renovation work, designs on request.

La Rochelle   Ripeau-Martel, 1 rue Solette   ☎ 05 46 41 63 83
                    🖳 *www.ripeau-martel.fr*
                    General building firm specialising in restoration work.

Rochefort   J.J. Gros, 22 Alfred Nobel,
                    Tonnay-Charente   ☎ 05 46 88 72 09
                    (next to the tip)

Royan   ABP, 132 avenue de Rochefort   ☎ 05 46 38 25 91

St Jean d'Angély   Cauillaud et Fils, 29 avenue du
                    Point du Jour   ☎ 05 46 32 34 44
                    Carpentry and building work.

Saintes   Serbat, Place St Louis   ☎ 05 46 90 10 08
                    General builder.

Carpenters

Jonzac   J.C. Riche, Chez Bascle,
                    route de Mirambeau   ☎ 05 46 48 10 94

La Rochelle   J. Savineau Ets. 69 rue des Saulniers   ☎ 05 46 27 11 39

Rochefort   TDM, 67 rue du Breuil   ☎ 05 46 83 66 65

Royan   Michelet Joël, 21 rue François Arago   ☎ 05 46 06 09 76
                    Windows, doors and parquet made and installed, free quotes.

St Jean d'Angély   Escap Menuiserie, 8 rue Breville,
                    la Petite Clie, St Julien de l'Escap   ☎ 05 46 26 63 29
                    Carpentry, plasterboard and partitioning.

Saintes	Dim'Sud Menuiseries, 2 rue Provence	☎ 05 46 92 06 58

Doors and gates, parquet flooring and kitchens.

Chimney Sweeps

Jonzac	Clean 17, Mirambeau	☎ 05 46 49 61 54
La Rochelle	Mr Guilbaud	☎ 05 46 42 31 30
Rochefort	David Franceschi, 12 rue de la Croix, Beaugeay	☎ 05 46 82 06 62
Royan	ABP, 132 avenue de Rochefort	☎ 05 46 38 25 91
St Jean d'Angély	ADC, 46 rue Dampierre	☎ 05 46 32 26 20
Saintes	Christian Montoroy, Les Barres, Ecurat	☎ 05 46 74 39 57

July to November.

Electricians & Plumbers

Jonzac	Sarl Maroc, avenue M. Chauvin	☎ 05 46 48 26 93
	Sarl Motard, 9 place Fillaudeau	☎ 05 46 48 18 42
La Rochelle	LS Elec, 68 avenue Maréchal Juin	☎ 05 46 07 49 37
	Pentecôte, 19 rue Maurice Ravel, ZA Plessis	☎ 05 46 27 05 50

Heating, plumbing, roofing and chimney sweeping.

Rochefort	BEL Entreprise, 6 avenue Dulin	☎ 05 46 87 68 82
Royan	Claude Roy, 55 boulevard Clémenceau	☎ 05 46 05 09 17
	Mandin Palissier, rue François Arago	☎ 05 46 05 65 76
St Jean d'Angély	Berthouin, 8 rue des Bancs	☎ 05 46 32 13 89

General electrics and plumbing as well as repairs of household electrical items.

	Alan Bailey, route de Poitiers, Aulnay	☎ 05 46 32 12 46

British plumber who works in and around Aulnay and St Jean.

Saintes	Brunet Drouillac, 24 rue Fougères ZI de l'Ormeau de Pied	☎ 05 46 93 07 52

🖳 *www.brunet-groupe.fr*
Electrics, heating, alarms and 24 hour call-out.

Mr Terry Duggan, 46 rue du Renferme,
la Guerinaille   ☎ 05 46 94 84 70
(south of Saintes in Varzay).
This British tradesman carries out electrical work, plumbing.

G. Dupré et Fils, 97 avenue Gambetta   ☎ 05 46 93 05 29
Plumbing heating, repairs and maintenance.

Translators & Teachers

French Teachers & Courses

Jonzac	Haute Saintonge Accueil, 41 rue des Carmes English/French conversation.	☎ 05 46 48 01 60
	Ecole des Arts de la Haute Saintonge le Paradis Courses in French held here and elsewhere.	☎ 05 46 48 31 26
La Rochelle	l'Univers des Langues, 1 avenue de Colmar 🖳 www.univers-langues.com	☎ 05 46 41 69 31
Rochefort	APP, 18 rue de la République	☎ 05 46 99 80 12
	Rochefort Accueil, quai Louisiane, Bassin Bourgainville (by the marina)	☎ 05 46 99 04 93
Royan	Centre Audiovisuel de Royan pour l'Etude des Langues, 48 boulevard Franck Lamy	☎ 05 46 39 50 00
St Jean d'Angély	Chris Devine, 31 Rue du Bourg, Courcelles ✉ ambervineclub@club-internet.fr Small groups or one-to-one lessons.	☎ 05 46 26 20 44
Saintes	'Get to Grips with French' One-to-one or small groups.	☎ 05 46 93 92 09
	Risiau, Maison de la Solidaritie	☎ 05 46 93 19 94

Translators

Jonzac	Alain Le Corroller, Le Ramet	☎ 05 46 48 22 94

| La Rochelle | Carolyne Occhuzzo, 21 rue Alfred Kastler | ☎ 05 46 30 23 10 |

| Royan | Isabel Verpeaux, Mortagne-sur-Gironde (on the coast south of Royan) | ☎ 05 46 90 54 03 |

| Saintes | Juristyle, 80 rue Emile Zola Legal translations. | ☎ 05 46 74 20 53 |

Utilities

Electricity & Gas

Électricité de France/Gaz de France (EDF/GDF) is one company for the whole of France but operates its gas and electricity divisions separately. The numbers below are for general information; emergency numbers can be found on page 56.

| General | Gaz de France, 6 rue Auguste Perret, Lagord (near La Rochelle) | ☎ 05 46 43 43 43 |

| | EDF Services Charente-Maritime 🖳 *www.edf.fr* | ☎ 08 10 17 60 00 |

EDF local offices are listed below (there are no direct telephone numbers for these offices; you must dial one of the above numbers).

La Rochelle	1 rue Marius Lacroix
Rochefort	2 boulevard Aristide Briand
Royan	9 avenue Maréchal Leclerc
Saintes	avenue Saintonge

Heating Oil

| Jonzac | Pierre Sardin, 35 avenue Kennedy | ☎ 05 46 48 02 36 |

| La Rochelle | Picoty Fioul Services, 6 rue Béthencourt | ☎ 05 46 01 50 15 |

| Rochefort | CPO, ZAC Fraternité, Tonnay Charente | ☎ 05 46 99 06 13 |

| Royan | Atlantique Fioul Services | ☎ 05 46 39 01 14 |

| St Jean d'Angély | CPO, 25 rue Elysée Loustalot | ☎ 05 46 32 06 77 |

| Saintes | Atlantique Fioul Services | ☎ 05 46 39 01 14 |

Water

The main water supply companies are listed below. If you aren't covered by one of these, your *mairie* will have details of your water supplier.

Compagnie des Eaux de Royan	1 avenue de Valombre, Royan	☎ 05 46 39 00 22
	emergencies	☎ 05 46 39 24 02
Régie des Services d'Eau	ZI Ormeau de Pied, BP551, Saintes	☎ 05 46 92 39 00
	emergencies	☎ 05 46 93 19 19
SAUR	avenue Louis Lumière, Périgny	☎ 05 46 44 29 11

Wood

Ile d' Oléron	La Forezienne du Littoral, rue des Aires, Grand Village Plage	☎ 05 46 47 51 97
La Rochelle	Aunis Bois, La Jarne (east of La Rochelle)	☎ 05 46 50 58 41
Saintes	Jean-Luc Vriet, Chemin Gatefer	☎ 05 46 92 07 31

4

Deux-Sèvres

This chapter provides details of facilities and services in the department of Deux-Sèvres (79). General information about most subjects can be found in **Chapter 1**. All entries are arranged alphabetically by town, except where a service applies over a wide area, in which case it's listed at the beginning of the relevant section under 'General'. A map of Deux-Sèvres is shown below.

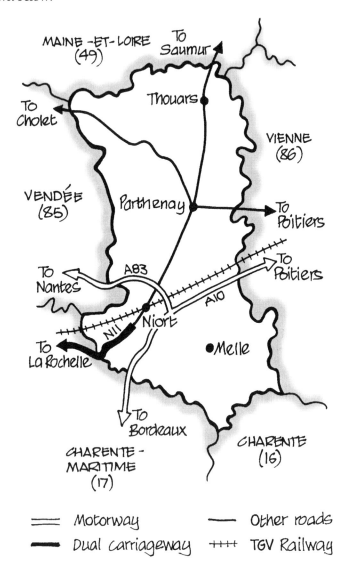

Accommodation

Camping

Melle	Camping Municipal, rue Villiers	☎ 05 49 29 18 04

Niort   Camping de Noron, boulevard
               Salvador Allende   ☎ 05 49 78 71 24
               Open April to September, bike hire and play area.

Parthenay   Château de la Clairière,
               La Clairière, Adilly   ☎ 05 49 95 19 59
               (just north-east of the town)

Thouars   Camping Municipal, 13 rue Grande
               Côte de Crevant   ☎ 05 49 66 17 99
               (500m from the town centre)
               Open 1st June to 30th September.

Châteaux

Amailloux   Château de Tennessus   ☎ 05 49 95 50 60
               💻 *www.tennessus.com*
               (just north of Parthenay)
               A 14th century château with round towers, surrounded by a
               moat and drawbridge, set in tranquil parkland. Three huge
               bedrooms (100m^2) with en-suite facilities from €115 per room;
               suites from €165. Fishing and punting possible in the moat.
               English is spoken and the château is open March to December.
               Booking required.

St Loup-Lamairé Château de Saint Loup   ☎ 05 49 64 81 73
               💻 *www.chateaudesaint-loup.com*
               (north of Parthenay in the Thouet valley alongside a village of
               timbered houses)
               This château is from the period of Henry IV to Louis XIII and is
               set in 50ha (125 acres) of ground, including a unique orangery.
               Three of the six bedrooms have canopy beds, and all have
               private bathrooms and sitting area. Rooms from €135 to €190,
               breakfast €15, evening meal €65, wine included. English is
               spoken and the château is open all year. Booking required.

Gîtes And Bed & Breakfast

Niort   15 rue Thiers   ☎ 05 49 24 00 42
               💻 *www.itea2.com/GDF/79*
               Gîtes de France listed. Bookings can be made by phone or via
               the internet.

Hotels

Hotels have been listed only for towns that have a limited number. All other main towns have a wide selection, including national chains such as those listed on page 45.

Melle	Les Glycines, 5 place René Groussard (in the centre of town) Double rooms from €46.	☎ 05 49 27 01 11
Parthenay	Hôtel Le Castille, 6 avenue 114ème RI Two-star hotel with parking. From €36 for two people.	☎ 05 49 64 13 67
	Hôtel le Commerce, 30 boulevard Edgard Quinet Two-star hotel and restaurant. From €38 for two people.	☎ 05 49 94 36 13
Thouars	Hotel de la Gare, 1 place de la Gare (in the centre of town) Rooms from €31 for two people.	☎ 05 49 66 20 75

Bars & Nightlife

A monthly publication, *Niort en Poche*, lists concerts, plays, films and other activities in Niort and the surrounding area.

Arçais	Le Saphir Disco, 15 rue du Vanneau (west of Niort) Open Fridays and Saturdays 11pm until 5am.	☎ 05 49 35 41 18
Coulonges-sur-l'Autize	The Retro, route Niort (north of Niort) A private club for the over 25s. In a distinctive building, half railway coach half aeroplane, containing three clubs. Open Thursdays, Fridays and Saturdays 10.30pm to 5am.	☎ 05 49 06 20 00
Forêt de l'Hermitain	L'Hacienda 🖳 *www.lhacienda.com*. A nightclub complex with three clubs, four bars, a garden and a pool, with various themes and events. Open Fridays, Saturdays and bank holidays 11pm to 4.30am.	☎ 05 49 76 04 00
Melle	Bowling, Loisirs Plus, 3 impasse Gaston Chérau	☎ 05 49 66 39 41
	Café du Boulevard, 2 place René Groussard (in the centre of town)	☎ 05 49 27 01 28

Leaflets are available giving full details of the coming month's live entertainment. English is spoken and there's a cyber café.

Moulin du Royou, Tillou ☎ 05 49 29 77 12
Pub disco between Melle and Chef-Boutonne that holds events such as 'Chippendale' evenings. Booking possible.

Niort

Amusement Arcade, 4 rue du Temple
Hosts 'events', such as table football tournaments, in the evenings. Open Mondays to Wednesdays noon to 8pm, Thursdays noon to 10pm, Fridays and Saturdays noon to midnight and Sundays 2 to 8pm. Open on bank holidays from 2pm.

Bowling, 169 terrasse avenue Nantes ☎ 05 49 09 26 26
Open every day, with bar and concerts.

Camino Café, place de la Brèche ☎ 05 49 08 05 32
(in the centre of the town)
This bar/restaurant is open every day 10am to 2am, closing only Sunday lunchtimes.

Jardin de La Brèche, place de La Brèche ☎ 05 49 24 24 78
A restaurant that holds a karaoke the first Friday of each month. Three-course meal with coffee, small carafe of wine and live entertainment €25. Open Mondays to Fridays and Saturday evenings.

White Ball, 104 rue de la Gare ☎ 05 49 28 59 19
French billiards, pool and snooker tables. Open every day 3pm to 2am.

During the summer there's a variety of free concerts on the square in front of the Moulin du Roc, including regular Thursday evening concerts starting at around 9pm.

Parthenay

Americ'n Blues, 12 rue Marne ☎ 05 49 94 11 13
Nightclub.
Diff'Art, 15 rue Prés Salvador Allende ☎ 05 49 94 67 10
Concert hall.

Saint-Gelais

Le Mylord Disco, Le Breuillat ☎ 05 49 75 00 00
(7km/4.5mi from Niort)
Retro, '80s and other themes. Open Thursdays to Saturdays 10.30pm to 5am. Over 25s.

Thouars

Loisirs Plus, 3 impasse Gaston Chérau ☎ 05 49 66 39 41
Bowling and leisure venue.

Le Café des Arts, 55 rue St Médard   ☎ 05 49 66 09 13
Bar and brasserie open Tuesdays to Saturdays (Fridays and
Saturdays until 2am).

Le Scénario, 33 avenue Victor Hugo   ☎ 05 49 66 21 64
(on the left as you descend the hill)
Modern bar and nightclub open every day 7pm to 2am.

Business Services

Computer Services

General   K. Humphreys, Chez Bouchet,
                Montalembert   ☎ 05 49 07 53 46
                ✉ *humphreyskeith@aol.com*
                This Briton deals with computer problems and sells hardware,
                software and upgrades, covering eastern Deux-Sèvres,
                northern Charente and southern Vienne.

Melle   Mellecom, 5 rue des Trois Marchands   ☎ 05 49 27 00 24
                💻 *www.mellecom.fr*
                Computer shop open Mondays to Saturdays. English spoken.

Niort   Médi@clic, 8 rue Porte St Jean   ☎ 05 49 28 31 31
                Sales, repairs and accessories, including home repairs.

Parthenay   Microgat Informatique,
                14 rue du Sépulire   ☎ 05 49 94 34 11
                Computers, repairs and accessories. Open Mondays to
                Saturdays 9am to noon, 2 to 7pm.

Thouars   Config Système, 21 place St Médard   ☎ 08 25 16 20 20
                (in the old town of Thouars)
                Computers made to order and repaired, as well as internet
                systems and accessories. Open Tuesdays to Saturdays 10am
                to 1pm, 2 to 7.30pm.

Employment Agencies

(see page 50)

Communications

Fixed Telephones

General   France Télécom: Dial 1014 or go to
                💻 *www.francetelecom.fr*
                Local shops are listed below.

Bressuire	23 rue Huchette
Niort	26 rue Victor Hugo
Parthenay	38 rue Jean Jaurès

Internet Access

Melle	Café du Boulevard, 2 place René Groussard	☎ 05 49 27 01 28
	Mellecom, 5 rue des Trois Marchands *www.mellecom.fr*	☎ 05 49 27 00 24
Niort	Médi@clic, 8 rue Porte St Jean	☎ 05 49 28 31 31
	Espace Culturel, Hyper Leclerc, avenue de Paris	☎ 05 49 17 39 10
Parthenay	La Mairie, 2 rue Citadelle	☎ 05 49 94 03 77
	Office de Tourisme, 8 rue Vau St Jacques A dedicated area for comfortable 'surfing'.	☎ 05 49 64 24 24

Note that all internet access in Parthenay is free.

| Thouars | Espace Tyndo, 6 rue de Président Tyndo Wednesdays 5 to 7pm, Fridays 5 to 8pm, Saturdays 2 to 5pm. | ☎ 05 49 68 15 47 |
| | Collège Marie de la Tour d'Auvergne, Place du Château Mondays, Tuesdays and Thursdays 5.30 to 7pm, Wednesdays 2 to 9pm, Fridays 5.30 to 7pm. | ☎ 05 49 67 19 24 |

Mobile Telephones

Melle	Cyber.com, Grand' Rue (tucked away in a small street beyond the market)	☎ 05 49 27 00 24
Niort	There are several mobile phone shops on rue Ricard, including:	
	Orange Mobistore, 32 rue Ricard	☎ 05 49 24 02 30
	Espace SFR, 1 rue Ricard	☎ 05 49 08 18 88
Thouars	Espace Communications, 73 avenue Victor Hugo Open Tuesdays to Saturdays.	☎ 05 49 68 08 35

Domestic Services

Curtain Making

General   Carol Weekes 'Les Petites Pommes',
                   Les Hâtes, Couture   ☎ 05 45 90 88 36
                   ✉ *dacawe@wanadoo.fr*
                   Curtains made to measure for addresses in Poitou-Charentes.

Equipment & Tool Hire

Niort   Loxam, 31 rue Henri Sellier   ☎ 05 49 09 08 28
                   🖥 *www.loxam.fr*

Thouars   Loca Ser, Le Motte des Justices   ☎ 05 49 67 84 26
                   (north of the town on the D938)
                   Equipment hire for all building work.

Garden Services

General   Garden Maintenance Services,
                   Champs-Viron, La Couarde   ☎ 05 49 06 03 53
                   🖥 *www.silkwarner.com/garden*
                   British-run company offering grass cutting, garden clearance
                   and maintenance within a 60km (40mi) radius of Melle.

Launderettes

Melle   Laverie Automatique, rue Raffinière
                   Open every day 7am to 9pm.

Niort   Laverie, 50 avenue de Limoges

Parthenay   Laverie, avenue François Mitterand
                   (beside Hyper U)
                   Open Mondays to Saturdays 8am to 12.30pm, Sundays 8am to 1pm.

Thouars   Pierre Lorigeon, 53 avenue Victor Leclerc
                   Open every day 8am to 8pm.

Septic Tank Services

General   AVSP, route de Thouars, Bressuire   ☎ 05 49 65 31 31
                   Emptying, cleaning and unblocking. Also has units in
                   Châtellerault, Couhé, Loudun, Poitiers and Yversay (all in Vienne).
                   SARP Sud Ouest, 65 rue Goise, Niort   ☎ 05 49 26 13 56
                   All tank-related services, including inspections.

                   Sanitra Fourrier, route de
                   Chardonchamp, ZA le Porteau,

Migné-Auxances (Vienne)　　　☎ 05 49 51 67 21
Also has units in Châtellerault, Loudun and Poitiers (Vienne).

Entertainment

Cinemas

Melle　　　Cinéma Le Méliès, place Bujault　　　☎ 05 49 27 08 59
💻 *www.allocine.fr*

Niort　　　Cinéma CGR, rue Sainte Marthe　　　☎ 08 36 68 04 45
💻 *www.cgrcinemas.com*
(in an arcade off an distinctive one-way street with 80ft long snakes along its edge)
Three screens.

Cinéma CGR, 7 avenue de la République　☎ 08 92 68 04 45
(on Place de la Bréche, the large square in the centre of Niort)
Six screens. Wheelchair access.

Parthenay　Cinéma Le Foyer, 1 rue Denfert
Rochereau　　　　　　　　　　　　☎ 05 49 64 05 30

Thouars　　Cinéma Familia, 7 place Boël　　　☎ 05 49 66 06 48

English Books

The libraries listed below have a selection of English books and are closed on Sundays and Mondays.

	Tue	Wed	Thu	Fri	Sat
Melle 3 place René Groussard ☎ 05 49 27 91 09	1.00–6.00	10.00–12.00 1.00–6.00	10.00–12.00 1.00–6.00	1.00–6.00	10.00–5.00 (4pm July and August)
Niort Le Moulin du Roc, Boulevard Main ☎ 05 49 78 70 71	3.00–7.00	2.00–7.00	closed	10.00–6.00	2.00–6.00
Thouars 20 boulevard Jergeon ☎ 05 49 66 41 86	3.00–7.00	2.00–7.00	closed	10.00–6.00	2.00–6.00

Festivals

July	Niort	
	Jazzy…si	☎ 05 49 78 71 78

A combination of international performers and undiscovered talent in a series of free open-air concerts in the centre of town – at noon in the François Mitterrand gardens and in the evenings inside the Centre Du Guesclin.

July	St Maixent l'École	
	Rencontres Internationales Folkloriques	
	Enfantines	☎ 05 49 76 13 77

Performances by 450 young artists from all over the world, who communicate their traditional folklore via their language and costumes, over eight days.

Parthenay
Festival des Jeux   ☎ 05 49 94 24 20
🖥 *www.jeux-festival.com*
Held annually this is a two-week festival of games, shows and toys, for both grown-ups and children.

Le Vanneau
Marché sur l'Eau   ☎ 05 49 35 99 29
In the Marais Poitevin a floating market is organised in the shade of the weeping willows in the small port of Vanneau. Artisans, producers and others offer products and specialities of the region in an ambiance of regional folklore.

November	Ménigoute	
	Festival International du Film	
	Ornithologique	☎ 05 49 69 90 09

🖥 *www.menigoute-festival.org*
Held each year during the holidays around 1st November, this festival includes nature films, art, conferences and outings.

Theatres

Bressuire	Théâtre du Bocage, 9 boulevard	
	Alexandre I	☎ 05 49 65 09 04

Niort	Moulin du Roc, 9 boulevard Main	☎ 05 49 77 32 30

🖥 *www.moulinduroc.asso.fr*
La Scène Nationale, including two concert halls and three exhibition galleries. The season runs from September to June and there's a wide variety of shows, drama, dance, classical music, opera, jazz and comedy, as well as a programme for youngsters.

	L'Espace Tartalin, Aiffres (on the outskirts of the town)	☎ 05 49 75 53 58
	Théâtre de Saint Florent, 202 avenue St Jean d'Angély	☎ 05 49 79 31 43
Parthenay	Palais des Congrès, 22 boulevard Meilleraye 💻 *www.cc-parthenay.fr* Shows, concerts and exhibitions.	☎ 05 49 64 85 10
Thouars	Association S'il Vous Plaît, 5 boulevard Pierre Curie (in the centre of town) Popular venue for shows and events.	☎ 05 49 66 24 24

Video & DVD Hire

Melle	Mellois Vidéo, 20 Grande Rue	☎ 05 49 27 18 18

Mondays 2 to 7.30pm, Tuesdays to Saturdays 10am to
12.15pm, 2 to 7pm (Fridays and Saturdays till 8pm).

There's a dispenser next to Weldom at Saint Léger.

Niort	Vidéo-Futur, 3 rue du Temple	☎ 05 49 28 20 84

Open Mondays 3 to 8pm, Tuesdays to Fridays 11am to
12.30pm, 3 to 8pm, Saturdays 11am to 1pm, 2.30 to 8pm,
Sundays and bank holidays 11am to 1pm, 4.30 to 7pm.
24-hour external dispenser for videos and DVDs.

Parthenay	108 Champ'Vidco, rue Jean Jaurès	☎ 05 49 64 34 78

Tuesdays to Fridays 2 to 8pm, Saturdays 10am to noon, 2 to
8pm, Sundays 3 to 8pm.

Thouars	Bourgognon, 29 rue Porte de Paris	☎ 05 49 96 65 29

Mondays to Saturdays 2.30 to 7.30pm.

Miscellaneous

Loudun	Ludothec'Astérix, 9 rue du Lion d'Or	☎ 05 49 98 27 18

Toys and games for hire or to borrow.

Leisure Activities

This section is not intended to be a definitive guide but gives a wide range
of ideas for the department. Prices and opening hours were correct at the
time of publication, but it's best to check before travelling long distances.

Art Classes

Niort   Esquisses et Couleurs, MCPT St Liguaire,
               25 rue du 8 Mai   ☎ 05 49 79 37 48
               Drawing, oils, acrylics, watercolours and pastels. Workshops
               Monday evenings.

               Autour de la Sculpture, Salle des Fêtes,
               St Liguaire   ☎ 05 49 73 96 76
               Modelling, plaster and bronzes. Meetings the first weekend of
               every month 9am to 6pm, conferences and exhibitions.

Thouars   Écoles d'Arts Plastiques, Ecuries du
               Château, rue de La Trémoïlle   ☎ 05 49 66 12 36

Ballooning

Chanteloup   ☎ 05 49 97 33 16
               Leisure flights in hot air balloons, taking off from Chanteloup or
               other suitable locations. For more information contact Mr
               Fuseau.

Bike Hire

Arçais   La Bicyclette Verte, route de St Hilaire ☎ 05 49 35 42 56
               💻 www.bicyclette-verte.com
               Bike hire including children's bikes and tandems. There are
               45km (30mi) of cycle paths across le Marais Poitevin, many of
               which are traffic free.

Chef-Boutonne Office de Tourisme, Château Jarvarzay ☎ 05 49 29 86 31
               (south-east of the town)

Boat & Train Rides

Marais Poitevin Embarcadère de l'Autize, St Sigismond ☎ 02 51 52 97 45
               (west of Niort on the D68)
               Barques are traditional wooden boats that can seat up to six
               people and are available to hire to explore the tranquil
               waterways of the Marais Poitevin, with or without a guide, from
               one hour to half a day.

               'Green Venice', 6 rue de l'Eglise, Coulon ☎ 05 49 35 14 14
               💻 www.maraispoitevin-evasion.com
               (west of Niort)
               A park offering punts, scenic trains and gondolas. Individual
               hire, guided tours or river cruises.

               'Le Pibalou' Tourist Train Marais
               Poitevin, Coulon   ☎ 05 49 35 14 14

Discover the history, flora and fauna of the marshes.

Boat Hire   ☎ 05 49 35 43 34
Punt and canoe hire are available at Arçais in the heart of
Marais. Punts can be hired with or without a guide. Booking
possible.

Bridge

Melle   Bridge Club Mellois, Foyer de la
                    Jabotière, 1 rue du Tapis Vert   ☎ 05 49 27 90 89
                    Tuesday evenings at 8.15pm.

Niort   Bridge Club Niortais, 47 rue de Ribray ☎ 05 49 73 47 31
                    Beginners, training and tournaments. Sessions every day 2 to 6pm.

Thouars   Foyer Laïque, boulevard de Hannut   ☎ 05 49 66 33 68
                    Free lessons for beginners.

Children's Activity Clubs

Parthenay   Centre de Loisirs Maurice Caillon,
                    22 rue des Tulipes   ☎ 05 49 64 33 55
                    This centre organises activities for 3 to 14-year-olds during the
                    school holidays.

                    Mercredis Découverte, 42 avenue
                    Pierre Mendès   ☎ 05 49 94 24 43
                    This group organises activities on Wednesdays during term time.

Thouars   La Chevalerie du Thouet, Aubigny   ☎ 05 49 69 88 20
                    Offers horse-drawn caravan rides in the Gâtine and runs
                    holiday camps for children and activity weekends for people of
                    all ages.

Circus Skills

Niort   Cirque en Scène, 4 rue du
                    Château St Hubert   ☎ 06 23 41 16 64
                    Introduction to and training for a variety of circus skills, and
                    production of shows for all ages.

Parthenay   Carnaboul'System   ☎ 05 49 71 04 48
                    Contact Cécile Magnien.

Crazy Golf

Sauzé-Vaussais   Plan d'Eau
                    (directly east of Melle, the *plan d'eau* is signposted to the left
                    as you pass through Sauzé-Vaussais, before you reach the

Super U supermarket)
Take your own putter out of season.

St Martin-de-Sanzay | Mini golf Paysagé de La Ballastière (directly north of Thouars) | ☎ 05 49 67 72 92

Dancing

Melle | Lycée Desfontaines (in the gym) | ☎ 05 49 29 04 05
Modern jazz with a show at the end of each year. Contact Mr Hervé Juin.

Vie Danse | ☎ 05 49 08 01 00
Introduction to dance for children with ballet and modern jazz for all.

Niort | Hop Là, 14 rue de Bas Sablonnier | ☎ 05 49 26 06 55
Jazz and contemporary dance.

Parthenay | Maison de Cultures de Pays, Quartier St Jacques | ☎ 05 49 95 00 47
Waltz and salsa classes.

Flying

Niort | Aéro Club des Deux-Sèvres, route de Limoges | ☎ 05 49 28 29 41
Planes, gliders and a model plane club.

Thouars | Aéro Club Thouarsais, L'Aérodrome, Missé | ☎ 05 49 66 04 73
Contact Mr Joël.

Gyms & Health Clubs

Melle | Squash St Pierre, 21 rue Guillotière | ☎ 05 49 27 09 36
Open Mondays to Saturdays 9am to 8pm for work-outs and various classes throughout the week. Squash also played.

Niort | Niort Tonic/Moving, 36 rue Gare | ☎ 05 49 28 09 27
💻 *www.moving.fr*
Heath club, beauty centre, aqua gym, tennis and squash.

Amazonia, 133 avenue de Paris | ☎ 05 49 05 64 34
Health club open every day 6am to 11pm.

Parthenay | Body Form, 41 rue Henri Dunant | ☎ 05 49 95 21 83

Gypsy Caravan Rides

Thouars | La Chevalerie du Thouet, Aubigny   ☎ 05 49 69 88 20
Horse-drawn caravan rides in the Pays de Gâtine, a scenic area around Parthenay in the north of the department.

Karting & Quad Bikes

Clave | Gating Ball, Bois de St Loup   ☎ 05 49 69 00 93
🖳 *www.gating-ball.com*
(west of Thouars)
Quad bikes, paint ball and two karting tracks.

Fontenay-le-Comte | Karting Vendee Loisirs, La Michetterie   ☎ 02 51 69 39 15
(north-west of Niort)

Moutiers-sous-Chantemerie | Boca Speed, La Boiriou   ☎ 05 49 65 73 15
An international track for both professionals and amateurs. Clubhouse with a bar serving fast food.

Lakes & Beaches

Ayron | Base de Loisirs du Pays Vouglaisien   ☎ 05 49 51 06 69
(west of Poitiers)
A park with a large lake and sandy beach, crazy golf, picnic area, play area, fishing, pedalos, canoes, kayaks, beach volleyball, table tennis and boules.

Cherveux-St-Christophe | Plan d'Eau   ☎ 05 49 75 01 77
Beach with bathing, crazy golf, tennis, fishing, pedalos and restaurant. The leisure area is open all year round but some of the activities are seasonal.

Secondigny | Lac des Effres
This lake has an outdoor pool, crazy golf, sailing, windsurfing and pedalos.
There are barbeques, picnic tables, a playground, paths and *boules* courts.

Verruyes | Plan d'Eau   ☎ 05 49 63 21 22
This large lake has fishing and swimming from the beach with a lifeguard in the summer. Pedaos, tennis, windsurfing, canoe/kayaks, picnic and games area and restaurant. Open all year with some activities seasonal.

Vitré | Plan d'Eau du Lambon   ☎ 05 49 79 90 41
This is a 7ha (17-acre) lake with a large sandy beach, changing rooms, cold drinks and ice creams. There's also fishing and canoeing, a volleyball court, table tennis, a restaurant with panoramic view over the lake and an adventure playground.

Music

Melle   Ecole de Musique du Pays Mellois,
                 12 bis rue St Pierre   ☎ 05 49 27 09 62
                 Tuition available on a wide range of instruments, as well as
                 choir, orchestra, rock and jazz workshops. For children and
                 adults.

Niort   Arc Musical, 29 rue de la Gare   ☎ 05 49 28 10 14
                 Music training, workshops and introduction to various
                 instruments. A variety of courses throughout the week.

                 Sliv Jazz Band, Centre du Guesclin   ☎ 05 49 69 17 65
                 Amateur jazz band giving concerts and taking part in shows.
                 Rehearsals on Thursdays 8.30 to 10.30pm.

Thouars   Ecole de Musique   ☎ 05 49 66 41 64
                 Contact Mr Lecain.

Paint Ball

Clave   Gating Ball, Bois de St Loup   ☎ 05 49 69 00 93
                 🖳 *www.gating-ball.com*
                 Two paint ball grounds as well as quad bikes and karting tracks.

Thouars   Paint Ball Club   ☎ 05 49 96 12 64
                 Contact Mr Bridier.

Photography

Niort   Pour l'Instant, MCPT Centre,
                 7 avenue de Limoges   ☎ 05 49 24 35 44
                 Promotion of photography, shows, courses and meetings.

Thouars   Photo Club de Grine   ☎ 05 49 68 13 24
                 Contact Mr Courtin.

Rollerskating & Skate Boarding

Melle   Melle Posse, Espace de Glisse de la
                 Fosse aux Chevals   ☎ 06 23 07 53 35
                 Free access to the park. BMX and skateboarding.
                 Contact David Chantecaille.

Niort   Pré-Leroy Skate Park, route Pré-Leroy   ☎ 05 49 24 09 96
                 Rollerskating and skate boarding.

                 Roller Club Niortais, 10 allée
                 Alphonse-Laveran   ☎ 05 49 24 90 70
                 Acrobatic and speed skating, as well as hockey on skates.

Scouts & Guides

Niort   Scouts de France, 42 rue Chabaudy   ☎ 05 49 73 52 90
                 Phone weekends between 2 and 5pm for details.

Thouars   Scouts de France   ☎ 05 49 96 73 47
                 Contact Mr Penneteir for details of local groups.

Social Clubs & Organisations

Thouars   Rotary Club   ☎ 05 49 66 11 74
                 Contact Philippe Morin for details of local meetings.

                 Round Table   ☎ 05 49 66 13 53
                 Contact Pascal Rambault for details of local meetings.

Town Twinning

Niort   Comité de Jumelage, 12 rue Joseph
                 Cugnot   ☎ 05 49 24 24 37
                 Niort is twinned with Wellingborough.

Stamp Collecting

Niort   Union Philatélique Niortaise,
                 12 rue Joseph Cugnot   ☎ 05 49 33 05 76
                 Meetings on the third Sunday of the month 10am to noon,
                 September to June inclusive.

Thouars   Club Timbrophile Thouarsais   ☎ 05 49 66 08 29

Vintage Cars

Niort   Les Belles d'Antan, 170 avenue
                 de Nantes   ☎ 05 49 79 49 12
                 Rallies, outings and festivals.

Walking & Rambling

The local tourist office holds guide books and data sheets for walkers.

Parthenay   Les Joyeux Randonners Gâtinais   ☎ 05 49 95 32 88
                 Regular organised walks, usually on Sunday mornings.

Thouars   Les Galopins du Thouet   ☎ 05 49 66 36 99
                 Contact Mr Renaudin for details.

Yoga

Melle   Centre d'Etude et de Pratique du Yoga,
                 13, place de la Poste   ☎ 05 49 27 06 91

| Niort | Equilibre
Contact Mme Croisé. | ☎ 05 49 04 07 78 |

| Thouars | Club de Yoga, Salle des Fêtes
Contact Mme Marchais at the above number or Louzy town hall
(☎ 05 49 66 20 16) for details of classes, which are held on
Monday evenings. | ☎ 05 49 66 14 31 |

Medical Facilities & Services

Ambulances

In the event of a medical emergency dial 15.

| Melle | ☎ 05 49 29 44 47 |

| Niort | ☎ 05 49 08 16 70 |

| Parthenay | ☎ 05 49 95 02 11 |

| Thouars | ☎ 05 49 96 13 59 |

Doctors

English-speakers may like to contact the following doctors.

| Melle | Dr Bertrand, 12 rue llément de Reigné | ☎ 05 49 27 00 21 |

| Niort | Dr Zaccheo, 20 rue Paul Gauguin | ☎ 05 49 09 99 55 |

| Parthenay | Dr Pinsembert, 40 boulevard
Anatole France | ☎ 05 49 94 34 44 |

| Thouars | Dr Désitter, 3 avenue Victor Hugo | ☎ 05 49 96 30 20 |

Dentists

English-speakers might like to contact the following dentists.

| Melle | Dr Touzard, rue de l'Ecole & La Mairie,
Chef-Boutonne | ☎ 05 49 29 62 92 |

| Niort | Dr Rheinart, 5 avenue Prés Wilson,
St Maixent d'Ecoles
(east of Niort) | ☎ 05 49 05 53 02 |

| Parthenay | Dr Lieumont, 17 avenue Général de Gaulle | ☎ 05 49 64 10 61 |
| Thouars | Cabinet Dentaire, 8 rue Hotel de Ville, St Varent
(south of Thouars) | ☎ 05 49 67 61 22 |

Emergency Services

Fire Brigade

Dial 18.

Gendarmerie Nationale

Some of the smaller gendarmeries are being merged with others may be open limited hours, but the local number will always put you through to the station that is on duty.

Melle	avenue Commandante Bernier	☎ 05 49 27 00 10
Niort	23 rue Général Largeau	☎ 05 49 28 63 00
Parthenay	4 boulevard Ambroise Paré	☎ 05 49 95 26 17
Thouars	19 rue Maurice Ravel	☎ 05 49 66 00 34

Health Authority

Local offices of the Caisse Régional Assurance Maladie Centre Ouest (CRAMCO) are listed below.

| Niort | 29 place du Port (main office) | ☎ 05 49 77 30 00 |
| Thouars | 4 rue Gambetta | ☎ 05 49 68 07 33 |

Hospitals

Niort	40 avenue Charles de Gaulle	☎ 05 49 32 79 79
Bressuire	rue Docteur Ichon	☎ 05 49 68 30 08
Melle	4 place Strasbourg Doesn't have an emergency department.	☎ 05 49 27 81 81
Parthenay	13 rue Brossard	☎ 05 49 68 31 55
Thouars	rue du Docteur Colas	☎ 05 49 68 30 52

Motoring

Breakers' Yards

Aiffres	Gouin Laurent, 111 rue Moulin (south-east of Niort)	☎ 05 49 32 15 96
Bressuire	Bressuire Récup' Auto, Champ Thibaud, route Poitiers, St Sauveur (east of the town)	☎ 05 49 74 00 10
Parthenay	Auto Pièces, 98 rue Atlantique, Le Tallud (just to the west of the town)	☎ 05 49 94 69 36

Car Dealers

Melle	Citroën, Sud Deux-Sèvres Autos, route Poitiers	☎ 05 49 27 00 29
	Fiat, Top Garage, St Léger	☎ 05 49 27 10 11
	Peugeot, Garage Bailly, route de Niort, St Martin Lès Melle	☎ 05 49 27 00 70
	Renault, Sarl Guibert, 33 avenue du Commandant Bernier	☎ 05 49 27 01 03
	Vauxhall/Opel, Garage Alain Brault, Le Perot, St Martin Lès Melle	☎ 05 49 27 04 46
Niort	Alfa Romeo, Garage de Paris, 55 bis rue Terraudière	☎ 05 49 17 30 30
	BMW, Emaud, 45 rue des Maisons Rouges	☎ 05 49 33 01 46
	Citroën, NASA Citroën, Espace Mendès France	☎ 05 49 17 85 00
	Chrysler/Jeep, Hav Auto, 132 avenue de Nantes	☎ 05 49 73 44 44
	Ford, Genève Automobile, 119 avenue Nantes	☎ 05 49 77 23 80
	Honda, Cachet Giraud Venise Verte, 10 boulevard de l'Atlantique	☎ 05 49 77 08 08

Hyundai, Sarah Sport, 132 avenue
de Nantes   ☎ 05 49 73 44 45

Jaguar, Garage Aumonier, 630 route
de Niort, Aiffres   ☎ 05 49 32 02 57
Also deals in Austin, Bedford, Land Rover, Lotus, MG and
Triumph.

Land Rover, Garage Juillet,
475 avenue Paris   ☎ 05 49 24 14 14

Peugeot, Peugeot Auto, Espace
Mendès France   ☎ 05 49 33 02 05

Renault, Saint Christophe,
214 avenue de Paris   ☎ 05 49 33 34 22

Rover, Garage Juillet, 475 avenue Paris   ☎ 05 49 24 14 14

Suzuki, Garage Gabardos,
9 rue de Vaumorin   ☎ 05 49 33 57 75

Vauxhall/Opel, Opel, Espace
Mendès France   ☎ 05 49 17 85 40

Volvo, 29 avenue St Jean d'Angély   ☎ 05 49 73 42 69

Parthenay   Audi/VW, ETS Chollet, 6 boulevard
de l'Europe   ☎ 05 49 64 15 51

Citroën, boulevard Bernard Palissy   ☎ 05 49 94 14 11

Fiat/Alfa, Marteau Philippe, 30 route
St Maixent, Pompaire   ☎ 05 49 64 04 03

Ford, Ford APS Automobiles,
boulevard Bernard Palissy   ☎ 05 49 64 10 91

Peugeot, Saga Automobiles,
81 rue des Loges   ☎ 05 49 71 15 15

Renault, Gâtine Espace, 114 avenue
Aristide Briand   ☎ 05 49 94 04 00

Vauxhall/Opel, Cadet Gérard,
6 rue Carnot   ☎ 05 49 64 27 98

Thouars	Audi/VW, Garage Philippe Blay, 76 rue Parthenay	☎ 05 49 66 15 53
	Citroën, SDA, 56 avenue Victor Leclerc	☎ 05 49 66 21 45
	Fiat, Noirault Automobiles, 6 rue Voltaire	☎ 05 49 96 31 85
	Ford, Garage Zola Auto, 141 avenue Emile Zola, Ste Verge	☎ 05 49 66 00 42
	Mazda, Guérin Eric, 66 rue Camille Guérin	☎ 05 49 96 29 31
	Nissan, BMSA, ZI Sainte Verge, route de Saumur	☎ 05 49 96 18 18
	Peugeot, Saga Automobiles, 14 route de Saumur	☎ 05 49 68 08 22
	Renault, Groupe Jean Rouyer, 142 avenue Emile Zola	☎ 05 49 66 21 78

Driving Lessons

| Chef-Boutonne | Auto Ecole 'Virage', 57 Grand' Rue du Commerce | ☎ 05 49 07 66 69 |

This driving school near Melle offers refresher courses and lessons for foreigners in adapting to driving on the right. It has both male and female driving instructors who speak English.

Tyre & Exhaust Centres

Melle	Le No. 1 du Pneu Mellois, 32 rue Beau Soleil	☎ 05 49 27 13 12
Niort	Pneu Center, 145 avenue de Nantes	☎ 05 49 26 29 50
Parthenay	Vulco, 8 place Marytrs de La Résistance	☎ 05 49 94 34 22
Thouars	Baudry Pneus, 26 boulevard Ernest Renan	☎ 05 49 66 06 52

Pets

Dog Training

| St Gelais | Complexe Canin, 1485 route Niort | ☎ 05 49 33 42 63 |

🖥 *www.complexe-canin.com*
Dog training, kennels, cattery and pet care.

Farriers

General   Philippe Rongieras, La Tenauderie,
                   La Chapelle Thireuil   ☎ 05 49 04 20 27

Horse Dentists

General   Christophe Gaillard   ☎ 06 11 63 37 61
                   Based just south of Poitiers, covering Deux-Sèvres and Vienne
                   and travelling south as far as northern Charente and Charente-
                   Maritime.

                   Guy Chatignol   ☎ 05 59 65 14 96
                   Covers southern Deux-Sèvres as well as Charente and
                   Charente-Maritime.

Kennels & Catteries

The facilities listed below accept cats and dogs unless otherwise stated.

Brulain   Pension Canine de la Douve d'Availles ☎ 05 49 26 48 56
                   (directly west of Melle)
                   Dogs only.

Moutiers-sous-   La Pension du Bocage, les Prés ☎ 05 49 65 04 63
Agenton   (west of Thouars)

St Gelais   Complexe Canin, 1485 route Niort ☎ 05 49 33 42 63
                   🖥 *www.complexe-canin.com*
                   Also offers dog training and pet care.

Verruyes   Ferland Dominique, Le Rocher   ☎ 05 49 63 21 66
                   (west of Parthenay)
                   Dogs only.

Pet Parlours

Melle   Caniclean, 33 avenue Poitiers,
                   Brioux-sur-Boutonne   ☎ 05 49 07 49 08
                   (directly south of Melle)

Niort   Toilettage de l'Octroi, 21 chemin
                   Gayolles   ☎ 05 49 33 25 55

Parthenay   Boîte à Toutou, boulevard des Sires
                   de Parthenay   ☎ 05 49 95 24 43
                   Appointments needed.

Thouars   Dandy Dog, 12 avenue Victor Leclerc   ☎ 05 49 96 30 54

Riding Equipment

Le Caravoine   23 rue Gare, Chauray   ☎ 05 49 08 25 21
(north-east of Niort)

SPA

Châtellerault   Valette   ☎ 05 49 21 61 11

Lagord   rue Guignarderie   ☎ 05 46 34 32 03

Poitiers   Grange des Prés   ☎ 05 49 88 94 57

Veterinary Clinics

Melle   Clinique Vétérinaire, 5 rue Pièce,
St Leger   ☎ 05 49 27 01 73
(on the outskirts of Melle, on the road to St Maixent)

Niort   Clinique Vétérinaire, 19 rue Pierre   ☎ 05 49 73 48 61
This surgery has a vet who speaks some English.

Parthenay   Cabinet Cougnon, 94 avenue
Aristide Briand   ☎ 05 49 71 01 65

Saintes   Dr Bétizaud, 5 avenue Saintonge
(Charente-Maritime)   ☎ 05 46 92 08 81
A specialist horse vet.

Thouars   Christian Colasson, 22bis avenue
Victor Hugo   ☎ 05 49 66 70 29

Places To Visit

This section isn't intended to be a definitive guide but gives a wide range of ideas for the department. Prices and opening hours were correct at the time of publication, but it's best to check before travelling long distances.

Châteaux

Chef-Boutonne   Château de Javarzay   ☎ 05 49 29 86 31
This château houses a museum of headdresses. Entrance €2.25 for adults and free for the under-12s. There's a large open space around the château, ideal for picnics, kite flying or just relaxing.

Coulonges	Château Coulonges, 4 place du Château ☎ 05 49 06 10 72

💻 *www.ville-coulonges-sur-lautize.fr*
A 16th century château with vaulted kitchens, a finely decorated ceiling and four ornamental chimneys. Renaissance-style meal served (booking required). Open 1st May to mid-June, weekends and bank holidays 3 to 7.30pm; mid-June to first weekend in September daily 9.30am to noon, 2.30 to 7.30pm; September to mid-November weekends and bank holidays 2.30 to 6pm.

Gilles de Rais   Château de Barbe-Bleue   ☎ 02 51 65 70 51
💻 *www.chateau-barbe-bleue.com*
Bluebeard's castle. Visit comprises three hours of animation and spectacle that takes you back to the Middle Ages. Open May, June and September Mondays to Fridays 10am to 12.30pm, 2 to 6pm (weekends and bank holidays 2 to 7pm); July and August every day 11am to 7pm. Adults €7, 6 to 13-year-olds €5.

Orion   Château d'Oiron   ☎ 05 49 96 51 25
Built in the 16th century by Henri II's grand equerry, the château was completely refurbished in the 17th century. The painted gallery houses a collection of contemporary works inspired by the curio rooms of the Renaissance. Closed 1st January, 1st May, 1st and 11th November and 25th December. Adults €5.50, children €3.50.

St Georges-de-Noisné   Château de St Loup-sur-Thouet   ☎ 05 49 95 40 13
A fine example of Louis XIII to Henry IV architecture. The gardens are being restored to classical 18th century designs. The château has an orangery, woodland park, vegetable garden and magnificent suites.

Thouars   Château des Ducs de la Trémoille   ☎ 05 49 66 17 65
Originally constructed in 1158, this château was rebuilt in 1635 and is one of the few remaining châteaux in the style of Louis XIII.

Museums & Galleries

L'Absie   Musée des Voitures Miniatures,
6 route de La Chapelle Seguin   ☎ 05 49 95 98 86
A museum retracing automotive history from its earliest days to the mid-'30s with an accompanying exhibition of old trades and crafts.

Bougon   Musée des Tumulus de Bougon   ☎ 05 49 05 12 13
Five tumuli with eight burial chambers, built around 4,500BC. An extensive collection of archaeological artefacts reflecting the history of the men who erected these monumental chambers and dolmens, a replica house from a Neolithic village and workshops demonstrating basket-making, weaving and pottery. Open February to December. Under 6s free.

Coulon	La Maison Des Marais Mouillés, Place de la Coutume	☎ 05 49 35 81 04

The 'wet marshes' museum. The region's characteristics are related by the history of the area, with 'marshscope' – a light and picture show on three screens. Open every day during the holiday season, 10am to noon, 2 to 7pm. May, June and September Mondays to Fridays 10am to noon, 2 to 7pm, weekends 10am to 1pm, 2 to 5pm. July and August every day 10am to 8pm.

La Mothe-St Héray	La Maison de la Haute Sèvre, Moulin du Pont l'Abbé	☎ 05 49 05 19 19

This eco-museum invites you to discover the mill with its paddle wheel, flour milling and the customs and traditions surrounding the theme of the innocent, reed-picking maiden (La Rosière). On the bank of the Sèvre Niortaise is a botanical garden with around 100 species of tree. Open Wednesdays to Mondays mid-June to mid-September 10.30am to 12.30pm, 2.30 to 6.30pm.

Niort	Donjon Museum, rue de Guesclin	☎ 05 49 28 14 28

The lower, 18th century rooms house an archaeological collection (Bronze and Copper Ages, Roman-Gallic period and Middle Ages.) There's also a reconstructed 1830s Poitevin-style interior, with costumes, headdresses and local jewellery. Open Wednesdays to Mondays 2nd May to 15th September 9am to 12pm, 2 to 6pm, closing at 5pm the rest of the year.

Prahecq	Musée Jardin des Ruralies	☎ 05 49 75 68 27

(10km/7mi south-east of Niort between Aiffres and Vouillé) A museum with both indoor and outdoor 'exhibits': a garden with over 500 identified species, an exhibition about the farming of bees; a mini-farm, animals and the history of agriculture. Open every day 10am to 6pm (7pm in the summer). Free entry.

St Maixent	Musée Militaire, Quartier Marchand	☎ 05 49 76 84 76

This is a museum of the non-commissioned officer, with several collections of uniforms, weapons and diverse souvenirs. The Souvenir Museum is at the same site and traces military life in St Maixent from 1881 to 1967.

Thouars	Le Musée Henri Barre, 7 rue Marie de la Tour d'Auvergne	☎ 05 49 66 36 97

Beautifully furnished salons housing a collection of important paintings and an exhibition of local history. €3.

Parks, Gardens & Forests

Le Bourdet	Sentier de la Maraîchine	☎ 05 49 04 80 43
	(south-west of Niort)	

This is a circular walk that takes you through a fragile
environment, including a park with a herd of marsh cattle and a
flock of Poitevin Marsh grey geese. Information boards show
the way along the walk, which also includes a botanical area.

Chizé   Forêt de Chizé   ☎ 05 49 77 17 15
                 Nature trails and information about local environmental work.
                 Picnic area.

Marais Poitevin Visitor Centre, 2 rue de l'Eglise, Coulon ☎ 05 49 35 15 20
                 🖳 *www.parc-marais-poitevin.fr*

                 Boat & Train Trips, 6 rue de l'Eglise,
                 Coulon   ☎ 05 49 35 14 14
                 🖳 *www.maraispoitevin-evasion.com*
                 (west of Niort)
                 'Green Venice' is a protected site that offers a maze of canals
                 and channels, a unique environment, carefully preserved.
                 There are many interesting villages in this area, including
                 Arçais, which has an 18th century castle overlooking its port,
                 Sansais/La Garette, a typical local 'market garden' village, and
                 Le Vanneau-Irleau, which holds traditional water markets.
                 There are scenic train rides, and punts and gondolas are
                 available for hire, with or without a guide.

Melle   Chemin de la Découverte
                 Contact the tourist office,
                 3 rue Émilien Traver   ☎ 05 49 29 15 10
                 Melle is an old town and there are maps available from the
                 tourist office suggesting walks around the town. One of these is
                 a 'route of discovery', with information given along the way on
                 the 1,000 or more species of shrub and rose from all over the
                 world. The route covers three areas, which can be separated
                 into three walks or completed in one go (a total of 6km/4mi),
                 each section taking around one and a half hours. There are
                 several access points and parking at various stages.

Niort   La Coulée Verte, Prélude au Marais Poitevin
                 (in the west of the town)
                 An area of gentle countryside forming a natural division
                 between the town and the Marais Poitevin, the Coulée Verte is
                 an ideal spot for families to walk or cycle, fish or participate in a
                 variety of watersports. There are numerous mills and foot
                 bridges across the locks. Near the public gardens is a
                 swimming pool, play area and skate park.

Zoos & Wildlife Parks

Pomperron-   Kangourou Parc   ☎ 05 49 69 07 30
Menigoute   A farm with a wide range of Australian animals, all extremely rare

in Europe, including emus, kookaburras, black swans and cockatoos as well as traditional farm animals. Open mid-February to the end of June 2 to 8pm; 1st July to 31st August 10am to 8pm (Sundays and bank holidays 10am to noon, 2 to 8pm); 1st September to the end of November 2 to 8pm.

Forêt de Chizé   Zoorama de Chizé, rue du
Chêne à Margot   ☎ 05 49 77 17 17
In the centre of the Forest of Chizé, a 25ha (60-acre) zoo with 600 European animals, mini-farm and a children's play area. Open May to August every day 9am to 7pm; February to March and September to November Wednesdays to Mondays 1 to 6pm. Adults €7.50, children €3.50.

Vasles   Maison du Mouton   ☎ 05 49 69 12 12
Twenty-three varieties of sheep in 6ha (15 acres). Headsets are available to provide explanations. There are demonstrations of shearing, sheepdog work, felt making and tapestry. Open March and April every day 10.30am to 6.30pm; May, June and September daily 1.30 to 6.30pm (Sundays and bank holidays 10.30am to 6.30pm); July and August daily 10am to 7pm; October and November Sundays, bank holidays and school holidays only 10.30 to 6pm. Adults €9, children €5.

Miscellaneous

Arçais   La Calèche d'Arçais,
64 rue de la Garenne   ☎ 05 49 35 40 29
Trips in a horse-drawn carriage through the unspoilt Marais Poitevin.

Boësse   Moulin   ☎ 05 49 65 96 56
An 18th century windmill that was operational until 1913. Now restored, it enables visitors to rediscover the miller's trade. Guided tours can be booked via the tourist office at Argenton-Château.

Celles-sur-Belle Abbaye Royale, rue des Halles   ☎ 05 49 32 14 99
A completely restored abbey and abbey church with formal gardens. Free access and guided tours.

Eglise Notre Dame
This gothic church has a Romanesque doorway with gargoyles and ornate stonework above it.

Champdeniers- Rivière Souterraine   ☎ 05 49 25 80 47
St Denis   Discovered in 1970, this underground river is approximately 800m long and consists of a main corridor and a number of caves of great interest to potholers.

Chantemerle   La Forêt de l'Aventure,
               rue Petit Château   ☎ 06 81 45 71 37
               💻 *www.foret-aventure.com*
               (near Pescalis – see below)
               An adventure forest with rope ladders, aerial runways,
               elevated platforms and other vertiginous methods of
               traversing the tree-tops. You must be over 1.40m (4ft 6in) tall
               and under 18s must be accompanied by an adult. Sports
               shoes required, safety equipment provided. Adults €19, under
               18s €11.50. Open every day 6th July to 1st September 10am
               to 7pm; September weekends only 10am to 7pm. Last arrival
               5pm. The site includes a play area, picnic area and marked
               footpaths.

Echiré   Coudray-Salbart   ☎ 05 49 25 71 07
               (north of Niort, but south of the A83)
               The impressive remains of Salbart Castle, empty for over 400
               years but neither demolished nor modified, are away from built-
               up areas. Open 1st April to 31st October 9am to 7pm; 1st
               November to 31st March 9am to noon, 2 to 5pm.

Melle   Eglises Saint-Hilaire, Saint-Pierre and Saint-Savinien
               Interesting Romanesque churches.

               Mines d'Argent   ☎ 05 49 29 19 54
               These silver mines, belonging to the Frankish kings, were
               worked from the fifth to the tenth centuries and are the oldest
               mines that can be visited in Europe. Carolingian methods of
               mining and minting money are explained, with an award-
               winning sound show. Open 1st March to 31st May and 1st
               October to 15th November weekends and public holidays 2.30
               to 6.30pm; 1st June to 30th September 10am to noon and 2.30
               to 7.30pm. Adults €6, children €3.

Moncoutant   Pescalis   ☎ 05 49 72 00 01
               💻 *www.pescalis.com*
               One hundred hectares (250 acres) of fishing catering for
               families, children and adults, plus indoor exhibitions and
               aquariums.

Thouars   Le Moulin de Crevant, promenade
               des Pommiers   ☎ 05 49 68 38 59
               Situated on the edge of the river Thouet, this mill was built
               in 1840 and was working until 1989. Guided tour of 1 hour
               and an exhibition area. Open 15th June to 15th September
               Wednesdays to Mondays 2.30 to 6pm with tours on the
               hour; 16th September to 31st December and 1st March to
               14th June the first and third Sunday of each month 2 to 6pm
               with tours at 2.30pm, 4pm, and 5.30pm.

Professional Services

Accountants

Niort   In Extenso Anjou et Maine,
Mr Lapicier, 9 avenue Jacques Bujault   ☎ 05 49 25 17 00
This firm works with British companies and has a fluent
English-speaking accountant in the office weekly.

Solicitors & Notaires

The following office has an English-speaking *notaire*.

Niort   Notaires Associés Brisset,
Pitre et Dagès, 16 avenue Limoges   ☎ 05 49 28 30 99

Religion

Anglican Services In English

La Merlatière   Parish Church
(on the D98, 6km west of Les Essarts)
The fourth Sunday of the month at 11.30am.

Puy de Serre   Parish Church
(on the D49 between St Hilaire de Voust and Foussais Payré)
The second Sunday of the month at 11am.

Details of the above services from John Matthews, the Vendée Fellowship of the Anglican Chaplaincy of Poitou-Charentes (☎ 05 49 75 29 71, ✉ *matthewsj@wanadoo.fr*). Each service is followed by refreshments and an optional bring-and-share lunch.

Melle   parish church of St Léger-de-la-Martinière
Holy Communion the first Sunday of the month at 10.30am.
Contact the Chaplain, the Reverend Michael Hepper, 19 avenue
René Baillargeon, Civray (☎ 05 49 97 04 21) for details.

Evangelical Churches

Niort   Eglise, 3 terrasse avenue
Normandie Niemen   ☎ 05 49 33 47 61

Protestant Churches

Melle   Eglise Réformée Presbytère Protestant,
10 rue Foucaudrie   ☎ 05 49 27 01 35

Moncoutant	Eglise Réformée, 80 avenue Maréchal Leclerc (south of Bressuire)	☎ 05 49 72 71 82
Niort	Eglise Protestante Baptiste, 17 rue Herse	☎ 05 49 77 58 06
St Maixent	Eglise Réformée, Pasteur, 63 rue Anatole France (north-east of Niort)	☎ 05 49 05 50 27

Synagogues

La Rochelle	Maison Communautaire Israélite, 40 cours Dames (in Charente-Maritime)	☎ 05 46 41 17 66

Restaurants

Celles-sur-Belle Hostellerie de l'Abbaye, 1 place des
Epoux Laurant ☎ 05 49 32 93 32
Situated next to a remarkable abbey, this restaurant is open all
week except Sunday evenings with an €11 lunch menu and
further set menus at €12 to €19.

Chef-Boutonne Restaurant des Voyageurs,
18 place Cail ☎ 05 49 29 73 13
Menu of the day, grills and à la carte menu. Open every day.
€10 lunch menu Mondays to Fridays, set menus from €14 to
€19.50. English spoken.

Coulonges Citronnelle, 10 rue du Commerce ☎ 05 49 06 17 67
Shaded terrace. Closed Sunday evenings and all day
Mondays. Set menus from €10 to €23.

Fontenille Le Colvert ☎ 05 49 29 82 22
Lunch and dinner menus, full English breakfast served
Tuesdays to Saturdays 10am to 2pm plus fish and chips on
Friday nights.

Massais Le Bois Joli, route de Nantes ☎ 05 49 96 82 54
(between Thouars and Argenton-Château)
Open every day but closed Sunday evenings. Seafood a speciality.

Melle Les Glycines
5 place René Groussard ☎ 05 49 27 01 11
Relaxing atmosphere in a 14th century house in the centre of
the town. English spoken.

Restaurant du Palais, 14 Grande Rue   ☎ 05 49 27 18 52
Traditional cuisine with dining under the trees by the church in the centre of Melle. Open Tuesday to Saturday evenings. €9 lunchtime menu, set menus from €13 to €16.

Moncoutant   Le Saint Pierre, rue Barillière   ☎ 05 49 72 88 88
Silver service restaurant with menus from €20 to €56. Closed Saturday lunchtimes and Sunday evenings.

Moutiers-sous-   La Carpe d'Or, Pescalis   ☎ 05 49 80 45 10
Chantermerie   Regional cuisine with fish a speciality, part of the Pescalis fishing complex (see page 249).

Niort   L'Atlas, 31 avenue St Jean d'Angély   ☎ 05 49 09 09 83
Moroccan restaurant open lunchtimes, Tuesdays to Sundays.

La Belle Etoile, 115 quai Métayer   ☎ 05 49 73 31 29
Situated on the banks of La Sèvre, with gardens and an attractive dining area on the outside terrace.

Buffalo Grill, avenue de Paris   ☎ 05 49 33 40 64
(in the east of the town, opposite Maaf)
A reliable steak house-style restaurant, part of a nationwide chain. Open every day 11am to 11pm.

Les Deux Chèvres, rue Basse   ☎ 05 49 05 10 44
Open lunchtimes and evenings Mondays to Fridays. Lunchtime menu €12.50, other set menus starting at €18.

L'Esterel, 5 rue Baugier   ☎ 05 49 73 42 42
A restaurant serving traditional Provencal cuisine. Open Mondays to Fridays until 11pm, Saturday evenings until midnight.

Les Relais d'Alsace, place de La Brèche   ☎ 05 49 17 84 60
On a corner of place de La Brèche, this restaurant is one of the few that serves meals throughout the day, seven days a week from noon to midnight. Seafood all year. Set menus from €9.90 to €16.60.

Le Saïgon, 8 rue E. Cholois,
Place St Hilaire   ☎ 05 49 77 54 86
Chinese and Vietnamese food. Take-away service available. Closed Sundays.

Le Sorrento, 7 avenue de Paris   ☎ 05 49 24 58 59
Specialises in seafood pizzas. Take-away service available. Open daily until midnight.

La Table des Saveurs, 9 rue Thiers   ☎ 05 49 77 44 35

A smart restaurant in front of the Hôtel de Ville. No set menu.
Fish and meat dishes range from €16 to €30.

Taj Mahal, 25 rue Basse   ☎ 05 49 24 47 36
(up a small street running north-east away from the covered
market; park by the covered market)
Indian food. Open every day except Monday lunchtimes. €7.50
lunch menu; other set menus from €11 to €17. Take-away
service available.

La Véranda du Dauzac,
80bis avenue de Paris   ☎ 05 49 24 29 29
Within the Mercure hotel, this calm and elegant restaurant has
inspired menus with prices from €16 to €25.

Parthenay   Auberge Des Voyageurs, 41 place de
               l'Hôtel de Ville, Beauvoir sur Niort   ☎ 05 49 09 70 16
               (close to the forest of Chizé)
               An inn since 1900. Closed Tuesday and Friday evenings and
               all day Wednesdays. Dogs are allowed and English is spoken.

               Le Bong Laï, 80 avenue Prés Wilson   ☎ 05 49 95 25 75
               Vietnamese food, Take-away service available. Closed
               Wednesdays, except in July and August.

               La Citadelle, 9 place Georges Picard   ☎ 05 49 64 12 25
               An intimate bistro by the Citadel gate. À la carte menu.

               Darna, rue de La Poste   ☎ 05 49 71 20 28
               Moroccan cuisine, including couscous, kebabs and tajine.

               La Dolce Vita, 4 place du Vauvert   ☎ 05 49 71 12 12
               Italian restaurant in the heart of the old town. Eat in or take
               away.

               Hotel du Nord, 86 avenue
               du Général de Gaulle   ☎ 05 49 94 29 11
               Local and regional food served in a pleasant dining room or on
               an outside terrace. English spoken.

               Le Relais du Château, 17 place des
               Marronniers, Orion   ☎ 05 49 96 54 96
               (200m from the château)
               Gastronomic cuisine with specialities of foie gras and fish.
               Menus from €13 to €35. Closed Sunday evenings, all day
               Mondays and during the February school holidays.

               La Truffade, place du 11 novembre   ☎ 05 49 64 02 26
               Closed Tuesdays and Wednesdays. €19.50 set menu. Menu
               available in English.

| St Généroux | Auberge du Vieux Pont,
2 rue du Vieux Pont | ☎ 05 49 67 29 24 |

(15km/10mi from Thouars)
Specialities include meat fondues and ostrich and kangaroo steaks. Open Fridays to Sundays and bank holidays. Menus €15 to €21.
Closed the first half of September.

| Thouars | L'Abattoir, 101 rue Camille Pelletan | ☎ 05 49 66 07 26 |

Traditional cuisine, open lunchtimes and evenings Mondays to Fridays.

Asia Restaurant, 18 avenue Victor Hugo ☎ 05 49 96 17 28
Chinese, Vietnamese and Thai cuisine. Open Tuesdays to Sundays noon to 2pm, 7 to 10pm.

Le Mohery, 8 rue Ricard ☎ 05 49 66 21 06
Traditional cuisine with set menus from €9.25 to €15. Open lunchtimes and evenings. Closed Wednesday and Sunday evenings.

Moopys Bay, 6 avenue Victor Leclerc ☎ 05 49 96 33 62
Pizzeria. Eat in or take away.

Le Pilote, 145 avenue Emile Zola ☎ 05 49 66 29 31
Brasserie serving grills and pizzas. Open Mondays to Saturdays.

Au Trésor Belge, rue Saugé ☎ 05 49 67 85 74
(in the old town)
Open lunchtimes and evenings until 11pm. Closed Wednesdays. Doesn't accept payment by cheque.

Rubbish & Recycling

Metal Collection

| Niort | Rouvreau, 201 rue Jean Jaurès,
ZI St Florent | ☎ 05 49 79 00 11 |

| Parthenay | Loca Récuper, 68 rue Pré Maingot,
Pompaire | ☎ 05 49 95 06 75 |

(just south of Parthenay)

Shopping

Alcohol

| Melle | Le Cépage, 39 route de Poitiers, |

St Léger   ☎ 05 49 29 11 38
(on the small parade of shops immediately past Intermarché on
the outskirts of Melle)
Tuesdays to Thursdays 9am to 12.15pm, 3 to 7pm, Fridays
and Saturdays 9am to 12.30pm, 2.30 to 7pm.

Niort   Cav O'Vin, 326 avenue de Paris   ☎ 05 49 33 17 69

Parthenay   La Grappe d'Or, 3 rue Marchioux   ☎ 05 49 64 04 69

Thouars   Les Bonnes Caves, 39 boulevard
               de La République   ☎ 05 49 96 30 11
               Open Tuesdays to Saturdays 9 to 12.30pm, 2.30 to 7pm.

Architectural Antiques

Chail   Les Vielles Pierres du Mellois,
               Les Cerizat   ☎ 05 49 29 31 23
               (on the D948 Melle to Sauzé-Vaussais road)
               Specialises in the sale of old building materials – mainly stone,
               but there's a large selection of reclaimed timbers in the far
               corner as you enter from the back.

L'Hotellerie- BCA Matériaux Anciens   ☎ 02 33 94 74 00
De-Flée   💻 www.bca-recyclage.com
               (on the route de Craon, in Maine-et-Loire)
               Antique floor tiles, antique floorboards, old oak beams, re-sawn
               beams, architectural antiques, reclaimed building materials.
               Fluent English spoken.

Naintre   Tavares   ☎ 05 49 90 15 32
               (on the ZI off the A10; take the exit for Châtellerault Sud)

British Groceries

L'Absie   L'Absie British Shop, 5 rue de la Poste   ☎ 05 49 95 80 57
               ✉ labsiebritishshop@wanadoo.fr
               Grocery, bar and tea room. Open every day 9am to 8pm.

Building Materials

Melle   Point P, ZI Baudroux   ☎ 05 49 07 47 00
               Mondays to Fridays 7.30am to noon, 1.30 to 6pm, Saturdays
               8.30am to noon.

Niort   Castorama, 10 rue R. Turgot,
               ZAC Mendès France   ☎ 05 49 04 45 00
               Mondays to Saturdays 9am to 8pm.

Parthenay   Mr Brico & Matériaux,
                 boulevard G. Clémenceau   ☎ 05 49 64 33 77
                 Mondays to Saturdays.

Thouars   Mr Bricolage & Matériaux,
                 route de Saumur, Sainte Verge   ☎ 05 49 68 10 00
                 Mondays to Thursdays 9am to 12.30pm, 2 to 7pm, Fridays and
                 Saturdays 9am to 7pm, north side of the town.

Camping & Caravanning

Niort   Niort Evasion, rue R. Turgot,
                 Espace Mendès France   ☎ 05 49 33 41 76

Department Stores

Niort   Nouvelles Galeries, 47 rue Victor Hugo ☎ 05 49 24 41 23
                 (in the centre of the town at the bottom of the 'serpent'-lined road)

DIY

Melle   Mr. Bricolage, St Léger   ☎ 05 49 27 08 47
                 (on the outskirts of town towards St Maixent)
Niort   Mr Bricolage, 270 avenue de
                 La Rochelle   ☎ 05 49 79 47 47

Parthenay   Brico Jardi Leclerc,
                 rue Léonard de Vinci   ☎ 05 49 64 58 88
                 (going out of Parthenay in the direction of Poitiers)

Thouars   Weldom, 8 rue Gambetta   ☎ 05 49 96 33 79

Fabrics

Niort   La Tissuterie, 21 rue Gare, Zone Géant,
                 Chauray   ☎ 05 49 24 17 88
                 (near Géant, east of the town)

Thouars   La Tissuterie, 145 avenue Emile Zola,
                 Sainte Verge   ☎ 05 49 67 66 18
                 Mondays 2 to 7pm, Tuesdays to Thursdays 9.30am to
                 12.15pm, 2 to 7pm, Fridays and Saturdays 9.30am to 7pm.

Fancy Dress

Parthenay   Rigaud Fabienne, 69 rue de
                 La Vau St Jacques   ☎ 05 49 63 14 45
                 (near the tourist office)
                 Specialising in period costumes. Open Tuesdays to Saturdays.

Frozen Food

Argenton l'Eglise   Argel, 200 boulevard G. Brassens   ☎ 05 49 67 03 08
Free home delivery. A catalogue can be ordered by phone.

Niort   Picard Surgelés, 283 avenue Paris   ☎ 05 49 08 27 76

Garden Centres

Melle   Gamm Vert, impasse de La Gare   ☎ 05 49 27 26 13

Niort   Jardiland, route de La Rochelle,
Bessines   ☎ 05 49 77 26 77
(on the way out of the town centre in the direction of La Rochelle)

Parthenay   Brico Jardi Leclerc, rue
Léonard de Vinci   ☎ 05 49 64 58 88
DIY store and garden centre. Mondays to Saturdays 8.45am to 7.30pm.

Thouars   Gamm Vert, 20 boulevard de Diepholz   ☎ 05 49 66 04 15
Tuesdays to Saturdays 9 to noon, 2 to 7pm.

Kitchens & Bathrooms

Niort   Schmidt, 53 boulevard Ampère,
Chauray   ☎ 05 49 08 21 43
Large kitchen showroom.

Gillest Boeuf, 12 rue Paul Sabatier   ☎ 05 49 79 02 74
Design and production of bathrooms.

Thouars   Schmidt, route de Saumur   ☎ 05 49 67 84 94
(next to the Leclerc hypermarket)

Markets

Bressuire   Tuesday market.

Brioux   Covered market every Thursday morning.

Chantonnay   Markets Tuesdays, Thursdays and Saturdays every week, with a fair on the second and fourth Tuesday of each month.

Chef-Boutonne   Market on Saturdays.

Coulonges   A large market on Tuesdays, when all the streets in the town centre are closed.

Lezay	Europe's third-largest market for cattle and calves. Tuesdays from 7 to 11am.
Melle	Market on Fridays.
Niort	Indoor food and flower market Tuesdays to Sundays from early morning until around 12.30pm. Main market Thursdays and Saturdays.
Parthenay	Market on Wednesdays.
Sauzé-Vaussais	Market on Thursdays.
Thouars	Markets on Tuesday and Friday mornings inside and outside the covered market hall. Tuesdays are mainly food, while on Fridays the market is much bigger with a wider variety of stalls. There's also a market on the second Sunday of each month.

Music

| Thouars | Music Fournier, 33 boulevard Pierre Curie ☎ 05 49 65 01 10 (on the main boulevard overlooking the marketplace) |

Organic Food

Coulonges	La Plantivore, rue du Commerce ☎ 05 49 06 03 87 (north of Niort on the D744) Open Tuesdays to Saturdays 9am to 1pm, 3 to 7pm.
Niort	Espace Bio, 36bis avenue Nantes ☎ 05 49 79 39 59 Mondays 3 to 7pm, Tuesdays and Fridays 9am to noon, 3 to 7pm, Wednesdays and Thursdays 9am to 7pm, Saturdays 9am to noon.
Sauzé-Vaussais	l'Essential, 6 rue de La Chevalonnerie ☎ 05 49 07 17 68 Wednesdays and Saturdays 9am to 12.30pm, Tuesdays, Thursdays and Fridays 9am to noon, 3 to 7pm.
Thouars	Diététique Cherel, 145 avenue Emile Zola, Ste Verge ☎ 05 49 96 16 30 (in the parade of shops to the left of Leclerc) Open Tuesdays to Fridays 9.30am to 7pm, closed Saturdays.

Retail Parks

| Niort | Espace Mèndes, route de Paris – with Géant hypermarket (in the east of the town on the road to Poitiers) ● BUT – furniture and accessories; ● Conforama – furniture, household appliances and accessories; |

- Fly – furniture;
- Jouetland – toys.

rue Jean Baptiste Colbert/avenue de Paris – with Leclerc
(east of the town)
- Casa – gifts and household accessories;
- Décathlon – sports goods;
- Pier Import – household goods;
- Saint Maclou – painting and decorating.

Thouars   Sainte Verge – with Leclerc hypermarket
(in the northern outskirts of Thouars)
- Cuisines Schmidt – kitchens;
- Diététique – organic foods;
- Hyper aux Chaussures – shoes;
- Mobis – electrical equipment and furniture;
- Mr Brico – DIY;
- La Tissuterie – fabrics.

Second-Hand Goods

Melle   La Brocalou, Chaignepain, Les Alleuds   ☎ 05 49 29 64 42
(on the D948 between Melle and Sauzé-Vaussais)

Niort   Galerie Royale, 8 rue Basse   ☎ 06 08 83 41 42
(near the market)
Closed Sundays and Mondays.

Salle de Dépôt Vente de Niort,
309 avenue de Paris   ☎ 05 49 33 36 38

Parthenay   l'Entrepot, avenue Aristide Briand   ☎ 05 49 64 06 28

Thouars   Troc à Faire, 31 rue Gambetta   ☎ 05 49 67 69 42
Closed Mondays and Wednesdays.

Sports Goods

Niort   Intersport, Espace Mendès France   ☎ 05 49 33 39 22
(on the retail park by Géant)

Décathlon, 1 rue Jean Baptiste Colbert   ☎ 05 49 33 34 97
🖳 *www.decathlon.fr*
(east of Niort near Leclerc)

Parthenay   Intersport, 24 boulevard Sires de
Parthenay   ☎ 05 49 64 21 02
(in the town centre near the open car park)

Thouars   Sport 2000, 8 avenue Victor Leclerc   ☎ 05 49 66 15 02
(behind the theatre)

Supermarkets & Hypermarkets

Niort   Géant, Niort Est, Chauray   ☎ 05 49 17 34 00
(in the east of the town on the road to Poitiers)
This centre has an SFR phone shop, chemist's, pet shop,
photo booth, key cutting, Crédit Agricole cash machine, dry
cleaner's and optician's. There's also a sports shop, a garden
centre and a toy superstore nearby. Open Mondays to
Saturdays 9am to 8.30pm (Fridays till 9pm).

Leclerc, 580 avenue Paris   ☎ 05 49 17 80 00
(on the right on the road to Poitiers)
Part of a large retail park (see above), the hypermarket building
includes a chemist's, travel agent's, café, jeweller's and
electronics shop. Open Mondays to Saturdays 9am to 8pm.

Carrefour, boulevard d'Atlantique   ☎ 05 49 79 15 11
(not on a main route like Leclerc and Géant but tucked away off
boulevard d'Atlantique as you leave the town centre south of
the river, heading west)
Open Mondays to Saturdays 8.45am to 9pm (Fridays till 9.30pm).

Parthenay   Hyper Leclerc, rue Léonard de Vinci   ☎ 04 59 64 58 88
This store has a bar, restaurant, newsagent's, florist, chemist's
and Crédit Agricole bank and separate cash machine. It also
has a fresh fish shop, dry cleaner's, photo booth, photocopier,
business card machine, post office and video hire shop. Open
Mondays to Saturdays 8.45am to 7.30pm (Fridays till 8pm).

Hyper U, 1 avenue François Mitterrand   ☎ 05 49 64 32 22
Although called a 'hyper' store, this is really only a large
supermarket.

Thouars   Hyper Leclerc, 145 avenue
Emile Zola, Sainte Verge   ☎ 05 49 68 11 33
Within this complex is a dry cleaner's, hairdresser's, baker's,
optician's, shoe and key kiosk, photo developing, cafés and gift
shops. Open Mondays to Saturdays 9am to 7.30pm (Fridays till
8pm).

Swimming Pool Equipment

La Crèche   Everblue, avenue de Paris   ☎ 05 49 05 34 35
(on the right going out of Niort towards St Maixent)
Spas, kit pools and design and installation of in-ground pools.
Open Mondays 2 to 6.30pm, Tuesdays to Saturdays 9am to
noon, 2 to 6.30pm.

| Niort | Piscines Magiline, route de Paris | ☎ 05 49 04 81 67 |

Swimming pools and supplies. Design and construction.

Sports

The following is just a selection of the activities available, the large towns having a wide range of sports facilities. Full details are available from tourist offices and *mairies*.

Vivez Niort is a leaflet worth looking out for, as it gives details of various events happening in and around Niort, from rollerskating through the streets to canoeing trips and horse riding through the forests. Available from the Niort tourist office.

Aerial Sports

Parachuting

| Niort | Paraclub des Deux-Sèvres, L'Aérodrome, avenue Limoges | ☎ 05 49 24 53 65 |

| Thouars | Centre de Parachutisme, L'Aérodrome, Missé
 (just east of Thouars) | ☎ 05 49 96 10 72 |

Archery

| Niort | Stade de Massujat, rue Massujat | ☎ 05 49 28 19 09 |

| | Archers Niortais, 43 rue Massujat | ☎ 05 49 24 15 28 |

Club offering equipment for hire.

| Thouars | Archers de La Trémoille | ☎ 05 49 66 27 04 |

Contact Mr Courtin

Badminton

| Melle | St Jo Sport | ☎ 05 49 29 04 05 |

Tuesdays and Thursdays 6 to 8pm.

| Niort | Niort Badminton Club,
 12 rue Joseph Cugnot | ☎ 05 49 35 02 77 |

Leisure and competitions, plus training at various locations across Niort. Minimum age ten.

Canoeing & Kayaking

| Niort | Base Nautique de Noron, Niort | ☎ 05 49 79 01 93 |

| Thouars | Les Alligators | ☎ 05 49 66 16 38 |

Canoes and kayaks for hire on the river Thouet. Contact Mr Proust.

Clay Pigeon Shooting

| Niort | Ball Trap Club Niortais, 6 impasse de La Minoterie | ☎ 05 49 73 44 57 |

| Thouars | Ball Trap Club Thouarais. | ☎ 05 49 67 72 37 |

Contact Mr Carrére

Climbing

| Melle | Brioux | ☎ 05 49 07 26 35 |

(just south of Melle)
Minimum age eight.

| Niort | Club Alpin Français | ☎ 05 49 28 31 27 |

Artificial walls at a variety of locations around Niort, as well as canyoning, caving and cross-country skiing. Minimum age 14.

| Thouars | The Grifférus Site | ☎ 05 49 65 96 56 |

(between Argenton Château and Thouars)
Two rock faces for experienced amateurs.

| | Escapade Verticale | ☎ 05 49 96 63 15 |

Climbing club.

Cycling

| Melle | Pédale St Florentaise Section Melle | ☎ 05 49 29 02 53 |

Competitions, mountain biking and road cycling.

| Niort | Amicale des Cyclos Niortais | ☎ 05 49 79 34 26 |

Leisure and competitive cycling. Rides on Sunday and bank holiday mornings, leaving the station car park at 9am in winter, 7.30am summer.

| Thouars | Brion Cyclotourisme | ☎ 05 49 68 00 61 |

Fencing

| Niort | Cercle d'Escrime Duguesclin,12 rue Joseph Cugnot | ☎ 05 49 24 89 27 |

Training at the Pissardant sports complex on Tuesdays and Fridays 6 to 9pm.

Fishing

| General | Fédération départementale de la Pêche | ☎ 05 49 09 23 33 |

There's over 1,900km (1,200mi) of waterways for fishing in Deux-Sèvres with facilities for both novice and experienced fishermen. Annual fishing permits (cartes) can be bought locally, such as at fishing tackle shops and tabacs close to fishing lakes (étangs). They also stock maps of local fishing sites and rivers.

Moncoutant	Pescalis ☎ 05 49 72 00 01

A 100ha (250-acre) site catering both families, children and adults in separate areas. Night fishing, lessons and equipment hire available. Fishing from €14 a day.

Niort Club Compétition de la Gaule Niortaise ☎ 05 49 08 01 77
Competitions, courses, fishing school and leisure angling. Fishing on the Sèvre Niortaise, Noron, les Chizelles and other waterways in the department.

Parthenay St Aubin-le-Cloud ☎ 05 49 95 35 08
(south-west of the town)
This fishing lake also has a picnic area and tennis courts.

Football

Football clubs can be found even in small villages and your *mairie* is the best place to obtain contact details for your local club.

Golf

Les Forges Forges Golf, Le Bourg ☎ 05 49 69 91 77
(south-east of Parthenay)
In gently rolling countryside this club has 27 holes designed as three 9-hole courses which can be combined to provide three different 18-hole par 72 courses of approximately 6,500m. Lessons, driving range, buggy hire and club house with restaurant. Open all year except 25th December. Green fees €30 to €36 for 18 holes.

Niort Golf Club Niortais, Chemin du
Grand Ormeau ☎ 05 49 09 01 41
A fairly flat course with narrow fairways and tall trees, 18 holes, par 71, 5,865m. Lessons, driving range, practice greens, buggy hire, pro shop and clubhouse with bar and restaurant. Open all year from 9am to 6pm in low season, 8.30am to 7pm in high season. Green fees €28.50 to €35.50.

Parcours Formule Golf, Le Petit Chêne ☎ 05 49 63 20 95
(between Niort and Parthenay)
This course is on a 60ha (150-acre) estate. 18 holes, par 72, 6,020m. Driving range, six-hole course, clubhouse with bar and restaurant. Hire of buggies, lessons and a pro shop. Open all year but closed Tuesdays in low season. Green fees €29 to €36.

Horse Riding

Melle	L'Etrier de Pays Mellois, Lavau, St Martin-lès-Melle	☎ 05 49 27 09 44
Niort	Centre Equestre, 340 route d'Aiffres Indoor and outdoor facilities.	☎ 05 49 24 76 39
Thouars	Centre Equestre Le Petit Mans, St Martin-de-Sanzay	☎ 05 49 67 72 40

Competitions, pony club and riding out. Minimum age four.

Parthenay	Parc Equestre de Parthenay, Château des Plans, rue Brossard	☎ 06 80 42 10 12

Ice Skating

Niort	103 avenue de la Venise Verte Open 1st September to 31st May.	☎ 05 49 79 11 08

Ice Hockey

Niort	Niort Hockey Club, Patinoire Municipale, avenue de la Venise Verte Training four times a week.	☎ 05 49 79 11 08

Motorcycle Riding

Melle	Amicale Moto Verte du Mellois Rallies, endurance tests and classes.	☎ 05 49 27 17 85
Niort	Moto Club Pirate 'Les Pucerons' Rallies, tours and weekly meetings.	☎ 05 49 24 01 97
Thouars	Moto Club Thouarsais contact Mr Eric Forthin	☎ 05 49 66 10 86
	Massais Motorbike Club, le Bois Joli	☎ 05 49 66 56 41

Martial Arts

Melle	Judo Club Mellois, Dojo du Pinier Activities and classes, Monday to Saturday evenings.	☎ 05 49 29 36 62
Niort	Judo Club Niortais, Salle Omnisports, rue Barra Training every day, competitions.	☎ 05 49 77 05 09
Parthenay	Comité des Deux-Sèvres de Judo et Ju Jitsu, 6 rue Ernest Pérochon	☎ 05 49 64 15 22

| Thouars | Judo Club Thouarsais et Argentonnais | ☎ 05 49 96 09 07 |

Potholing

| Niort | Club Alpin Français | ☎ 05 49 28 31 27 |

Minimum age 14.

Rowing

| Niort | Niort Aviron Club, Base Nautique de Noron | ☎ 05 49 79 01 93 |

From beginners to international competitions. Wednesdays 2 to 6pm, Saturdays 9am to noon. Minimum age ten.

Sailing

| Niort | Yachting Club Niortais Voile, Base Nautique de Noron | ☎ 06 87 27 89 05 |

Scuba Diving

| Melle | Club de Plongée Mellois | ☎ 05 49 07 18 94 |

Training, lessons and dives throughout the year, from the Ile d'Oléron to Spain. Contact Mr Billondeau.

| Thouars | Club Subaquatique de Thouars | ☎ 05 49 66 05 40 |

Contact Mr Parfait.

Shooting

| Niort | Stade Niortais Tir | ☎ 05 49 33 12 21 |

Minimum age ten.

| Parthenay | Ligue Rég Tir Poitou-Charentes, 93 rue Jean Jaurès | ☎ 05 49 94 15 59 |

| Thouars | Tir à la Carabine | ☎ 05 49 66 03 91 |

Contact Mr Olivier.

Snooker, Pool & Billiards

Some bars listed under **Bars & Nightlife** on page 224 also have billiards, pool or snooker tables.

| Melle | Billard Club Mellois | ☎ 05 49 07 23 04 |

French billiards. Open practice in the foyer of la Jabotière, Melle. Annual membership fee €15. Free lessons on request. Contact Mr Martin.

| Niort | Académie Niortaise de Billard, impasse du Colombier, 19 avenue de Paris | ☎ 05 49 28 10 15 |

French billiards.

Squash

| Melle | Squash St Pierre, 21 rue Guillotière | ☎ 05 49 27 09 36 |

Also has facilities for dance, gym and weight training.

| Niort | Squash Niortais, 22 chemin de Pied de Fond | ☎ 05 49 79 52 30 |

Open every day. Minimum age ten.

| Parthenay | Cocktail Sportif, rue Léonard de Vinci | ☎ 05 49 71 15 47 |

| Thouars | Loisirs Plus, 3 impasse Gaston Chérau | ☎ 05 49 66 39 41 |

Squash and outdoor tennis.

Swimming

| Melle | Piscine Municipale, route Roche | ☎ 05 49 27 02 83 |

This outdoor pool is open mid-June to the end of August.

| | Piscine Couverte, rue Guillotière | ☎ 05 49 27 01 91 |

Closed during the summer months.

| Niort | route Pré-Leroy | ☎ 05 49 24 09 96 |

Indoor and outdoor pools.

| | rue de Champommier | ☎ 05 49 24 59 19 |

Indoor pool.

| Parthenay | 8 rue Clément Ader | ☎ 05 49 64 24 88 |

Indoor pool open all year.

| Thouars | 7 boulevard du 8 Mai | ☎ 05 49 66 26 69 |

Indoor pool open September to June.

| | 11 rue Grande Côte de Crevant | ☎ 05 49 66 06 08 |

Outdoor pool open July and August.

Tennis

| Melle | Tennis Club de Melle, chemin du Pinier | ☎ 05 49 29 18 78 |

| Niort | Tennis Centre, 162 rue St Symphorien | ☎ 05 49 73 00 52 |

Five indoor and five outdoor courts.

| Thouars | Tennis Club de Thouars | ☎ 05 49 68 04 77 |

Contact Serge Guillemin.

Waterskiing

| Niort | Base Nautique de Noron | ☎ 05 49 79 01 93 |

Tourist Offices

General   Comité Départemental du Tourisme
                 en Deux-Sèvres   ☎ 05 49 77 19 70
                 💻 *www.tourisme-deux-sevres.com*

Melle   3 rue Emilien Traver   ☎ 05 49 29 15 10
                 💻 *www.paysmellois.org*
                 Tuesdays to Fridays 10am to 12.30pm, 2.30 to 5.30pm,
                 Mondays 2.30 to 5.30pm, closed Saturdays and Sundays. In
                 the summer the office is also open Saturday, Sunday and
                 Monday mornings.

Niort   16 rue de Petit-St-Jean,
                 Place Martin Bastard   ☎ 05 49 24 18 79
                 💻 *www.niortourisme.com* & 💻 *www.vivre-a-niort.com*
                 (to the left of the Donjon, in front of the Hôtel de Ville)
                 Mondays to Fridays 9.30am to 6pm, Saturdays 9.30am to
                 12.30pm, plus Saturday afternoons in spring and autumn; July
                 and August Mondays to Saturdays 9.30am to 7pm and
                 Sundays 10am to 1pm.

Parthenay   8 rue Vau St Jacques   ☎ 05 49 64 24 24
                 💻 *www.cc to parthenay.com*
                 (at the very bottom of the cobbled street, rue Vau St Jacques,
                 near the towers – not easy to find without a street map!)
                 Mondays 2 to 6pm, Tuesdays to Fridays 9.30am to 12.30pm,
                 2 to 6pm, Saturdays 9.30am to 12.30pm. In the summer it's open
                 from 8.30am to 12.30pm, 2 to 6pm Mondays to Fridays and
                 weekends. Comfortable seating area to the side with free
                 Internet access.

Thouars   3bis boulevard Pierre Curie   ☎ 05 49 66 17 65
                 With limited information on display, this isn't a very good
                 office for browsing, so you need to know what you want and
                 ask for it. Mondays to Fridays 9.30am (Tuesdays 10am) to
                 12.30pm, 1.30 to 6.30pm, Saturdays 9.30am to 12.30pm
                 all year.

Tradesmen

Architects & Project Managers

General   Adams Gautier Poitou-Charentes   ☎ 05 49 64 42 96
                 💻 *www.adamsgautier.com*
                 This is a British/French team that are experienced architects
                 and also organise surveys and building permits and carry out
                 project management, new construction, renovation,
                 landscaping and pool installation.

Mr Louis Albagnac, Le Bourg,
St Fraigne   ☎ 05 45 96 56 08
This French architect speaks English.

Eric Archaimbault   ☎ 06 77 13 41 41
✉ *archaimbaulteric@wanadoo.fr*
Bilingual project manager using only registered French
tradesmen and covering the whole region of Poitou-Charentes.

Builders

Melle   STPM, Mardre, St Léger   ☎ 05 49 29 17 60
               (on the right as you leave Melle past Rhodia towards Limoges)
               General building work.

Niort   AB Construction, Espace Mendès
               France, rue Boëtte   ☎ 05 49 33 24 40
               New and renovation work, plumbing and heating.

Parthenay   Sogem GE Sarl, 29 rue Louis Braille   ☎ 05 49 64 58 75
               General builders.

Thouars   Les Maisons FL, 28 place du Boël ☎ 05 49 66 01 66
               New and renovation work.

Carpenters

Melle   Entreprise Tanvier, route de la Roche   ☎ 05 49 27 03 44
               Carpentry, joinery and cabinet making.

Niort   Fabrix, 481 route Limoges   ☎ 05 49 28 47 43
               (near the aerodrome on the main road into Niort from Melle)

Parthenay   Menuiserie Bodin, 39 rue Henri Dunant   ☎ 05 49 64 05 72

Thouars   Menuiserie-Charpente, 16 place de Boël   ☎ 05 49 66 31 66

Chimney Sweeps

Melle   Yves Delouche, 41 avenue Gare, Brioux   ☎ 05 49 75 56 84

Niort   Bodin Service, 14 avenue Mr de Lattre
               de Tassigny   ☎ 05 49 73 33 11

Parthenay   Michel Rambaud, 16 rue Bourg Belais   ☎ 05 49 64 34 11

Thouars   Yves Ferchaud, 2 place Abbaye,
               St Jean de Thouars   ☎ 05 49 66 45 64

Electricians & Plumbers

Melle	Ribot Sarl, route de Niort, St Martin Lès Melle	☎ 05 49 27 91 54
	(on the right leaving Melle in the direction of Niort) Plumbing, heating and electrics. Pro & Cie outlet.	
Niort	Garnault Entreprise, 23 boulevard des Rochereaux, Chauray	☎ 05 49 33 01 54
	Heating, plumbing and electrics.	
Parthenay	Gatinelec Sarl, 27 rue Michelet	☎ 05 49 64 07 07
	General electrician.	
	Francis Juin, 23 allée de La Mélusine	☎ 05 49 94 63 30
	Heating and plumbing.	
Thouars	Rateau Sarl, 105bis avenue Emile Zola	☎ 05 49 96 37 84
	Heating, bathrooms and electrics.	

Translators & Teachers

French Teachers & Courses

Melle	CFPPA	☎ 05 49 27 24 44
	This education centre runs courses of two hours a week for 20 weeks.	
Montcoutant	Euro-Communication	☎ 05 49 80 64 68
	(north-west of Parthenay) Contact Hélène Rivaleau, La Guêlerie, Largeasse. This organisation offers French lessons for adults, both beginners and intermediate.	
Niort	ABC Formation, route du 14 juillet	☎ 05 49 28 06 09
Parthenay	Greta, 2 rue Perochon	☎ 05 49 94 67 06
	This government organisation offers French lessons for foreigners.	
St Romain	Tournesol Language School	☎ 05 49 87 45 23
	Just over the border into Vienne, this organisation takes beginners, improvers and advanced classes. One-to-one, group and intensive courses.	
Thouars	Mme. Nigot, Espace Tyndo, 6 rue du Président Tyndo	☎ 05 49 68 15 47
	Courses on Tuesday, Thursday and Friday mornings.	

Translators

Bressuire   David Poppleton, 33 rue Thude   ☎ 05 49 65 22 33

Sauzé-Vaussais ASCOM, 1 impasse Terrage les Jarriges ☎ 05 49 07 77 43
                (east of Melle)

Utilities

Electricity & Gas

Électricité de France/Gaz de France (EDF/GDF) is one company for the whole of France but operates its gas and electricity divisions separately. The numbers below are for general information; emergency numbers can be found on page 56.

EDF GDF Services Vienne et Sèvres   ☎ 08 01 07 90 86
💻 www.edf.fr

EDF local offices are listed below (there are no direct telephone numbers for these offices; you must call the above number).

Bressuire   43 rue Chachon
Melle   rue Simplot
Niort   28 rue Boule d'Or
Parthenay   26 rue Alsace Lorraine
Poitiers   74 rue Bourgogne (head office)
St Maixent-
l'Ecole   4 rue Aristide Briand

Heating Oil

Melle   Garage Chaillois, Bellevue, Chail   ☎ 05 49 29 36 44

Niort   CPO, route Limoges   ☎ 05 49 77 11 80

Parthenay   Esso Fioul, ZA Le Poirier   ☎ 05 49 64 04 55

Thouars   Shell, 22 boulevard Ménard   ☎ 05 49 68 09 15

Water

The main water supply companies are listed below. If you aren't covered by one of these, your *mairie* will have details of your water supplier.

Générale des
Eaux   3 rue Marcel Sembat, Nantes   ☎ 08 11 90 29 02

Lyonnaise des Eaux	Le Retord, La Peyratte	☎ 08 10 38 73 87
Régie d'Eau	Impasse de La Croix Thibault, Thouars	☎ 05 49 66 69 05
SAUR	Frontenay Rohan Rohan	☎ 05 49 04 68 00

Wood

Ferrière-en-Parthenay	Les Bois du Poitou, 64 avenue de Nantes (east of Parthenay)	☎ 05 49 63 04 83
Niort	Jérome Muller, 13 rue Arsenal	☎ 05 49 06 15 12

Montmorillon

5

Vienne

This chapter provides details of facilities and services in the department of Vienne (86). General information about each subject can be found in **Chapter 1**. All entries are arranged alphabetically by town, except where a service applies over a wide area, in which case it's listed at the beginning of the relevant section under 'General'. A map of Vienne is shown below.

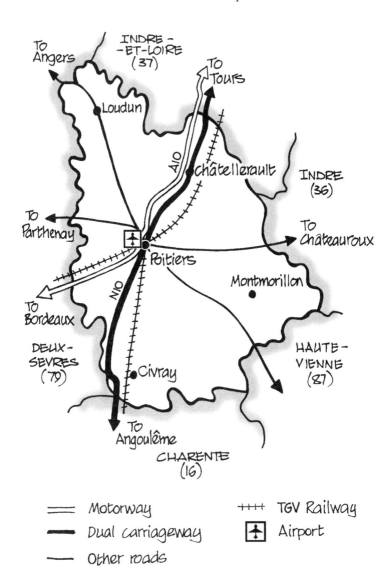

═══ Motorway	┼┼┼┼ TGV Railway
▬▬ Dual carriageway	✈ Airport
─── Other roads	

Accommodation

Camping

Châtellerault	Camping Valette, route d'Antran	☎ 05 49 02 06 27

Four-star campsite open mid-May to the beginning of September.

Civray	Les Aulnes, route de Roche	☎ 05 49 87 17 24

Site alongside the Charente river. Open April to mid-October.

Loudun	Beausoleil, chemin de l'Etang	☎ 05 49 98 14 22

Three-star campsite for tents, caravans and campervans.

Montmorillon	Camping Municipal, 31 avenue Fernand Tribot	☎ 05 49 91 02 33

This three-star site is open from March to the end of October.

Poitiers	Camping St-Cyr, St-Cyr (close to Futuroscope)	☎ 05 49 62 57 22

On the banks of a lake in a 300ha (750-acre) leisure park.

Châteaux

General	Bienvenue au Château	

🖥 *www.bienvenue-au-chateau.com*
This website is available in English and gives details of château accommodation in western France.

Ternay	Château de Ternay	☎ 05 49 22 97 54

🖥 *www.chateau-de-ternay.com*
(west of Loudun)
In the same family for 200 years this 15th and 19th century château is the birthplace of Admiral de Ternay. Three bedrooms and one suite available. Rooms from €80 to €103, suite €140, including breakfast. English spoken.

Vouneuil-sous-Biard	Le Grand Mazais	☎ 05 49 53 40 31

(on the eastern outskirts of Poitiers)
An elegant mansion built at the end of the 17th century. Three spacious rooms with en-suite facilities and dressing rooms. Dinner available if booked 48 hours in advance. Open all year round. €80 for two people, €105 for a four-person suite, dinner €40, including aperitifs, wine and coffee. No pets. English spoken.

Gîtes And Bed & Breakfast

Poitiers	1bis rue Victor Hugo	☎ 05 49 49 59 11

🖥 *www.gitesdefrance-vienne.com*

Gîtes de France listed. Bookings can be made by phone or via the internet.

Hotels

Civray	Le Cheval Blanc, rue du Temple €44 per night for a room for two people.	☎ 05 49 87 02 51
	Hôtel du Commerce, 5 rue Pont des Barres €40 for a room for two people.	☎ 05 49 97 03 97
Loudun	Le Ricordeau, place de la Boeuffetérie (in the town centre) Rooms from € 35 per night for two people.	☎ 05 49 22 67 27
	Le Cheval Blanc, 11 avenue Poitou Rooms for two people from €25.	☎ 05 49 98 02 00

Bars & Nightlife

Availles-Limouzine	Le Bimbo, route de l'Isle Jourdain Two rooms. Open Fridays and Saturdays.	☎ 05 49 48 37 33
Châtellerault	Armelle Brouard , 47 rue Soyecourt French billiards tables.	☎ 05 49 02 08 99
	Le Bar de l'Industrie, 103 boulevard Blossac Live events and themed evenings.	☎ 05 49 21 23 60
	Before Café, 19 avenue John Kennedy A bar aimed at 20 to 40-year-olds with themed music each night: Tuesdays jazz, Wednesdays '80s, Thursdays Salsa/Latino, Fridays house, Saturdays current. Open Tuesdays and Wednesdays noon to midnight, Thursdays to Saturdays noon to 2am, Sundays noon to 8.30pm.	☎ 05 49 20 32 67
	La Havane, 11 rue des Scieurs Disco. Open Thursdays to Sundays.	☎ 05 49 21 01 98
	Le Pam Club, 30 Grand Rue, Châteauneuf Bar with shows (jazz, tango and dancing). Open Tuesdays to Saturdays 9pm to 4.30am.	☎ 05 49 21 48 93

La Roche-Posay	Casino de la Roche-Posay, route de Vicq ☎ 05 49 86 20 10

Roulette, blackjack, restaurant, etc. Open every day 10am to 3am (Saturdays till 4am).

Le Pianocktail, Les Loges du Parc   ☎ 05 49 19 40 80
(beneath les Loges du Parc in the centre of the town)
This evening venue has a piano bar and holds karaoke, dances and '70s and '80s evenings. Open April to September Tuesdays to Saturdays 9.30pm to 2am. Free entry.

Loudun	Le Castillo, Arcay ☎ 05 49 98 29 1

(just south-west of Loudun)
Club/disco open Friday to Sunday evenings.

Montamisé	Relais de la Moulière, Le Grand Recoin ☎ 05 49 01 06 01

(north-east of Poitiers)
Afternoon tea dances Thursdays 3 to 8pm but not every week.

Montmorillon	Le Buvard, rue Montebello, Cité de l'Ecrit ☎ 05 49 83 82 55

A 'pub' in the old writing quarter.

Poitiers	Bar le Charleston, 10 rue Eperon ☎ 05 49 41 13 36

Karaoke Tuesdays to Fridays.

Bar O'Kinou, 177 rue Faubourg du Pont Neuf   ☎ 05 49 46 22 93
Cocktail brasserie.

The Black House, 195 avenue du 8 Mai 1945   ☎ 05 49 57 08 21
Open Tuesdays to Sundays, with techno, house and '60s to '90s music.

Bowling Poitiers Beaulieu, Géant Centre, 2 avenue Lafayette   ☎ 05 49 01 92 33
Bowling alleys, snooker tables, electronic games, restaurant and pizzeria.

Le Cod'Bar, 10 Grand Rue   ☎ 05 49 50 72 55
Open Mondays to Saturdays 9am to 2am, concerts, themed evenings, games and competitions.

L'Eclipse, 55 promenade des Cours   ☎ 05 49 88 34 21
Disco. Open Thursdays to Saturdays.

La Grand Goule Disco, 46 rue du Pigeon Blanc   ☎ 05 49 50 41 36
Three areas with different ambiances. Open every day all year.

Le Loft, 85 promenade des Cours ☎ 05 49 41 04 37
Groove, disco, house and R 'n' B. Wednesdays and Thursdays
11pm to 4am, weekends 11pm to 5am.

Le Pince Oreille, 11 rue des Trois Rois ☎ 05 49 60 25 99
Concert café with a full programme of events. Tuesdays to
Thursdays 5.30pm to 2am, Fridays 5.30pm to 3am and
Saturdays 9pm to 3am.

Studio Club, 3 boulevard René Descartes ☎ 05 49 49 70 80
(near Futuroscope)
Disco/club.

St Germain   VIP Club, route du Blanc ☎ 05 49 84 15 79
Disco for the over 25s.

St Macoux   Le Quincy, Le Pont de La Claude ☎ 05 49 87 67 61
(near St Macoux, close to the N10 exit for Les Maison Blanches)
Disco. Open Fridays, Saturdays and bank holidays 10pm to
5am. Free entry before midnight.

Business Services

Computer Services

General   K. Humphreys, Chez Bouchet,
               Montalembert ☎ 05 49 07 53 46
               ✉ *humphreyskeith@aol.com*
               This Briton deals with computer problems and sells hardware,
               software and upgrades, covering southern Vienne as well as
               northern Charente and eastern Deux-Sèvres.

Châtellerault Alliance Net Info, 6 rue Roffay de Pallus ☎ 05 49 02 03 04

Civray   Cré@thlon Informatique, La Gare,
               St Saviol ☎ 05 49 87 54 93
               (west of the town)
               Sale and repair of computers, including British computers, and
               training available at home.

Loudun   Loudun Computer Services,
               7 rue Mairie ☎ 05 49 98 59 39
               Sales, internet contracts, computer spares and accessories.
               Closed Mondays.

Montmorillon   Montmorillon Informatique,
               6 Grand' Rue ☎ 05 49 91 25 97
               Computer spares, repairs and assistance. Open mornings
               Tuesdays to Sundays.

Poitiers	Futur & Soft 86, 6 rue Eugène Chevreuil	☎ 05 49 55 42 98

Camera and computer specialist.

	Micro Tech Informatique, 55 boulevard Pont Achard	☎ 05 49 30 03 10

Computer Training

Châtellerault	Micro-Chatel, Maison Pour Tous, 69 rue Creuzé	☎ 05 49 93 01 23

Introduction to IT, the internet and use of various packages.

Civray	Club Informatique	☎ 05 49 87 39 08

Contact Mr Renoux.

Loudun	Informatique – RND186, 1 rue Housse Galant	☎ 05 49 98 39 20

Introduction and training at the workshops.

Poitiers	Club Informatique de St Benoît	☎ 05 49 52 92 84

Employment Agencies

(see page 50)

Communications

Fixed Telephones

General	France Télécom: Dial 1014 or go to 🖥 *www.francetelecom.fr* Local shops are listed below.	

Châtellerault Poitiers	73 boulevard Blossac rue Salvador Allende 18 rue Marché Notre Dame	

Internet Access

Châtellerault	Cyber Planète, 16 rue St Jean	☎ 06 77 65 67 48

Closed Mondays and Tuesdays, open Sunday afternoons.

	Espace Multimédia, 4 rue Aimé	☎ 05 49 21 32 03

Closed Sundays all day and Monday and Saturday mornings.

Civray	La Maison de la Nature, route de Roche	☎ 05 49 87 11 80

Loudun	Centre de Resources Internet	☎ 05 49 98 17 30

	(behind the library) Closed Mondays.	
Montmorillon	Médiathèque, 9 avenue Pasteur Closed Mondays.	☎ 05 49 91 78 09
Poitiers	ADN Games, 42 rue Magenta Open Mondays to Saturdays noon to 2am.	☎ 05 49 50 18 59
	Cyber Café Poitiers, 171 Grand' Rue	☎ 05 49 39 51 87

Mobile Telephones

Châtellerault	SFR, 54 rue Bourbon Closed Mondays.	☎ 05 49 85 80 30
Loudun	Espace'Com, 3 rue Marchands Closed Mondays.	☎ 05 49 22 99 66
Montmorillon	SFR, 13 Grand' Rue Open Mondays to Saturdays.	☎ 05 49 91 58 88
Poitiers	Boutique Bouygues 13 rue Marché Notre Dame Closed Monday mornings.	☎ 05 49 00 04 42
	Espace SFR, 37 rue Gambetta Closed Monday mornings.	☎ 05 49 45 00 14

Domestic Services

Curtain Making

General	Carol Weekes 'Les Petites Pommes', Les Hâtes, Couture ✉ *dacawe@wanadoo.fr* Curtains made to measure for addresses in Poitou-Charentes.	☎ 05 45 90 88 36

Equipment & Tool Hire

Civray	Blanchard, ZA Savigné Small diggers to chainsaws and ride-on lawn mowers.	☎ 05 49 87 11 77
Poitiers	Loxam, rue Thalweg, ZI de La République 💻 *www.loxam.fr*	☎ 05 49 88 33 90

Garden Services

Civray	Jardin Moine, Epanvilliers, Blanzay	☎ 05 49 97 03 77

(north-east of the town)
This company carries out garden maintenance and tree surgery.

Launderettes

Châtellerault   Lavamatic, 159 Grand Rue

Loudun   rue de La Porte du Chinon
Open every day 7am to 9pm.

Montmorillon   Lina Bouhet, 9 place Haut Poitou
(set back in the parade of shops opposite Hyper U)
Open every day 7am to 9pm.

Poitiers   Lavomatique, 5 rue René Descartes
Open every day 7am to 9pm.

Septic Tank Services

General   AVSP, ZA de Braille Ouaille, Yversay,
Neuville de Poitou   ☎ 05 49 51 52 17
Units in Châtellerault, Couhé, Loudun and Poitiers.

Sanitra Fourrier, route de Chardonchamp,
ZA le Porteau, Migné-Auxances   ☎ 05 49 51 67 21
Units in Châtellerault, Loudun and Poitiers.

Entertainment

Cinemas

Châtellerault   Les 400 Coups, 4 rue Aimé Rasseteau   ☎ 05 49 93 37 77

Cinéa, 58 boulevard Blossac   ☎ 05 49 21 08 36

Civray   7 rue Louis XIII   ☎ 05 49 87 82 40
(just off the main square)

Loudun   Cinéma Corny, rue de l'Abreuvoir   ☎ 05 49 98 56 70

Montmorillon   Cinéma Majestic, 52 boulevard
Strasbourg   ☎ 05 49 84 01 43

Poitiers   Cinéma CGR, Castille, 24 place
Maréchal Leclerc   ☎ 08 92 68 04 45
💻 www.cgrcinemas.com
Eight screens.

English Books

All the libraries detailed below have a selection of English-language books and are closed on Mondays.

	Tue	Wed	Thu	Fri	Sat
Châtellerault rue Gaudeau Lerpinière ☎ 05 49 21 11 28	1.30–7.00	3.00–6.00	9.00–12.00 1.30–6.00	1.30–6.00	9.00–5.00
Civray rue Victor Hugo ☎ 05 49 87 88 77	10.00–12.15 1.15–4.00	3.00–6.00	closed	10.00–11.00 4.00–7.00	11.00–12.00 3.00–5.00
Loudun place Sainte Croix ☎ 05 49 98 30 26	10.00–12.00 2.30–6.30	10.00–6.30	closed	2.30–7.00	10.30–12.30 2.30–6.30
Montmorillon 9 avenue Pasteur ☎ 05 49 91 78 09	1.00–6.00	10.00–12.00 2.00–6.00	1.00–6.00	1.00–6.00	10.00–12.00 2.00–6.00
Poitiers* Médiathèque 4 rue Université ☎ 05 49 52 31 51	11.00–10.00	11.00–6.00	11.00–10.00	11.00–6.00	11.00–5.00

* This is the main library in Poitiers, although there are also separate children's and multi-media libraries.

Festivals

May	**Châtellerault** Jazzellerault	☎ 05 49 93 03 08

This summer festival is new on the jazz scene, with regional, national and international artists. There are concerts in halls and open-air in the centre of the town.

June/July	**Poitiers** Festival Hip Hop & Co.	☎ 05 49 88 05 55

A week of hip hop and rhythm, dance shows, rap concerts with DJs and many different hip hop artists. The stages are in the centre of the city, which is busy both day and evening.

June to September	**Poitiers** Summer Festival 🖳 *www.mairie-poitiers.fr*	☎ 05 49 41 21 24

More than 60 shows are put on over the summer months, including theatre, cinema, music, concerts and dance, many of which are open-air in the heart of the city.

| August | Charroux | ☎ 05 49 87 60 12 |

Artists in the Street
During the first weekend in August the streets of the town are
full of artists. Competitions, exhibitions and activities.

Theatres

Châtellerault   Ateliers Theatre de Châtellerault   ☎ 05 49 93 59 30
Production of comedies and musicals and workshops.
Minimum age seven.

Nouveau Théâtre, 1 rue Chanoine
de Villeneuve   ☎ 05 49 93 03 08

Théâtre Populaire de Châtellerault,
rue Taupanne   ☎ 05 49 93 59 30

Loudun   Théâtre de La Reine Blanche,
rue du Bourg-Joly.   ☎ 05 49 98 17 87
Café/theatre.

Montmorillon   Théâtre de la Cité, 15 rue Champien   ☎ 05 49 48 47 97

Poitiers   Le Théâtre Scène Nationale,
1 place Mar Leclerc   ☎ 05 49 39 40 00
🖥 *www.letheatre-poitiers.com*
(in the city centre)

Le Salle de Spectacles de Saint-Benoît,
La Hune, 1 avenue du Champ
de la Caille   ☎ 05 49 37 77 88
🖥 *www.ville-saint-benoit.fr*
A large modern venue on the southern outskirts of Poitiers that
shows comedy, plays, musicals, jazz, opera and classical
theatre.

Video & DVD Hire

Châtellerault   Vidéo Cinebank, 24 avenue
Adrien Treuille   ☎ 05 49 19 46 24
Open Mondays, Tuesdays, Wednesdays, Fridays and
Saturdays 4 to 8pm.

Civray   There's an automatic dispenser for both DVDs and videos
in the car park at Intermarché.

Loudun   Station Esso Video Club, 5 place
Portail Chaussé   ☎ 05 49 98 11 95
DVDs and videos.

| Montmorillon | Cinébank, Grand' Rue | ☎ 06 64 15 47 77 |

Shop open Mondays 4 to 6pm, Wednesdays 10am to 1pm, Saturdays 5.30 to 8pm. 24-hour automatic dispenser.

| Poitiers | Cinébank, 300bis avenue de Nantes | ☎ 05 49 42 88 49 |

Videos and DVDs also available 24 hours a day via an external dispenser.

Miscellaneous

| Loudun | Ludothec'Astérix, 9 rue du Lion d'Or | ☎ 05 49 98 27 18 |

Toys and games for hire and to borrow.

Leisure Activities

Astrology

| Poitiers | Aujourd'hui l'Astrologie | ☎ 05 49 56 41 20 |

Contact Mr Diringer.

Art Classes

| Angles-sur-l'Anglin | Hôtel Lyon d'Or | ☎ 05 49 48 32 53 |

Courses in special paint effects for interior decorating.

| Châtellerault | Ecole Municipale d'Arts Plastiques, 12 rue de La Taupane | ☎ 05 49 93 03 12 |

| Loudun | Atelier d'Arts Plastiques de Loudun, 9 rue Lion d'Or | ☎ 05 49 98 6 77 |

Oils, drawing, painting and pastels.

Ballooning

| Châtellerault | Balade en Montgolfières, 86 avenue Camille Pagé | ☎ 05 49 21 52 98 |

Bike Hire

| Lathus | Centre de Plein Air, La Voulzie | ☎ 05 49 91 83 30 |

Open all year 9am to 6pm. Booking required.

| Poitiers | Vélomania, 195 avenue de Bordeaux | ☎ 05 49 59 96 91 |

Adult and child bike hire, classic and mountain bikes. Open Mondays to Saturdays.

| Roiffé | Domaine St Hilaire | ☎ 05 49 98 78 06 |

(north of Loudun)
Adult and child bikes. Open all year

Romagne   Garage Guillemin   ☎ 05 49 87 71 16
                 (north of Civray)
                 Open all year Mondays to Saturdays.

Bridge

Châtellerault   Bridge Club Châtelleraudais,
                 22 rue St André   ☎ 05 49 21 74 25
                 Beginners welcome, tournaments Monday and Wednesday
                 afternoons from 2.15pm and Thursday evenings from 8.15pm.

Civray   Club de Bridge de Civray, Espace
                 F. Mitterand   ☎ 05 49 87 02 30
                 (behind the Syndicat l'Initiative)
                 Every Friday 8.15pm and Wednesdays at 2pm, September to
                 June inclusive. Regular tournaments.

Loudun   Bridge Club Loudunais, Centre Culturel
                 de Loudun, boulevard Maréchal Leclerc ☎ 05 49 98 56 40
                 Matches 8pm Wednesdays; open to all Fridays from 3pm.

Montmorillon   Bridge Club de Montmorillon   ☎ 05 49 91 16 55

Poitiers   Club de Bridge de Poitiers   ☎ 05 49 47 01 72
                 Contact Mr Caillaud.

Bungee Jumping

l'Isle Jourdain Viaduct   ☎ 06 82 81 86 26
                 Weekends from June to October.

Children's Activity Clubs

Loudun   Les 12 Singes, Mille Club, allée des
                 Rosiers and Espace Jeunes, boulevard
                 Loche et Matras   ☎ 05 49 22 52 11
                 Concerts, open-air camps, sporting activities and games.

                 la Capucine, 9 rue du Lion d'Or   ☎ 05 49 22 40 32
                 Tuesdays to Fridays 8.30am to 5.30pm. €2 per hour, €12 all
                 day plus €15 a year membership.

Crazy Golf

Montmorillon   rue des Tennis   ☎ 05 49 91 22 46
                 (next to the tennis courts)

Dancing

Châtellerault   Prestige de La Danse, 141 rue Bourbon ☎ 05 49 21 38 30
                 Ballet, jazz and fitness classes for children and adults.

Association Danse 86, 11 rue Gustave
Courbet   ☎ 05 49 20 13 21
Rumba, twist, rock, Charleston, waltz and tango. Couples,
children and youngsters.

Montamisé   Relais de la Moulière, Le Grand Recoin   ☎ 05 49 01 06 01
                (north-east of Poitiers)
                Afternoon tea dances. Some Thursdays 3 to 8pm.

Payré   Guinguette des Bords de Dive,
                Les Iles de Payré   ☎ 05 49 42 88 38
                (on the N10 south of Poitiers)
                Tea dances Sunday afternoons, 3 to 8pm, 1st June to end of
                September.

Poitiers   Association Culture-Danse,
                29 avenue Libération   ☎ 05 49 53 26 85
                Classic, jazz and modern dance taught. Minimum age four.

                Ballet Jazz Cagine   ☎ 05 49 61 27 90
                Contact Mme Le Bihen.

                Patricia Moyon, 5ter rue Basse   ☎ 05 49 46 02 32
                Modern jazz and tap.

Flying

Le Blanc   Association De Vol à Voile, Aérodrome
                Bergeraux   ☎ 02 54 37 90 47
                (just north of Vienne)
                Hang gliding and flying lessons.

Châtellerault   Aéro Club Chatelleraudais, Aérodrome
                Targe   ☎ 05 49 93 12 13
                The club meets at the aerodrome on Saturday afternoons.

Couhé   Aéro Club de Couhé/Brux,
                Couhé Aérodrome   ☎ 05 49 37 97 98
                (on the N10 south of Poitiers)

Loudun   Aéro Club Loudunais, Aérodrome
                Veniers   ☎ 05 49 98 12 81
                Sightseeing flights, trial flights and lessons. Open weekends,
                and mid-week if arranged in advance.

Poitiers   Aéro Club du Poitou, Biard   ☎ 05 49 58 22 14
                A wide selection of aerial sports available.

Gypsy Caravan Holidays

Martaize   La Chevalerie du Thouet, Martaize   ☎ 05 49 69 88 20
                  Horse-drawn caravan holidays. Weekend for five people from
                  €200.

Gyms & Health Clubs

Châtellerault   CSAC, rue Abbé Lalanne   ☎ 05 49 02 85 20
                  (behind le Centre Aquatique)

Montmorillon   Espace Forme, Centre Commercial
                  Hyper U   ☎ 05 49 84 08 40
                  (on the first floor inside the Hyper U complex)
                  Offers a wide range of classes, including step, fitness and body
                  sculpture. For €30 a month you can attend as many classes as
                  you like. Dance classes also available, including jazz and tap.

Poitiers   Ener Gym, Parc Commercial Grand
                  Large, 50 avenue 11 novembre,
                  Saint Benoît   ☎ 05 49 46 17 58
                  Gym, health club and a variety of step, aerobic and stretch
                  classes.

Karting & Quad Bikes

Châtellerault   Piste Privée des Trois Chênes, Usseau ☎ 05 49 85 12 61

Loudun   Circuit National de La Boule d'Or   ☎ 05 49 98 75 12
                  (on the D147 going north out of the town)

Poitiers   Loisir Center, avenue Loge,
                  Migné Auxances   ☎ 05 49 51 23 71
                  650m circuit, open noon to 8pm Wednesdays to Sundays.

Lakes & Beaches

Ayron   Base de Loisirs du Pays Vouglaisien   ☎ 05 49 51 06 69
                  (east of Poitiers)
                  A park with a large lake, sandy beach, picnic area and play
                  area offering crazy golf, fishing, pedalos, canoes, kayaks,
                  beach volleyball, table tennis and boules.

Crémault-   Parc de Loisirs   ☎ 05 49 85 08 62
Bonneuil-   (north-east of Poitiers, south of Châtellerault)
Matours   Lake for swimming, with lifeguards in July and August, crazy
                  golf, playground, fishing, tennis, volleyball, roller skating and
                  canoe hire. Free access all year.

Moncontour   Base de Loisirs, Lake du Gué de Magne ☎ 05 49 98 91 60
                  (on the border with Deux-Sèvres)

The lake has a beach with lifeguards (summer only) and offers a water toboggan, pedalos, a small karting circuit, boats and fishing as well as a playground. Open 1st May to mid-September from 10am to 6pm. Adults €2, under 12s €1.

St Cyr   Lake Saint Cyr, parc de Saint Cyr   ☎ 05 49 62 57 22
                      (just north of Poitiers near Futuroscope)
                      A large lake with a very large beach (lifeguard in July and August), offering kayak hire, sailing, windsurfing, cycle trails and volleyball, plus a nearby golf course.

Vivonne   Parc de Vounant   ☎ 05 49 43 46 42
                      (south of Poitiers off the N10)
                      A leisure park that has an outdoor pool, 30m water chute and lots of surrounding space for relaxing and playing games. Open June to September.

Music

Châtellerault   Ecole Nationale de Musique et de Danse,
                      8 rue de La Taupanne   ☎ 05 49 21 38 44

Civray   Ecole de Musique   ☎ 05 49 87 47 82
                      Contact Mme. Bonneau.

Loudun   Ecole de Musique de Loudun,
                      1 rue Gambetta   ☎ 05 49 98 14 66
                      Contact Dominique Busson (director).

Poitiers   Musique du CEP   ☎ 05 49 41 12 89
                      Music school and orchestra.

Paint Ball

Civray   ☎ 05 49 87 10 37
                      Contact Mr Jolly.

Le Blanc   Quai Andé-Liesse   ☎ 02 54 37 19 21
                      🖳 www.coteauxloisirs.free.fr
                      (just north of Vienne)
                      €19 per person. English spoken.

Photography

Châtellerault   Club Photos des Minimes,
                      19 rue des Minimes   ☎ 05 49 02 18 50
                      Competitions, exhibitions, meetings with other clubs, courses and group work.

Lussac-les-   Atelier Photo Numérique,
Châteaux   21 route de Montmorillon   ☎ 05 49 48 29 46

(west of Montmorillon)
A workshop for digital photography, held 2 to 4pm the second
Saturday of each month.

Poitiers   Les Amis de l'Image   ☎ 05 49 57 03 12
                    Contact Mr Decoray.

Scouts & Guides

Civray   Scouts de France   ☎ 05 49 87 30 58
                    Contact Mme Rocher.

Loudun   ☎ 06 24 73 86 35
                    Boys and girls from 8 to 12.

Montmorillon   Scouts d'Europe   ☎ 05 49 91 00 83
                    Contact Mr Rochon.

Poitiers   Scouts Unitaires de France1   ☎ 05 49 53 26 08
                    Contact Mme Varenne.

Social Clubs & Organisations

Rotary Clubs

Châtellerault   Hôtel du Croissant, 13 avenue Kennedy ☎ 05 49 21 04 38

                    Club de Châtellerault, Hôtel Ibis,
                    RN10 sud   ☎ 05 49 02 18 18

Loudun   22 rue du Palais   ☎ 05 49 98 09 60
                    Contact Mr Berton.

Town Twinning

Châtellerault   Comité des Jumelages, 2 rue de Verdun ☎ 05 49 23 54 17
                    Twinned with Corby in England and Hamilton in Scotland.

Civray   Comité de Jumelage   ☎ 05 49 87 08 81
                    Twinned with Swaffham in Norfolk.

Poitiers   Relations Internationales, St Benoît   ☎ 05 49 37 44 00
                    South of Poitiers, St Benoît is twinned with Cookham in
                    Berkshire.

Stamp Collecting

Châtellerault   Amicale Philatélique Chatelleraudaise,
                    Salle de l'Ancien Musée, rue Clémenceau ☎ 05 49 93 60 16

Regular meetings, buying and exchanging of stamps, exhibitions and festivals.

Loudun   Mairie   ☎ 05 49 22 84 50
                Organised by Mr Bourdeau, this club has members who collect
                postcards and money as well as stamps.

Tree Climbing

Le Blanc   2 quai André Liesse   ☎ 02 54 37 19 21
                Aerial slides, suspended bridges and other paraphernalia for
                exploring the tree tops. Safety equipment provided. Contact
                Mme Franchaud.

Migné-Auxances Alma, Gymnase, route de Poitiers   ☎ 05 49 51 04 11
                (north-west of Poitiers)
                Exploring the tree canopy (*accrobranche*), canyoning, bungee
                jumping and climbing.

Poitiers   Auberge de Jeunesse   ☎ 05 49 30 09 70
                Minimum eight people.

Vintage Cars

Châtellerault   Ecurie Châtellerault Voitures
                Anciennes Centre, Café de l'Industrie,
                103 boulevard Blossac   ☎ 05 49 21 23 60

Loudun   Vehicules Anciens du Loudunois   ☎ 05 49 98 15 91
                Organised by Mr Vaucelles, this club organises trips and shows
                around Loudun and the region for vintage cars.

Walking & Rambling

The Vienne Valley has a variety of marked trails, from 6 to 30km (4 to 19mi), for those on foot, horseback or mountain bike (*VTT*). A brochure giving details and the routes is available from tourist offices in the area. Local tourist offices also hold guide books and data sheets for ramblers, or you can contact:

General   Comité Régional de Randonnée Pédestre,
                22 place Charles-de-Gaulle, Poitiers ☎ 05 49 88 93 48
Poitiers   Horizons et Nature, Centre
                Socio-Culturel de Beaulieu,
                boulevard Savari   ☎ 05 49 58 03 16
                Local walking/rambling group.

Yoga

Châtellerault   Various locations across the town   ☎ 05 49 93 08 82

| Loudun | Salle 1 at the Mairie | ☎ 02 47 95 76 62 |
| | Classes taken by Anne Viviani. | |

| Poitiers | Association de l'Enseignement du Yoga, | |
| | Carré bleu, 2 bis rue de Nimègue | ☎ 05 49 58 10 19 |

Medical Facilities & Services

Ambulances

In the event of a medical emergency dial 15.

Châtellerault	☎ 05 49 90 29 22
Civray	☎ 05 49 87 39 70
Loudun	☎ 05 49 98 00 00
Montmorillon	☎ 05 49 91 12 52
Poitiers	☎ 05 49 88 12 34

Doctors

English-speakers may like to contact the following doctors.

Châtellerault	Dr David, 34 rue Angelarde	☎ 05 49 21 11 97
Civray	Dr Chambeau, 42 avenue Henri Rocher	☎ 05 49 87 92 50
Loudun	Dr Villette, 4 rue Gambetta	☎ 05 49 98 06 98
Montmorillon	Dr Néraudeau, 3 boulevard Terrier Blanc	☎ 05 49 91 00 37
Poitiers	Dr Roquejoffre, quart Beaulieu,	
	6 place Rochemaux	☎ 05 49 01 91 87

Dentists

English-speakers might like to contact the following dentists.

Châtellerault	Dr Pierrefitte, 7 boulevard Blossac	☎ 05 49 21 98 13
Civray	Dr Flambeaux, place Gambetta	☎ 05 49 87 00 33
Loudun	Dr Rivault, 9 avenue Leuze	☎ 05 49 98 04 20
Montmorillon	Centre Médical, 31 Grand' Rue	☎ 05 49 91 12 12
Poitiers	Dr Aboucher, 3 rue Gibauderie	☎ 05 49 00 05 20

Emergency Services

Fire Brigade

Dial 18.

Gendarmerie Nationale

Some of the smaller gendarmeries are being merged with others and may be open limited hours, but the local number will always put you through to the station that is on duty.

Châtellerault	rue Chevalier de Ternay	☎ 05 49 20 17 33
Civray	2A route Limoges	☎ 05 49 87 00 32
Loudun	9 avenue Gare	☎ 05 49 98 00 40
Montmorillon	13 avenue Europe	☎ 05 49 91 10 44
Poitiers	1 rue Petit Polygone	☎ 05 49 44 02 02

Health Authority

Local offices of the Caisse Régional Assurance Maladie Centre Ouest (CRAMCO) are listed below.

Civray	Mairie, 12 place Général de Gaulle A CRAMCO representative visits every Tuesday from 1.30 to 4.30pm.	
Montmorillon	5 boulevard Gambetta Tuesdays and Thursdays 9am to 12.15pm, 1.30 to 4pm, Wednesdays 9am to 12.15pm and Fridays 1.30 to 4pm.	☎ 05 49 83 01 13
Poitiers	27 rue Bignoux (main office)	☎ 05 49 11 97 65

Hospitals

All the hospitals below have an emergency department.

Châtellerault	Centre Hospitalier Camille Guérin, Rocade Est	☎ 05 49 02 90 76
Loudun	Centre Hospitalier Théophraste Renaudot, 3 rue Visitandines	☎ 05 49 98 42 43
Montmorillon	Centre Hospitalier de Montmorillon, 2 rue Henri Dunant	☎ 05 49 83 83 83

| Poitiers | Centre Hospitalier Universitaire, rue de la Milétrie | ☎ 05 49 44 44 98 |

Spas

| La Roche-Posay | Les Thermes Saint-Roch, 4 cours Pasteur | ☎ 05 49 19 49 49 |

This thermal resort is the European capital of climatic dermatology and over 10,000 patients come every year for treatment. A huge range of treatments and breaks is available. Open mornings Mondays to Saturdays from 20th January to 21st December.

Motoring

Breakers' Yards

| Châtellerault | Bohan Pascal, ZI route Nonnes | ☎ 05 49 02 67 59 |

| Couhé | Starter, ZI Le Tranchis, Couhé (off the N10 south of Poitiers) | ☎ 05 49 30 34 74 |

| Montmorillon | Casse Auto-Jalladeau, 14 rue Raoul Mortier | ☎ 05 49 91 14 77 |

Open afternoons only Mondays to Fridays and Saturday mornings.

Car Dealers

| Châtellerault | Citroën, Raison, RN10 Sud | ☎ 05 49 21 32 22 |

| | Fiat, Touzalin, 107 rue d'Antran | ☎ 05 49 20 03 80 |

| | Ford, Tardy Automobiles, 40 boulevard d'Estrées | ☎ 05 49 20 44 44 |

| | Land Rover, Auto Sport, 9 avenue Honoré de Balzac, RN10 | ☎ 05 49 20 19 55 |

| | Peugeot, Georget, 17 avenue Honoré de Balzac, RN10 | ☎ 05 49 20 00 80 |

| | Renault, Garage Morosini, 136 rue Antran | ☎ 05 49 93 28 12 |

| | Rover, Auto Sport, 9 avenue Honoré de Balzac, RN10 | ☎ 05 49 20 19 55 |

	Toyota, Touzalin, 114 rue d'Antran	☎ 05 49 20 03 80
	Vauxall/Opel, Auto Diffusion, ZI Sanital, 9 rue Thomas Edison	☎ 05 49 23 24 24
Civray	Citroën, Vienne Sud Automobiles, route de Poitiers	☎ 05 49 87 00 20
	Fiat/Alfa Romeo, Mr Chauvergne, 15 boulevard Carnot	☎ 05 49 87 01 71
	Peugeot, Guenole, 5 avenue Henri Rocher	☎ 05 49 87 01 77
	Renault, Jean-Lois Bujon, 61 avenue Henri Roucher	☎ 05 49 87 03 91
	Vauxhall/Opel, Contact Autos, route de Limoges, Savigné	☎ 05 49 87 00 55
Loudun	Citroën, Blanchin Janick, 20 rue Artisans	☎ 05 49 98 34 30
	Peugeot, Saga Automobiles, 28 boulevard Jean Pascault	☎ 05 49 98 30 30
	Renault, Garage Delacote, 2 boulevard Guy Chauvet	☎ 05 49 98 12 93
	Toyota, Garage Boilaive, 47 avenue Val de Loire	☎ 05 49 98 05 87
	Vauxall/Opel, Garage Boilaive, 47 avenue Val de Loire	☎ 05 49 98 05 87
Montmorillon	Audi/VW, Garage Sarrazin, ZI Est La Barre, 10 rue Artisans	☎ 05 49 91 31 40
	Citroën, Montmorillon Auto, route Lussac les Châteaux	☎ 05 49 91 00 05
	Ford, Navarre Debiais, ZI Est	☎ 05 49 91 12 59
	Peugeot, Garage GMGA, 55 boulevard Gambetta	☎ 05 49 91 11 33
	Renault, F. Robuchon et Fils, 1 avenue de l'Europe	☎ 05 49 91 06 44

Poitiers	Alfa/Lancia, 166 avenue du Plateau des Glières	☎ 05 49 03 12 34
	Audi, Brillant Automobiles, Rocade Sud	☎ 05 49 37 60 60
	BMW, Futurauto, 147 avenue du 8 Mai 1945	☎ 05 49 54 04 04
	Citroën, DAP, 151 avenue du 8 Mai 1945	☎ 05 49 55 80 80
	Fiat/Lancia, J.F. Goutard, Porte de Paris	☎ 05 49 41 25 00
	Ford, Garage Belliard, 26 rue Bignoux	☎ 05 49 61 20 08
	Honda, Garage de l'Avenue, 1 rue Claude Berthollet	☎ 05 49 88 80 40
	Hyundai, 166 avenue du Plateau des Glières	☎ 05 49 03 12 34
	Mazda, Mazda Motors, route de Saumur, Migné Auxances	☎ 05 49 51 61 00
	Mercedes-Benz, Garage Etoile 86, 230 route Paris	☎ 05 49 37 37 73
	Mitsubishi, MMC Poitiers, 12 rue Torchaise, Vouneuil-sous-Biard	☎ 05 49 88 72 00
	Nissan, Espace des Nations, 17 avenue Loge, Migné Auxances	☎ 05 49 57 10 07
	Peugeot, SCAP, RN10, 149 avenue du 8 Mai 1945	☎ 05 49 30 03 30
	Renault, SACOA des Nations, 33 boulevard du Pont Archard	☎ 05 49 37 63 63
	Rover, Auto Sport, avenue Loge, Migné Auxances	☎ 05 49 51 57 57
	Skoda, Foucreau, 35 avenue Loge, Migné Auxances	☎ 05 49 54 25 26
	Suzuki, Suzuki Automobiles, 1 rue de l'Aérodrome, Biard	☎ 05 49 18 20 00

	Toyota, SNDA, 2 rue Proust, ZI République	☎ 05 49 69 24 46
	Vauxhall/Opel, Opel Poitiers, route de Saumur, Migné-Auxances	☎ 05 49 54 21 21
	Volvo, Cachet Giraud, rue de l'Aérodrome, Biard	☎ 05 49 37 29 15
	VW, Brillant Automobiles, Rocade Sud	☎ 05 49 37 60 60

Car Repairs & Service

General   Cole et Fils, 1 rue St Antoine, Charroux ☎ 05 49 87 72 40
British mechanic offering car servicing and repair, conversions from British to French, breakdown recovery and 'man with a van' service.

Driving Lessons

Chef-Boutonne Auto Ecole 'Virage'
57 Grand' Rue du Commerce   ☎ 05 49 07 66 69
This driving school gives refresher courses to Britons and lessons to help them adapt to driving on the right. It has male and female driving instructors who speak English.

Tyre & Exhaust Centres

Châtellerault	SiliGom, 3–5 rue Paix	☎ 05 49 02 02 12
Civray	Auto Marché, route de Limoges, Savigné	☎ 05 49 87 92 55
Loudun	Euro Tyre/Baudry Pneus, ZI Nord	☎ 05 49 98 19 39
Montmorillon	Ago Pneus, 101 avenue du Général de Gaulle (near the station) Closed Saturday afternoons.	☎ 05 49 91 38 16
Poitiers	Euromaster, 27 boulevard Pont Joubert	☎ 05 49 39 51 11

Pets

Dog Training

Naintré   Aniparc, 1 rue Bois Thevenault   ☎ 05 49 90 19 98
Dog training, kennels and dog breeding.

Quinçay   Despretz Syssi,15 rue Abineaux   ☎ 05 49 60 44 94

Farriers

Châtellerault   Patrick Begou, La Bougrière, Colombiers ☎ 05 49 90 28 44
                 (south-west of the town)
                 Covers the surrounding area.

Horse Dentists

General   Christophe Gaillard   ☎ 06 11 63 37 61
                 Based just south of Poitiers, Mr Gaillard covers Vienne, Deux-
                 Sèvres and northern Charente and Charente-Maritime.

Kennels & Catteries

The facilities listed below accept cats and dogs unless otherwise stated.

Benassay   Pelletreau, La Couinière   ☎ 05 49 43 75 74
                 (west of Poitiers)

Chauvigny   Au Toutou'Net, Epran   ☎ 05 49 01 76 30

La Pinolière-   Pension de La Pinolière des Bois, Payre ☎ 06 81 63 50 81
des-Bois

Pet Parlours

Châtellerault   Au Palais du Toutou et du Matou,
                 56 rue de Trois Pigeons   ☎ 05 49 20 43 19

Civray   Au Toutou Câlin, 6 rue Commerce   ☎ 05 49 87 28 93

Loudun   Elegance Canine, rue de La Porte de
                 Chinon   ☎ 05 49 98 21 89

Montmorillon   Les Aristochiens, 33 Grand' Rue   ☎ 05 49 91 96 57

Poitiers   Beauté Canine, 30 rue Grand Maison,
                 St Benoît   ☎ 05 49 01 18 17
                 (near Leclerc to the south of the town)

Riding Equipment

Poitiers   Horse Wood, 7 allée Haut Poitou, Chasseneuil-du-Poitou
                 ☎ 05 49 62 56 22
                 🖳 *www.horsewood.com*
                 (on the retail park north of the town, beside the Buffalo Grill
                 restaurant)

SPA

Châtellerault	Valette	☎ 05 49 21 61 11
Poitiers	Grange des Prés	☎ 05 49 88 94 57
	These are also both kennels.	

Veterinary Clinics

Châtellerault	Clinque Vétérinaire, 117 avenue Maréchal Leclerc	☎ 05 49 23 23 23
	(east out of the town centre, behind the station)	
Civray	Rai el Balhaa, 8 rue Duplessis	☎ 05 49 87 01 29
	(near the bridge) A small surgery.	
Loudun	Clinque Vétérinaire, 56 rue Porte de Chinon	☎ 05 49 98 00 55
	(set back on the main road near the wine shop)	
Montmorillon	Oliver de Russe, 5 boulevard Terrier Blanc	☎ 05 49 91 15 10
	(on the eastern outskirts of the town)	
Poitiers	Clinque Vétérinaire, 96 avenue 8 Mai 1945	☎ 05 49 53 01 67
	(on the main road into the south-west of the city from the N10)	
Saintes	Dr Bétizaud, 5 avenue Saintonge (Charente-Maritime)	☎ 05 46 92 08 81
	A specialist horse vet.	

Places To Visit

This section isn't intended to be a definitive guide but gives a wide range of ideas for the department. Prices and opening hours were correct at the time of publication, but it's best to check before travelling long distances.

Châteaux

Angles-sur-l'Anglin	Château Fort	☎ 05 49 48 61 20

Although in ruins, this imposing château on the edge of high cliffs dominates the valley of l'Anglin and is near one of the most beautiful villages in the region. Open every day except Tuesdays 10.30am to 12.30pm, 2.30 to 6.30pm. **Care should be taken if you're with young children.**

Gençay | Château Médiéval de Gençay ☎ 05 49 59 47 37
An imposing ruin of a military fortress, constructed in the 13th century and undergoing restoration. Guided tours last around 45 minutes and can be booked via the Gençay tourist office. Adults €2, under 16s free.

Gizay | Château de Chambonneau ☎ 05 49 42 94 07
💻 *www.chambonneau.com*
A prestigious fort from the 14th and 17th centuries, open every day in July and August from 1 to 7pm. Adults €4, under 12s €3.

Magné | Château de La Roche ☎ 05 49 59 31 07
This Renaissance château has a chapel, a museum and gardens. Open 1st June to 30th September every day 9 to 11.30am, 2 to 6pm; 1st April to 31st May, October and November 2 to 6pm; December to March by appointment. Adults €5.50, children 7–12 €3. Gardens only: adults €2.50, children €1.

Ternay | Château de Ternay ☎ 05 49 22 97 54
A 15th century château with an extraordinary gothic chapel. 1st April to 1st October every day except Thursdays and Saturdays; guided tours at 5pm. Adults €6.20, children €3.50.

Churches & Monuments

Charroux | Abbaye St Sauveur de Charroux ☎ 05 49 87 62 43
Once one of the most powerful Benedictine abbeys of Carolingian Europe, it was constructed in the eighth century and altered for the next 300 years. Its unusual octagonal tower with Gothic carvings and treasury makes it one of the most important medieval sites of the Poitevin region. Open June and September 10am to 12.30pm, 2 to 6.30pm; July and August 9.30am to 12.30pm, 2 to 6.30pm; 1st October to 31st May 10am to 12.30pm, 2 to 5.30pm. Closed Mondays and bank holidays all year. Adults €4, under 18s free.

Civray | Eglise St Nicolas
With its rectangular West Front decorated with carvings of the signs of the zodiac, the farming year and the wise and foolish virgins, this church, in the corner of the town square, is the only one of its kind in Poitou-Charentes.

Nouaille-Maupertuis | Abbaye de Nouaille-Maupertuis ☎ 05 49 55 35 69
An outstanding collection of 11th and 12th century abbey buildings and a medieval garden. It was here that King John the Good was defeated by the Black Prince in 1356. Free entry all year round. There are guided tours on Tuesdays in July and August: €3.50.

Museums & Galleries

Châtellerault   Auto Moto Vélo de Châtellerault
La Manu   ☎ 05 49 21 03 46
A museum for discovery, experimentation and fun. Experience simulators, try your skills against the clock on a bicycle and test your knowledge of road safety. The car museum has one of the largest public collections of motorbikes in France. Suitable for all ages, with explanations in English. Open 1st May to 30th September every day 10am to 12.30pm, 1.30 to 7pm; 1st October to 30th April Tuesdays to Sundays 2 to 6pm. Adults €4.80, free for under 18s and for everyone on the first Sunday of each month.

Musée Municipal Hotel Sully   ☎ 05 49 21 01 27
Archaeological collections relating to the story of Châtellerault plus fine arts, ceramics, weapons, hairstyles and costumes from the 18th and 19th centuries. Open 2 to 6pm every day except Tuesdays and bank holidays. Adults €2.60, free for under 18s and for everyone the first Sunday of the month.

Chauvigny   Musée de Traditions Populaires et
d'Archeologie   ☎ 05 49 46 35 45
A 16th century Poitevin house containing hairstyles, clothes and everyday objects from the 14th century. Open 15th June to 31st August Mondays to Fridays 10am to 12.30pm, 2.30 to 6.30pm, Saturdays and Sundays 2.30 to 6.30pm; 1st April to 14th June and 1st September to 31st October every day from 2 to 6pm. Adults €1.50, under 14s free.

Lussac-les-
Châteaux   Musée de Pré-histoire   ☎ 05 49 48 43 51
An exhibition of archaeological artefacts and objets d'art from the Palaeolithic period. Open February, March, October and November Sundays only 2 to 6pm; April to September Wednesdays to Sundays and bank holidays 10.30am to noon, 2 to 6pm (July and August until 6.30pm). Adults €3, under 18s free.

Poitiers   Musée Sainte Croix, 3bis rue Jean Jaurès ☎ 05 49 41 34 93
🖥 *www.musees-poitiers.org*
A museum illustrating the history of Poitou-Charentes from prehistoric times to the present day. Fine arts, archaeology, ethnology and a variety of exhibitions throughout the year. Adults €3.50, free for under 18s and for everyone on Tuesdays and the first Sunday of the month.

Parks, Gardens & Forests

Couhé   Les Iles de Payré   ☎ 05 49 59 10 55
(north of Couhé, on the N10)
A 22ha (55-acre) site with miniature port, electric karts, golf,

swimming, fishing, picnic areas and an open air café June to the end of August. Free access all year round.

Loudun	**Jardin Botanique**	☎ 05 49 98 15 96

Botanical garden around the ancient ramparts of the château. Route signposted and explanations given along the way. Open all year round and free access.

Lusignan	**Promenade de Blossac**	☎ 05 49 43 61 21

An 18th century French garden within the site of the château of Lusignan. Open all year, free access.

Smarves	**Les Bois de Saint Pierre**	☎ 05 49 88 54 77

(just off the D741 Gençay to Poitiers road)
250ha (600 acres) of forest to walk or cycle through, with trails throughout. There's pony trekking, crazy golf, an outdoor swimming pool (open July and August), a picnic area and a snack bar. An animal park is open 10am to 12.15pm, 2 to 7pm (till 4.45pm October to April inclusive) with free entrance.

Zoos & Wildlife Parks

Champagne St Hilare	**Le Haras de Saint Hilaire**	☎ 05 49 37 33 72

A 100ha (250-acre) stud owned by Edmond de Rothschild, where you can see some of his 100 trotting horses, their stables and training centre and a forge. Two-hour guided tours from 1st May to 30th September weekends at 2.30pm. Adults €7, 6 to 12-year-olds €4.

Chauvigny	**Les Géants du Ciel, Château des Aigles**	☎ 05 49 46 47 48

Eagles, falcons, condors, multi-coloured toucans and kookaburras. March to November falconry displays at 2.30 and 4pm plus 11.15am and 5.30pm weekends and bank holidays; July and August every day at 11.15am, 2.30pm, 4pm and 5.30pm. Show lasts 45 minutes. Adults €8, 5 to 12-year-olds €5.

La Trimouille	**L'Ile aux Serpents**	☎ 05 49 91 23 45

🖳 *www.ileauxserpents.com*
'Snake Island', with crocodiles, iguanas, tortoises and other reptiles as well as snakes. Open July and August 10am to 6pm; 1st December to end February 2 to 6pm; rest of the year 10am to noon, 2 to 6pm (closed bank holidays). Adults €7, children €5.

Linazay	**Cabrilia**	☎ 05 49 87 01 02

🖳 *www.cabrilia.com*
The world of goats: a wide variety of different breeds and a 300m² exhibition explaining their care and breeding, their milk and cheese, the history of goat farming and the technologies involved. Mid-June to mid-September, every day 10am to 7pm; April to mid-June and mid-September to the end of October,

Sundays, school holidays and bank holidays 10am to 6pm.
Adults €7, children €4.

Loudun   Aquarium, boulevard Maréchal Leclerc ☎ 05 49 22 34 01
Exotic fish from Africa, America and Asia. June to September
10.30am to noon, 3 to 7.15pm. Weekends 11am to 1pm, 3 to
8pm; October to May Wednesdays and Thursdays 2.30 to
6.30pm, Fridays 6 to 11pm and weekends 11am to noon, 2 to
6.30pm. Adults €4; 10 to 16-year-olds €2.50; six to ten-year-
olds €1.50.

Romagne   La Vallée des Singes   ☎ 05 49 87 20 20
💻 *www.la-vallee-des-singes.fr*
'Monkey Valley', a unique monkey park, with over 25 species of
primate and 250 other animals in a natural environment. Open
mid-March to September 10am to 6pm (till 7pm July and
August; till 5pm October and November). Adults €9, 5 to 12-
year-olds €6.

Vaux-en-Couhé   La Ferme des Autruches Gueffé   ☎ 05 49 87 72 29
Ostrich farm including an explanation of the birds and breeding
and farming methods and a shop selling ostrich meat, eggs
and leather products. Open April to June and September
weekends, bank holidays and holidays 2 to 6pm; July and
August every day 10am to noon, 1.30 to 6pm. Adults €3, 10 to
16-year-olds €2, under 10s free.

Miscellaneous

General   The vineyards of Haut-Poitou have 20 centuries of history, the
land and the traditions having been passed down from father to
son. There's a marked wine route, la Route des Vins, of which
details can be obtained from the Cave du Haut-Poitou, Poitou
(see below).

Cenon-sur-   Mini Port   ☎ 05 49 21 33 07
Vienne   Four-person electric boats for hire on the river. Mid-May to mid-
September Sundays and bank holidays 2 to 6pm; July and
August every day 2 to 6pm. €10.50 for half an hour, €32 for two
hours.

Charroux   Cité aux Trésors   ☎ 05 49 87 60 12
A thriving medieval village with timbered houses and a central
covered market. L'Abbaye Saint Sauveur, one of the largest
Benedictine abbeys in the western world, with the distinctive
Charlemagne Tower at its centre, was of major importance in
medieval times. In the summer there are painters in the streets
and on market day (Thursday) the pavements, cafes and
market stalls are bustling with activity.

Hippodrome   ☎ 05 49 87 60 12
Horse and trap racing in the summer.

Chasseneuil-du-Poitou	**Futuroscope** ☎ 05 49 49 59 06	

Chasseneuil-du-Poitou — **Futuroscope** ☎ 05 49 49 59 06
💻 *www.planete-futuroscope.com*
One of France's most popular attractions, with a variety of 'rides' including one through 'outer space'. Open high season from 9am to end of evening spectacular, low season 9am to 6pm. Closed from mid-November to mid-February.Prices vary with the season: adults €21 to €30, children €16 to €22. Evening tickets available in the summer from 6pm: adults €15, children €9.

Châtellerault — **Chocolaterie Henri IV, 26 avenue de M. Leclerc** ☎ 05 49 23 40 20
This master chocolate maker allows you to enter the world of chocolate, discover the history of chocolate-making in the region and see the transformation of cocoa into the finished product. Tasting and shop. By appointment all year round 9am to noon, 2.30 to 7pm. Three price 'formulas': 'traditional' €2.20, 'historic' €2.70, 'tasting and history' €3.70.

Chauvigny — **Le Vélo-Rail, rue de La Folie** ☎ 05 49 41 08 28
An unusual way to see the countryside, by cycling along a railway line on specially designed platforms. March, April and October 2 to 6pm; July and August 10am to 9pm; May, June and September 2 to 7pm; November 1 to 5pm. Booking recommended in the summer months. €20 for two hours, €22 in July and August. Minimum age four.

Lavausseau — **La Cité des Tanneurs, place de la Mairie** ☎ 05 49 43 77 67
A tannery that uses traditional methods, with an explanation of its history. Guided tours from 2nd May to 15th November: Tuesdays to Saturdays at 2.30pm, Sundays and bank holidays at 2.30pm and 4.30pm. Adults €5, children €3.50, under 7s free.

Le Vigeant — **Circuit du Val de Vienne** ☎ 05 49 48 86 38
💻 *www.circuit-valdevienne.com*
(east of Civray)
A 3,757m racetrack that hosts a wide range of motor sport events – one of the six best tracks in France.

Montmorillon — **Cité de l'Ecrit**
💻 *www.citedelecrit-montmorillon.com*
This is an area of Montmorillon to the west of the main square, overlooked by the Eglise Notre-Dame, where many shops are dedicated to books – new and second-hand – and there are book-related craft workshops. The shops themselves are old and characterful.

Poitou — **Cave du Haut-Poitou, 32 rue Plault, Neuville-du-Poitou** ☎ 05 49 51 21 65
(north-west of Poitiers)

Open Mondays to Saturdays 9am to noon, 2 to 7pm, Sundays 9am to 12.30pm.

Romagne	Le Labyrinthe Végétal	☎ 05 49 87 45 27

A 7ha (17-acre) maize maze. Open Tuesdays to Saturdays from 5th July to 31st August 10am to 7pm. Adults €6, 6 to 15-year-olds €5.

Sanxay   Gallo-Romain de Sanxay, route
                de Ménigoute   ☎ 05 49 53 61 48
Built in the second century, this theatre could seat 6,500 people. Its remains, along with those of a temple and baths, are open 1st September to 30th April Tuesdays to Sundays 10am to 12.30pm, 2 to 5.30pm; May and June daily 9.30am to 12.30pm, 2 to 6.30pm; July and August daily 9.30am to 6.30pm. Guided tours available.

Voulême   Moulin de l'Etourneau   ☎ 05 49 87 44 71
A working mill that produces walnut oil and bread flour. Guided tours by appointment. €2.25 for adults, free for children, just south-west of Civray.

Professional Services

Accountants

Poitiers   Charon-Saurois, 30 boulevard Solférino ☎ 05 49 01 83 56
Has an English-speaking accountant.

Solicitors & Notaires

The following office has an English-speaking *notaire*.

Poitiers   Résidence Cordeliers, 3 rue
                Paul Guillon   ☎ 05 49 88 10 11

Religion

Anglican Services In English

Magné   Holy communion in the parish church of St Médard
                (near Gençay)
Third Sunday in the month (November to March at the Salle de Réunion, St Nicholas de Civray) at 10.30am. Contact the Chaplain, the Reverend Michael Hepper, 19 avenue René Baillargeon, Civray (☎ 05 49 97 04 21) for details.

Evangelical Churches

Châtellerault	Centre Chrétien, Le Pautron	☎ 05 49 93 52 56
Montmorillon-	Eglise Protestante Evangélique, 5 rue Nouvelle	☎ 05 49 91 06 33
Poitiers	Eglise Chrétienne de Poitiers, 11 place Charles de Gaulle	☎ 05 49 50 07 61

Protestant Churches

Châtellerault	Eglise Réformée de Châtellerault, 1 rue Adrienne Duchemin	☎ 05 49 21 08 56
Poitiers	Eglise Reformé Protestante, 5 rue des Ecossais	☎ 05 49 41 12 91
	Eglise Protestante Baptiste, 47 rue Condorcet	☎ 05 49 41 62 33
St Sauvant	Pasteur, 9 rue Temple, St Sauvant (south-west of Poitiers on the Deux-Sèvres border)	☎ 05 49 59 70 32

Synagogues

La Rochelle	Maison Communautaire Israélite, 40 cours Dames (in Charente-Maritime)	☎ 05 46 41 17 66

Restaurants

Angles-sur-l'Anglin	Lyon d'Or, route de Vicq	☎ 05 49 48 32 53

Within a hotel this restaurant is tucked away in a beautiful village. Set menus from €15 to €30. Closed Monday and Tuesday lunchtimes and annually in January and February.

Châtellerault	Arlequin, 1 rue de Cheval Blanc	☎ 05 49 21 74 28

(tucked away between the main street and the river)
Specialities of Italian pasta and desserts. Set menus from €9.70 to €14.90 Take-away service available. Closed Sundays.

Auberge du Lac, 53 avenue Camille Pagé   ☎ 05 49 21 59 54
Beef a speciality. Set menus from €12.50 to €34. Closed Sunday evenings, all day Mondays and for two weeks in February and four weeks in July and August.

La Boîte à Crêpes, rue des Mignons   ☎ 05 49 21 35 69
Crêperie closed Sunday evenings and all day Mondays.

La Charmille, 74 boulevard Blossac   ☎ 05 49 93 33 00
Within a three-star hotel this restaurant has a €10.50 menu of
the day and gourmet menus from €22 to €45, including
vegetarian options. Closed Saturday lunchtimes, Sunday
evenings and all day Mondays.

Les Trois Daguets, 1 rue St Exupéry   ☎ 05 49 19 44 00
Regional and traditional cuisine. English spoken.

L'Univers, 4 avenue George Clémenceau   ☎ 05 49 21 23 53
(in the centre of the town)
Open every day for lunch and dinner. Set menus from €15 to
€35.

Civray   Auberge de Civray, route de Limoges   ☎ 05 49 87 01 11
Menus from €12 to €15. Closed Sunday evenings.

Hôtel de Commerce, 5 rue du
Pont des Barnes   ☎ 05 49 97 03 97
Menus from €10 to €23.

Gençay   Le Vieux Château, route de Poitiers   ☎ 05 49 36 01 55
Traditional cuisine with a lunchtime menu at €8.90 and evening
menus from €10 to €38. Children's menu €7. Parking in the
supermarket car park opposite.

La Trimouille   Terre des Andes, place du Champ de
Foire   ☎ 05 49 91 60 44
Open lunchtimes Sundays to Fridays. Monday to Friday lunch
menu from €9.50. For Sunday lunch a seafood platter is
available with dessert for €23, which must be booked at least
four days in advance.

Le Vigeant   La Grimolée, Port de Salles   ☎ 05 49 48 75 22
Relaxing surroundings while you enjoy the creative and
authentic cuisine offered by this three-star hotel.

Linazay   Le Clos de La Borderie, Cabrilia   ☎ 05 49 87 75 47
(within the Cabrilia complex, exit Linazay off the N10)
Regional and traditional cuisine.

La Sirène, Le Bourg   ☎ 05 49 87 75 38
British-run fish and chip shop. Open Thursdays 5 to 10pm,
Fridays and Saturdays noon to 3pm, 5 to 10pm.

Loudun   Le Crapouillot, 1 place de La
Poulaillerie   ☎ 05 49 98 28 46
Crêperie and grill with a large *à la carte* menu. Closed
Mondays.

Hostellerie de la Roue d'Or,
1 avenue d'Anjou   ☎ 05 49 98 01 23
Award-winning restaurant, with private parking and
accommodation. Set menus from €13 to €34.50. Closed all day
Saturday and Sunday evenings.

L'Indochine, 19 rue Porte de Chinon   ☎ 05 49 98 67 09
Chinese, Vietnamese and Thai cuisine. Lunch menus from
€9.90 to €13. Closed Wednesdays.

Le Ricordeau, place de La Boeuffeterie   ☎ 05 49 22 67 27
(in the centre of the town)
Set menus from €14.45 to €31.90. Closed Sunday evenings
and Mondays out of season and for a week in February.

Montmorillon   Le Bistrot, 4 boulevard de Strasbourg   ☎ 05 49 84 09 09
(alongside the Hôtel de France)
Set menu €13.50. Open Sunday evenings to Saturday
lunchtimes.

Bonheurs d'Asie, 39 boulevard Gambetta   ☎ 05 49 84 01 19
Chinese, Vietnamese and Thai cuisine. Closed Mondays.

Crêperie du Brouard, 1 rue Montebello   ☎ 05 49 91 18 61
This *crêperie* offers shaded dining beside the river. Closed
Mondays.

Restaurant Pakistanais, place du
Maréchal Leclerc   ☎ 05 49 83 08 36
(on the first floor, beside the tourist office in the town centre)
Set menus at €8.50 and €13 as well as *à la carte* and
vegetarian options.

Le Lucullus, 4 boulevard de Strasbourg ☎ 05 49 84 09 09
Within the Hôtel de France, this restaurant offers refined
cuisine based on regional and seasonal produce. Set menus
from €22 to €45, including a vegetarian menu. Closed Sunday
evenings and all day Mondays. Booking advisable.

Le Minaret, 10 place Haut-Poitou   ☎ 05 49 91 27 43
(set back opposite Hyper U on the outskirts of the town)
Moroccan cuisine. Closed Mondays and Tuesdays. Take-away
service available.

Le Pont de Bois, 2 rue Puits Chausés   ☎ 05 49 91 14 30
(in the old town)
Brasserie serving traditional cuisine, open lunchtimes
Tuesdays to Saturdays, evenings by appointment.

Le Roman des Saveurs, 2 rue Montbello   ☎ 05 49 91 52 06
Set menus from €13.50 to €25. Open lunchtimes from noon
and evenings from 7.30pm. Closed Sunday evenings.

Poitiers

L'Aquarium, 2 rue de La Croix Blanche ☎ 05 49 88 92 33
This fish restaurant is open Mondays to Saturdays with set
menus starting at €14.

Buffalo Grill, Chasseneuil-du-Poitou   ☎ 05 49 62 56 58
(in the large retail park north of Poitiers)
A reliable steak house-style restaurant – part of a nationwide
chain.

Château du Clos de La Ribaudière,
10 place du Champ de Foire,
Chasseneuil-du-Poitou   ☎ 05 49 52 86 66
(just north of Poitiers)
A gastronomic restaurant in a beautiful hotel with set menus
from €28 to €47.

Chinois Shanghai, 23 avenue de
Bordeaux, Jaunay Clan   ☎ 05 49 52 05 60
(off the N10 near Futuroscope)
A Chinese restaurant. Lunchtime menus from €10 and evening
menus from €13.50.

La Dent Creuse, 185 faubourg du
Pont Neuf   ☎ 05 49 46 69 61
Traditional French cuisine. A wide range of set menus starting
at €9. Closed Sundays.

La Fibule d'Eden, 185 Grand' Rue   ☎ 05 49 41 48 46
Moroccan and Mediterranean cuisine with oriental dancing
Friday evenings. Open Tuesdays to Sundays.

L'Istanbul, 14 place Charles de Gaulle ☎ 05 49 41 02 78
A Turkish restaurant open every lunchtime and evening.

Le Marrakech, 9 boulevard Pont Achard ☎ 05 49 58 52 20
(opposite the station)
Indian restaurant. Open every day until 10.30pm. Take-away
service available.

Le Poitevin, 76 rue Carnot   ☎ 05 49 88 35 04
Fine, regional cuisine. Set menus from €10 to €35.

La Serrurerie, 28 rue des Grandes Écoles ☎ 05 49 41 05 14
This bistro is open every lunchtime and evening, with 'brunch'
served from 11.30am to 3pm at weekends for those who like to
faire la grasse matinée.

La Tartignolle, 2 rue des Quatre Roues   ☎ 05 49 88 75 48
Traditional French cuisine. Set menus from €18 to €29. Closed
Sundays and Mondays.

La Taverne de Maître Kantes
24 rue Carnot   ☎ 05 49 50 10 80
(opposite the Hôtel de Ville)
One of the few restaurants in the town serving food
continuously from noon to midnight.

St Macoux   Le Dravir, Comporté   ☎ 05 49 87 31 95
(between St Saviol and St Macoux)
A hotel and restaurant on the banks of the river with a varied
menu, including vegetarian.

Savigné   Relais du Pays Civraisien, route de
               Limoges   ☎ 05 49 87 75 75
(just east of Civray)
Regional cuisine using local produce. Closed Thursday
evenings.

Verrières   Le Comme Chez Soi, place du Champ
               de Foire   ☎ 05 49 42 05 44
Traditional regional cuisine with set menus from €12.50 to €29.
Open lunchtimes and evenings from Tuesday to Sunday
lunchtime. Closed for a week in both March and September.
English spoken.

Rubbish & Recycling

Metal Collection

Chauvigny   Camille Moginer, Charron   ☎ 05 49 46 45 58
(directly east of Poitiers)

Poitiers   Bonnin Ets, 55 rue Poitiers,
               Migné Auxances   ☎ 05 49 51 71 73

Shopping

Alcohol

Châtellerault Cave du Roc, 16 place Croix Rouge   ☎ 05 49 21 76 17

Civray   Cave Languedoc, 2 place Gambetta   ☎ 05 49 03 27 11
Next to the estate agent's and easy to miss.

| Loudun | Les Bonnes Caves, 4 place Porte de Chinon | ☎ 05 49 98 55 99 |

| Montmorillon | Le Pressoir, place Haut Poitou | ☎ 05 49 91 29 15 |

(opposite Hyper U on the outskirts of town)
Open Tuesdays to Saturdays 9.30am to 12.30pm, 2.30 to 7pm.

| Poitiers | La Cave du Grand Large, 62 avenue du 11 novembre | ☎ 05 49 03 12 00 |

Architectural Antiques

| Chail | Les Vielles Pierres du Mellois, Les Cerizat | ☎ 05 49 29 31 23 |

(on the D948 Melle to Sauzé-Vaussais road)
Specialises in old building materials: mainly stone, but there's a large selection of reclaimed timbers in the far corner as you enter from the back.

| L'Hôtellerie-De-Flée | BCA Matériaux Anciens, route de Craon (in Maine-et-Loire) | ☎ 02 33 94 74 00 |

🖥 *www.bca-recyclage.com*
Antique floor tiles, oak beams and wooden flooring, architectural antiques and other reclaimed building materials, as well as re-sawn beams. Fluent English spoken.

| Naintré | Tavares | ☎ 05 49 90 15 32 |

(on the ZI near the A10; take the exit for Châtellerault Sud)

Building Materials

| Châtellerault | Brico Depot | ☎ 05 49 62 92 76 |

(on the N10 between Châtellerault and Futuroscope)
A large depot used by tradesman and private individuals.

| Civray | Pinault, route Niort, St Pierre d'Exideuil | ☎ 05 49 87 03 11 |

| Loudun | Point P, avenue Coopération | ☎ 05 49 98 00 09 |

🖥 *www.pointp.fr*

| Montmorillon | Big Mat, ZI Est, route de La Trimouille | ☎ 05 49 91 21 39 |

| Poitiers | Lepeyre, avenue de Paris | ☎ 05 49 00 47 10 |

🖥 *www.pepeyre.fr*
Sells everything from ready-made staircases to cement and screws.

Camping & Caravanning

| Auxances | Azur 86, avenue Châtellerault, Migné | ☎ 05 49 62 50 10 |

(just north-west of Poitiers)

A permanent display of caravans. Servicing and repairs available.

Department Stores

Poitiers   Au Printemps de Paris, 14 place
                  Maréchal Leclerc   ☎ 05 49 55 56 57
                  (in the city centre, near the theatre and Hôtel de Ville)
                  Open Mondays to Saturdays 9.30am to 7pm.

DIY

Châtellerault   Mr Bricolage, ZI Sanital   ☎ 05 49 02 35 10

Civray   Brico Marché, route Limoges, Savigné   ☎ 05 49 97 01 01

Loudun   Weldom, 17bis 19 boulevard
                  Loche et Matras   ☎ 05 49 09 00 08

Montmorillon   Mr Bricolage, 25 avenue de l'Europe   ☎ 05 49 84 00 04

Poitiers   Leroy Merlin, Chasseneuil-du-Poitou   ☎ 05 49 62 81 81
                  (on the retail park just south of Futuroscope on the N10)
                  This is a large store selling DIY materials and equipment,
                  furnishings, bathroom and kitchen fittings, and plants and
                  gardening equipment. Open Mondays to Saturdays 9am
                  to 8pm.

Fabrics

Châtellerault   Tiss'Affaires, 6 rue Alexandre Rivière   ☎ 05 49 21 84 62
                  (on a side street between the river and boulevard Blossac)

Montmorillon   Tapisserie-Decoration, boulevard
                  de Strasbourg   ☎ 05 49 91 27 54
                  Curtains and furnishings hand-made in this small workshop.
                  Fabric swatches available.

Poitiers   Mondial Tissus, Chasseneuil-du-Poitou ☎ 05 49 61 29 26
                  (on the retail park north of the city on the N10)
                  A large fabric store.

Frozen Food

Poitiers   Picard Surgelés, 1 route Gençay   ☎ 05 49 56 54 05

                  Thiriet Glaces, 10 rue du Commerce,
                  Chasseneuil-du-Poitou   ☎ 05 49 30 36 27

Garden Centres

Châtellerault   Jardinerie Auban Lélias, Naintré   ☎ 05 49 23 12 76
(just south of the Auchan retail park on the N10)

Loudun   Gamm Vert, 13 avenue Anjou   ☎ 05 49 22 48 06
(in the north of the town, on the road to Saumur)

Montmorillon   Robin Jardinerie,
1 boulevard Terrier Blanc   ☎ 05 49 91 08 64
(on the left as you leave Montmorillon in the direction of La Trimouille)
Open Mondays 2 to 7pm (6pm in winter), Tuesdays to Saturdays 9.30am to noon, 2 to 7pm (6pm in winter).

Poitiers   Vive le Jardin, 3 rue de Châlons   ☎ 05 49 61 19 49
(on the ring road east near the Parc des Expositions)
Open Mondays to Saturdays 9am to noon, 2 to 7pm, Sundays 10am to noon, 2.30 to 6.30pm.

Kitchens & Bathrooms

Poitiers   Lapeyre, avenue de Paris   ☎ 05 49 00 47 10
🖳 *www.lapeyre.fr*
DIY store with kitchen and bathroom fittings and furniture.

Mobalpa Poitou Concept, les Portes du
Futur, 56 allée du Haut Poitou   ☎ 05 49 30 07 09
🖳 *www.mobalpa.com*
(north of the city)
Bathrooms and kitchens.

Markets

Angles-sur-
l'Anglin   Saturdays and Sundays.

Availles-
Limouzine   Thursdays, with a fair on the 17th of each month.

Charroux   Thursdays, with a fair the first Saturday of the month.

Châtellerault   Tuesdays, Wednesdays and Thursdays, and a Thursday fair at boulevard Blossac.

Chauvigny   Tuesdays, Thursdays and Saturdays, with a fair the second Tuesday of the month.

Civray   Large market on Tuesdays closing off the centre of the town to traffic, and a smaller one on Fridays. A fair on the first Tuesday of the month.

Gençay	Thursdays, with a fair on the second and last Thursday of the month.
Isle Jourdain	Tuesdays, Fridays and Saturdays, with a fair on the 20th of each month.
La Roche-Posay	Main market on Tuesdays with smaller, food markets on Wednesdays, Fridays and Saturdays. The fair is on the 9th of each month from November to March and on the 10th from April to October.
Loudun	Main market on Tuesdays, smaller ones on Fridays and Saturdays and a fair the first and third Mondays of the month.
Montmorillon	Saturdays and Wednesdays, with a fair on the fourth Wednesday of each month.
Poitiers	Saturdays at place Notre-Dame-la-Grande, Sundays and Wednesdays at Zup des Couronneries, Tuesdays at Place Notre-Dame and Bellejouanne, Thursdays at place Notre-Dame and au Clos Gaultier, and Friday afternoons at rue Magenta.
Tournon-St-Martin	Tuesday and Friday mornings, with a fair on the third Tuesday of each month.

Music

Loudun	La Pibole, rue de La Porte de Chinon ☎ 05 49 22 47 99 Open Tuesdays, Wednesdays, Fridays and Saturdays.

Organic Food

Châtellerault	Le Pois Tout Vert, avenue Camille Pagé ☎ 05 49 02 71 41
Poitiers	Espace Nature, centre Géant ☎ 05 49 01 92 37 (on the east side of the city) Plants, cosmetics and other organic products. Open all day, closing at 7pm.

Second-Hand Goods

Civray	La Sigalière, 30 avenue René Baillargeon ☎ 05 49 87 24 19 Open Tuesdays, Thursdays, Fridays and Saturdays, and afternoons of the second and third Sundays of the month.
	Paul Priou Brocante, 10 rue du Commerce ☎ 05 49 97 05 86

Montmorillon   Dépôt Vente de la Gartempe,
                9 rue de la Fuie   ☎ 05 49 91 20 10

Poitiers   Futurotroc, 11 rue du Commerce,
                Chasseneuil-du-Poitou   ☎ 05 49 52 08 88
                (north of the city)

                La Trocante, 24 boulevard Grand Cerf   ☎ 05 49 60 77 55
                (near the station)
                Tuesdays to Saturdays 10am to noon, 2 to 7pm, Sundays and
                bank holidays 3 to 7pm.

Sports Goods

Châtellerault   Intersport, 11 rue Pierre Pleignard   ☎ 05 49 85 44 56

Loudun   Twinner Sports, 4 avenue Coopération   ☎ 05 49 98 18 36

Montmorillon   Intersport, 52 boulevard de Strasbourg ☎ 05 49 91 02 17
                Open Tuesdays to Saturdays.

Poitiers   Décathlon, centre Commercial Auchan,
                Chasseneuil-du-Poitou   ☎ 05 49 52 80 11
                💻 www.decathlon.fr
                (north of the city)

Supermarkets & Hypermarkets

Montmorillon   Hyper U, avenue de Provence   ☎ 05 49 84 08 40
                Open Mondays to Saturdays 8.30am to 7.30pm (till 8pm on
                Fridays).
                In the foyer is a dry cleaner's, post office, florist's, electrical
                store, hairdresser's, newsagent's, chemist's, café, cash
                machine, photo booth and battery recycling unit.

Poitiers   Auchan, Chasseneuil-du-Poitou   ☎ 05 49 90 36 36
                (alongside Futuroscope)
                Open until 10pm Mondays to Saturdays.

                Leclerc, 93 route Gençay   ☎ 05 49 42 20 00
                (off the south ring road, in the St Benoît area of Poitiers)
                Open Mondays to Saturdays 9am to 8.30pm.

                Géant, 2 avenue Lafayette, Centre
                Commercial Beaulieu   ☎ 05 49 44 84 00
                (just off the ring road in the east)
                Mondays to Fridays 9am to 8.30pm, Saturdays 9am to
                9.30pm.

Swimming Pool Equipment

Montmorillon   Desjoyaux Vienne, route de Moulismes   ☎ 05 49 91 35 04
💻 *www.desjoyaux.fr*
Pool design, kit pools, products and accessories.

Poitiers   Hydrosud Soatec, Les Portes de
l'Auxances, Avenue Loge, Migné
Auxances   ☎ 05 49 36 03 60
(north-west of the city)
Construction, renovation, maintenance, products and accessories.

Azur Piscines 86, 8 rue Puy Joubert,
St Benoît   ☎ 05 49 46 14 67
(on the southern outskirts off the ring road)
Construction, renovation and maintenance.

Sports

This is just a selection of the activities available, the large towns having a wide range; full details are available from the tourist office or the Mairie.

Aerial Sports

Gliding & Hang-Gliding

Le Louroux   ☎ 02 47 65 43 13
(just north of Vienne)

Parachuting

Le Blanc   Centre Ecole Régional de Parachutisme,
Aérodrome, Le Blanc   ☎ 02 54 37 05 90
💻 *www.cerpco.com*
Open 1st February to 15th December.

Loudun   Aérodrome Veniers   ☎ 06 08 46 03 58
Solo and tandem jumps.

Poitiers   Parachute Club de Vienne   ☎ 05 49 58 25 81
Contact Mr Julienne.

Archery

Châtellerault   Les Archers, Salle de Tir à l'Arc,
La Manu   ☎ 05 49 21 41 19
(next to the Musée Auto-Moto)
Minimum age ten.

| Loudun | Cie des Archers | ☎ 05 49 90 25 81 |

| Poitiers | Les Archers de Poitiers Sud | ☎ 05 49 00 53 99 |
Contact Mr Bisserier.

Badminton

| Châtellerault | Gymnase Jean Mace | ☎ 05 49 02 44 18 |
Mondays 8 to 11pm, Thursdays 6.30 to 8.30pm.

Canoeing & Kayaking

| Châtellerault | Bonneuil-Matours | ☎ 05 49 85 20 47 |
(south of the town)
Canoes can be hired by the day (€16) or half day (€9.50).

| Civray | Camping les Aulnes, bord de la Charente | ☎ 05 49 87 17 24 |
Open from Easter to the end of October.

| Lathus | Centre de Plain-Air MJC 'La Voulzie' | ☎ 05 49 91 83 30 |
Permanent slalom course.

| Poitiers | Parc de St Cyr | ☎ 05 49 62 57 22 |
(just north of Poitiers on the N10)

Canoë Kayak Club Poitevin, avenue de Lorch, St Benoît   ☎ 05 49 52 98 64
Open Wednesdays and Saturdays all year; July and August every day.

Base Canoë Kayak, Moulin de Chasseigne, 47 boulevard Chasseigne   ☎ 05 49 88 84 48

Climbing

| Châtellerault | Club Alpin Français Section Poitou | ☎ 05 49 20 41 52 |
Meet at the gymnase of the Collège Descartes, boulevard Blossac.

| Lathus | Site du Roc d'Enfer, Lathus | ☎ 05 49 91 83 30 |
Open access to this site, 30 climbs of 10 to 20m.

| Le Blanc | Base de Plein Air, Le Blanc | ☎ 02 54 37 36 85 |
(just north of Vienne)
Individuals and groups. Booking required.

| Loudun | Near La Trésorerie | ☎ 05 49 98 29 55 |

| Poitiers | Gravite, 27 route de l'Ormeau, Buxerolles | ☎ 05 49 56 97 20 |

(just north of the city)
300m² of climbing area, including artificial walls and natural sites.
Individuals and group courses with qualified instructors.
Minimum age six.

Cycling

The Vienne Valley has a variety of marked trails, from 6 to 30km (4 to 19mi), for those on foot, horseback or mountain bike (*VTT*). A brochure giving details and the routes is available from tourist offices in the area. Local tourist offices also hold guide books and data sheets for ramblers.

| Brion | Centre d'Environnement Nordique de Brion, Les Pommeraies | ☎ 05 49 36 05 77 |

'Husky cycling' – a sport involving 'riding' a bike or tricycle while being pulled by dogs (!). Open every day 15th March to 20th December by appointment.

| Châtellerault | Avenir Cycliste Châtelleraudais | ☎ 05 49 23 17 94 |

Adults and over 12s meet at the place de l'Europe on Wednesdays at 2.15pm, 6 to 12-year-olds meet at the Parc Chillou d'Ozon on Saturdays at 2.15pm during term time.

| Civray | Cycle Amical Civraisien | ☎ 05 49 87 55 59 |

Contact Mr Moinet.

| Loudun | Cyclotourisme | ☎ 05 49 98 32 70 |

Non-competitive rides in the local area.

| Poitiers | Le Cycle Poitevinq | ☎ 05 49 00 58 20 |

Contact Mr Faugeroux.

Fencing

| Châtellerault | Salle Fernand Benoist, Le Manu | ☎ 05 49 85 94 80 |

(by the Musée Auto-Moto)
Minimum age seven.

Fishing

There's over 2,000km (1,250mi) of waterways for fishing in Vienne with facilities for both novice and experienced fishermen. Annual fishing permits (*cartes*) can be bought locally, e.g. at fishing tackle shops and *tabacs* close to fishing lakes (*étangs*). They also stock maps of local fishing sites and rivers. For further information contact:

| General | FDAAPPMA de Vienne, 178 rue Georges Guynemer, Poitiers | ☎ 05 49 37 66 60 |

Football

Football clubs can be found even in small villages; the *mairie* is the best place to obtain details of your nearest clubs.

Golf

La Roche-Posay Golf du Connétable, Parc Thermal   ☎ 05 49 86 25 10
🖳 *www.golfconnetable.free.fr*
This 18-hole, par 72, 6,014m course has narrow, winding fairways and dog's legs requiring both technical and tactical skill. Lessons, driving range, buggy hire, pro shop and clubhouse with a bar serving fast food. Closed the last two weeks in December and the first week in January. Green fees from €21 to €32.

Mignaloux-   Golf de Mignaloux-Beauvoir   ☎ 05 49 55 47 47
Beauvoir   🖳 *www.manoirdebeauvoir.com*
(east of Poitiers on the wooded Beauvoir estate)
This 18-hole, par 71, 6,032m course has wide fairways and is suitable for all levels. Lessons, driving range, four-hole beginners' course, buggy hire, pro shop and clubhouse. Open all year. Green fees from €29 to €37.

Roiffe   SAEM Golf de Loudun, Domaine
                  Saint Hilaire   ☎ 05 49 98 78 06
🖳 *www.france-in.com*
An 18-hole, par 72 course measuring 6,400m. Practice holes and both covered and open driving range, pro shop, buggy hire, clubhouse with bar and restaurant and a two-star hotel. Open all year: 9am to 6pm November to March, 9am to 7pm April, June, September and October and 8am to 8pm July and August. Green fees of €23 to €34 with special rates for couples and juniors.

St Cyr   Golf du Haut-Poitou   ☎ 05 49 62 53 62
(on the edge of the Saint Cyr lake and leisure park)
18-hole (par 73, 6,590m) and 9-hole courses designed by Harold J. Baker. The 9-hole course is ideal for beginners while the 18-hole course provides a varied game. Lessons, driving range, buggy hire, pro shop and clubhouse with both quick and gourmet restaurants. Open all year except 25th December and 1st January. Green fees for 18 holes from €25 to €37.

Horse Riding

The Vienne Valley has a variety of marked trails, from 6 to 30km (4 to 19mi), for those on foot, horseback or mountain bike (*VTT*). A brochure giving details and the routes is available from tourist offices in the area. Local tourist offices also hold guide books and data sheets for ramblers.

Châtellerault   l'Eperon, Naintré   ☎ 05 49 90 27 61

(just south of the town)
Open all year from 8am to noon, 2 to 8pm.

Civray	Ferme Equestre des Boutiers, Lizant	☎ 05 49 87 65 39

Hacking, lessons, week courses and night time rides in the
summer. Open all year.

Loudun	Poney Club de la Buissonniere, Monts-sur-Guenes	☎ 05 49 22 85 18

(just south-east of the town)
Open all year for rides in the forest or lessons in the indoor
riding school.

Montmorillon	Centre Equestre, rue St Nicolas	☎ 05 49 91 01 52

Open September to June.

Poitiers	Centre Equestre Municipal, 1 route de Chauvigny	☎ 05 49 46 28 38

Lessons by the hour, courses and stabling. Open Mondays to
Saturdays, for adults and children.

Ice Skating

Châtellerault	La Manu	☎ 05 49 21 09 40

Open 1st October to mid-May each year. There's an ice hockey
club at this rink.

Poitiers	54 avenue Jacques Cœur	☎ 05 49 46 26 68

Open mid-September to Mid-May. Adults €4.50, children €3.05.

Martial Arts

Châtellerault	Dojo Municipal	☎ 05 49 20 14 07

(various locations)
Minimum age four.

Civray	Judo Club de Civray	☎ 05 49 87 36 07
Loudun	Judo Club Loudunais, Gymnase du Stade	☎ 05 49 98 53 11

Tuesday, Wednesday and Friday evenings.

Montmorillon	Judo Club, 3 Grand' Rue	☎ 05 49 91 24 81
Poitiers	Judo Club du Poitou, 16 rue Victor Hugo	☎ 05 49 62 57 02

Judo, karate and ju-jitsu. Minimum age six.

Off-Roading

Availles	Centre Tout Terrain des Beaupinières	☎ 05 49 48 50 90

Limouzine   Drive a 4x4 Land Rover on a demanding 40km circuit. Open all
                   year. Booking required.

Potholing

Châtellerault   Spéléo-Club Châtelleraudais,
                   15 rue de La Gornière   ☎ 05 49 22 49 72
                   Beginners and training in alpine potholing techniques, with
                   outings to caves all over France.

Le Blanc   Base de Plein Air   ☎ 02 54 37 36 85
                   (just north of Vienne)

Rowing

Châtellerault   Société Nautique,15 rue Charlotte
                   Perdrige   ☎ 05 49 21 01 97
                   1st July to 15 August at Plan d'Eau de La Gornière, 1 rue Henri
                   Boucher. Every day from 2 to 4pm and Saturdays also 9am to
                   noon.

Poitiers   Comité Départemental Aviron 86 ☎ 05 49 21 01 97
                   Contact Mr Leclerc.

Scuba Diving

Châtellerault   Cap'taine Nemo, La Piscine,
                   21 rue Abbé Lalanne   ☎ 05 49 90 06 73
                   Minimum age ten.

Poitiers   Remora – Club Poitiers   ☎ 05 49 88 87 40
                   Contact Mr Garborit.

                   La Plongée, 123 route Poitiers, St Benoît ☎ 05 49 45 06 26

Shooting

Châtellerault   La Manu   ☎ 05 49 85 95 83
                   (by the Musée Auto-Moto)
                   10m, 25m and 50m ranges.

Loudun   'La Populaire', Carrière de St Leger   ☎ 05 49 22 40 83

Poitiers   France Liberté – Tir Olympique Poitevin,
                   Halle de Sports, 39 route de la Cassette ☎ 05 49 43 73 86

Snooker, Pool & Billiards

General   Some bars listed under **Bars & Nightlife** on page 276 also
                   have billiards, pool or snooker tables.

| Poitiers | Billard Club Pictave, 119 avenue Nantes ☎ 05 49 58 65 74
French billiards. |

Squash

| Poitiers | Association Squash Club 86, route
de Chauvigny, Mignaloux-Beauvoir ☎ 05 49 44 01 37
(east of Poitiers)
Six courts. |

Swimming

| Châtellerault | Centre Aquatique, 'La Piscine',
rue Aimé Rasseteau ☎ 05 49 21 14 83
Water park open all year with a 'lazy river', 65m toboggan run,
three pools, a sauna, solarium and café. |

| | Naintré ☎ 05 49 90 03 65
A conventional indoor pool. |

| Civray | place du 14 juillet ☎ 05 49 87 03 62
Outdoor pool with aqua gym, scuba diving and waterpolo sessions.
Open June to August inclusive. |

| Loudun | rue Roches ☎ 05 49 98 14 92
Indoor pool. |

| | boulevard 8 Mai 1945 ☎ 05 49 98 13 77
Outdoor pool. Aqua gym, lessons and a swimming club. |

| Montmorillon | Piscine Municipale, 21 avenue
Fernand Tribot ☎ 05 49 91 03 73
25m covered water slide, spa, indoor and outdoor pools,
solarium and a bar. Open all year, except one week at both
Easter and Christmas. |

| Poitiers | Piscine de La Ganterie, rue de La
Ganterie ☎ 05 49 46 27 28
Indoor pool open all year. |

Tennis

| Châtellerault | Stade Montée Rouge, 89 avenue Stades ☎ 05 49 23 41 41
Open all year. Court hire from €7.90 per hour. Week's courses
available in summer (☎ 05 49 85 95 83). |

| Civray | Tennis Club du Pays Civraisien ☎ 05 49 87 13 33 |

| Loudun | Tennis Club de Loudun ☎ 05 49 98 06 11
Two indoor and four outdoor courts. |

| Montmorillon | Tennis Club de Montmorillon, rue des Tennis | ☎ 05 49 91 22 46 |

Three outdoor and three indoor courts. Open 9.30am to 10pm Mondays to Saturdays and 9.30am to 7pm Sundays. Group and individual lessons available.

| Poitiers | Halle Tennis, rue Devinère | ☎ 05 49 47 02 06 |

Waterskiing

| l'Isle Jourdain | Lac de Chardes | ☎ 05 49 48 70 50 |

Every day in July and August.

Waterpolo

| Châtellerault | La Piscine, 21 rue Abbé Lalanne | ☎ 05 49 85 95 83 |

| Civray | place du 14 juillet | ☎ 05 49 87 03 62 |

Outdoor pool with water polo sessions. Open June to August inclusive.

| Loudun | ASNL Natation | ☎ 05 49 98 14 92 |

(at the municipal pool on boulevard 8 Mai 1945 – see **Swimming** above)

Tourist Offices

| General | Comité Départmental du Tourisme, La Maison du Tourisme, 33 place Charles de Gaulle, Poitiers | ☎ 05 49 37 48 48 |
| | Comité Régional du Tourisme | ☎ 05 49 50 10 50 |

🖳 *www.poitou-charentes.vacances.com*

| Châtellerault | 2 avenue Treuille | ☎ 05 49 21 05 47 |

🖳 *www.agglo-pays-chatelleraudais.fr*
(on the corner of boulevard Blossac)
Saturdays all year 9am to 12.15pm, 2 to 6pm. Easter to mid-September Mondays to Fridays 9am to 12.30pm, 1.30 to 7pm. mid-September to Easter Mondays to Fridays 10am to 12.15pm, 2 to 6pm.

| Civray | place Maréchal Leclerc | ☎ 05 49 87 47 73 |

June to October Mondays to Saturdays 10am to noon, 2 to 6pm; November to May Tuesdays and Saturdays 9.30am to12.30pm, 2 to 6pm.

| Loudun | 2 rue des Marchands | ☎ 05 49 98 15 96 |

Summer: Mondays to Saturdays 9am to 12.15pm, 2 to 7pm,

Sundays 3 to 7pm. Out of season: Mondays 2.30 to 6.30pm,
Tuesdays to Saturdays 9.15am to 12.15pm, 2.30 to 6.30pm.
Closed bank holidays all year round.

Montmorillon   2 place du Maréchal Leclerc   ☎ 05 49 91 11 96
Open mid-September to mid-June Mondays to Saturdays
10am to noon, 2 to 6pm; 15th June to 15th September
Mondays to Saturdays 9.30 to 1pm, 2 to 6.30pm, Sundays and
bank holidays 3 to 6pm.

Poitiers   45 place Charles de Gaulle   ☎ 05 49 41 21 24
🖳 *www.ot-poitiers.fr*
Open mid-June to mid-September Mondays to Saturdays
9.30am to 11pm, Sundays and bank holidays 10am to 6pm,
7.30 to 11pm; mid-September to mid-June Mondays to
Saturdays 10am to 6pm, closed Sundays and bank holidays.

Tradesmen

Architects & Project Managers

General   Adams Gautier Poitou-Charentes   ☎ 05 49 64 42 96
🖳 *www.adamsgautier.com*
A British/French team that are experienced architects and also
organise surveys, obtain building permits and carry out project
management. New build, renovation, landscaping and pools.

Eric Archaimbault   ☎ 06 77 13 41 41
✉ *archaimbaulteric@wanadoo.fr*
Bilingual project manager using only registered French
tradesmen and covering the whole of Poitou-Charentes.

Builders

General   Poitou-Charentes Renovations,
La Bayette de Bioussac   ☎ 05 45 85 46 78
✉ *huckstepp.lee@wanadoo.fr*
This British-run company covers the southern part of Vienne,
including Charroux and Civray, and works with a team of
French-registered British tradesmen, including electricians,
plumbers and roofers.

Châtellerault   Dupuy Sarl, 136 avenue de Lattre de
Tassigny   ☎ 05 49 21 21 14
🖳 *www.dupuybat.com*
Construction and renovation.

Civray   J.C. Baussant, 1 route de Montmorillon,
Savigné   ☎ 05 49 87 16 30
Building, roofing and renovation.

Loudun	Boucher Ets, route Chauleries, Guesnes	☎ 05 49 22 82 27

New and renovation work undertaken.

Montmorillon	J.M. Hebras, 37 rue du Haut-Poitou	☎ 05 49 91 20 11

Building, roofing, carpentry and tiling.

	Marcadier Sarl, 52 rue Abel Pinaud	☎ 05 49 91 11 78

General building work.

Poitiers	SNBM, Vouneuil-sous-Biard	☎ 05 49 37 50 00

(near the airport)
New building and renovation.

Carpenters

Châtellerault	Alubois 86, 3 rue B. Palissy, ZI Sanital	☎ 05 49 93 53 54

Windows and doors, gates and shutters.

	Dupuy Sarl, 136 avenue de Lattre de Tassigny	☎ 05 49 21 21 14

💻 *www.dupuybat.com*
Made-to-measure windows, doors and stairs.

Civray	Menuiserie Bonnet, 10 rue Victor Hugo	☎ 05 49 87 64 19
Loudun	Bourdon SA, 45 rue Artisans	☎ 05 49 98 13 85
Montmorillon	Mr Lancereau, 17 rue d'Anjou	☎ 05 49 91 24 24
	Mr Blanconnier, 7 allée du Général de Gaulle	☎ 05 49 91 12 30
Poitiers	Guilleminaud Fabien, 37 rue Soleil Levant	☎ 05 49 03 38 13

Chimney Sweeps

Châtellerault	Gaëtan Brosse, 16 chemin Herse	☎ 05 49 23 48 42
Civray	Giraud Serge et Fils, ZA route Limoges, Savigné	☎ 05 49 87 17 50
Loudun	J.M. Barray, Beaussay, Mouterre Silly	☎ 05 49 22 31 59

Chimney sweeping and maintenance of heating systems.

Lussac-les-Châteaux	Rémy Bernier, Villeneuve	☎ 05 49 48 49 98
Poitiers	Chauffage Schweitzer Jean, 10 rue Gué Sourdeau	☎ 05 49 38 26 83

Electricians & Plumbers

There are many tradesmen who do both electrics and plumbing, so they've been combined under this heading and do both unless otherwise stated.

Châtellerault	Aucher Electricité, 8 rue Prieuré, Usseau	☎ 05 49 02 35 79
	General electrics.	
	Brunet, 21 rue André Boulle, ZI Nord	☎ 05 49 93 20 59
	Electrics, plumbing and heating, installation, repairs and maintenance.	
Civray	Giraud et Fils, 10 route Limoges, Savigné	☎ 05 49 87 17 50
	Plumbing, heating, roofing, kitchens and bathrooms.	
Loudun	Brunet, 7 bis boulevard Maréchal Leclerc	☎ 05 49 98 04 01
	Electrics, plumbing and heating. Installation, repair and maintenance.	
Montmorillon	Demazeau Frères, 20 boulevard Strasbourg	☎ 05 49 91 04 40
	Heating, plumbing and electrics.	
	Beauchesne Sarl, 8 rue du Chemin des Dames	☎ 05 49 91 25 26
Poitiers	Pradeau Sarl, 3 avenue Europe, Chasseneuil-du-Poitou	☎ 05 49 52 02 51
	The proprietor deals with electricity, heating and bathrooms and speaks some English.	
	Proxiserve, 19 route de l'Ormeau, Buxerolles	☎ 05 49 47 59 05
	Repair and maintenance of plumbing and all types of heating.	

Translators & Teachers

French Teachers & Courses

Châtellerault	Richard Wimberley, 13 rue des Mignons	☎ 05 49 23 33 75
	🖳 *www.on-speaking-terms.com.* Spanish and Italian lessons also available.	
Civray	Tournesol Language School, St Romain	☎ 05 49 87 45 23
	(just north of Civray) For beginners, improvers and fluent speakers with an emphasis on communication. One-to-one, group and intensive courses.	

Loudun	Mme Saulnier, 16 rue du Collège	☎ 05 49 98 10 45

Montmorillon	Laurent Geneix, 1 rue de La Poêlerie	☎ 05 49 83 82 54

Individual and group lessons, here or at your home. Once enrolled, clients are entitled to help liaising with artisans.

Poitiers	Centre d'Etude des Langues, 2 avenue René Cassin	☎ 05 49 49 48 48

(near Futuroscope)
Individual lessons only.

Translators

Châtellerault	Richard Wimberley, 13 rue des Mignons	☎ 05 49 23 33 75

🖳 *www.on-speaking-terms.com*

Civray	Tournesol Services, St Romain	☎ 05 49 87 45 23

(north of the town)
This company helps communicate with tradesmen.

Couhé	Pierre Bruce, 3 place Marne	☎ 05 49 89 04 36

(just off the N10 south of Poitiers)

Montmorillon	Continental Horizons, 2 impasse des Millepertuis, Malliers	☎ 05 49 84 17 73

(just north of the town)

Poitiers	Edith Tapia, 1 allée Brouette du Vinaigrier	☎ 05 49 46 38 87

Utilities

Electricity & Gas

Électricité de France/Gaz de France (EDF/GDF) is one company for the whole of France but operates its gas and electricity divisions separately. The numbers below are for general information; emergency numbers can be found on page 56.

General	EDF GDF Services Vienne et Sèvres, 2 rue Marcel Paul, Châtellerault	☎ 08 10 07 90 86

🖳 *www.edf.fr*

	Gaz de France, 6 rue Auguste Perret, Lagord	☎ 05 46 43 43 43

(near La Rochelle, in Charente-Maritime)

EDF local offices are listed below (there are no direct telephone numbers for these offices; you must call the above number).

Châtellerault	2 rue Marcel Paul
Loudun	13 boulevard Loches et Matras
Montmorillon	3 rue Varennes
Poitiers	74 rue Bourgogne

Heating Oil

Châtellerault	Auchan Fioul, avenue Jean Moulin, RN10	☎ 05 49 23 48 85
Civray	Rodière Lancereau, 3 rue Moulin Neuf	☎ 05 49 87 00 47
Loudun	CPO, 9 avenue Leuze	☎ 05 49 98 05 00
Montmorillon	CPO, 87 avenue Fernand Tribot	☎ 05 49 91 00 65
Poitiers	Fuel 2000, ZI La Richaumoine, Neuville de Poitou	☎ 05 49 51 34 71

Water

The main water supply companies are listed below. If you aren't covered by one of these, your *mairie* will have details of your water supplier.

Générale des Eaux	8 rue Marcel Dassault, Châtellerault	☎ 08 11 90 29 02
Service des Eaux	40 avenue Fernand Tribot, Montmorillon	☎ 05 49 91 02 66
SIAEA	1 rue Chemin Vert, Civray	☎ 05 49 87 04 38
SIGEP	2 Champ du Soleil, Lathus	☎ 05 49 91 87 05
SIVEER	55 rue Bonneuil Matours, Poitiers	☎ 05 49 61 16 90
Syndicat d'Eau de Charroux	2 quart St Laurent, Charroux	☎ 05 49 87 84 48

Wood

Civaux	Jacquart Bois, 11 route Rivalières Ribes	☎ 05 49 48 28 60
Migné-Auxances	Rives et Bois, Malaguet (north-west of Poitiers)	☎ 05 49 54 43 51

328 Poitou-Charentes Lifeline

INDEX

P

R

S

T

W

U

V

ORDER FORM 1

Qty.	Title	Price (incl. p&p)*			Total
		UK	**Europe**	**World**	
	The Alien's Guide to Britain	£6.95	£8.95	£12.45	
	The Alien's Guide to France	£6.95	£8.95	£12.45	
	The Best Places to Buy a Home in France	£13.95	£15.95	£19.45	
	The Best Places to Buy a Home in Spain	£13.95	£15.95	£19.45	
	Buying a Home Abroad	£13.95	£15.95	£19.45	
	Buying a Home in Florida	£13.95	£15.95	£19.45	
	Buying a Home in France	£13.95	£15.95	£19.45	
	Buying a Home in Greece & Cyprus	£13.95	£15.95	£19.45	
	Buying a Home in Ireland	£11.95	£13.95	£17.45	
	Buying a Home in Italy	£13.95	£15.95	£19.45	
	Buying a Home in Portugal	£13.95	£15.95	£19.45	
	Buying a Home in Spain	£13.95	£15.95	£19.45	
	Buying, Letting & Selling Property	£11.95	£13.95	£17.45	
	Foreigners in France: Triumphs & Disasters	£11.95	£13.95	£17.45	
	Foreigners in Spain: Triumphs & Disasters	£11.95	£13.95	£17.45	
	How to Avoid Holiday & Travel Disasters	£13.95	£15.95	£19.45	
	Costa del Sol Lifeline	£11.95	£13.95	£17.45	
	Dordogne/Lot Lifeline	£11.95	£13.95	£17.45	
	Poitou-Charentes Lifeline	£11.95	£13.95	£17.45	
				Total	

Order your copies today by phone, fax, mail or e-mail from: Survival Books, PO Box 146, Wetherby, West Yorks. LS23 6XZ, UK (☎/▤ +44 (0)1937-843523, ✉ orders@ survivalbooks.net, 🖥 www.survivalbooks.net). If you aren't entirely satisfied, simply return them to us within 14 days for a full and unconditional refund.

Cheque enclosed/please charge my Amex/Delta/MasterCard/Switch/Visa* card

Card No. ＿ ＿ ＿ ＿　＿ ＿ ＿ ＿　＿ ＿ ＿ ＿　＿ ＿ ＿ ＿

Expiry date ＿＿＿＿＿＿＿ Issue number (Switch only) ＿＿＿＿＿＿＿＿＿＿＿

Signature ＿＿＿＿＿＿＿＿＿＿＿＿ Tel. No. ＿＿＿＿＿＿＿＿＿＿＿＿＿

NAME ＿＿＿＿＿＿＿＿＿＿＿＿＿＿＿＿＿＿＿＿＿＿＿＿＿＿＿＿＿＿＿

ADDRESS ＿＿＿＿＿＿＿＿＿＿＿＿＿＿＿＿＿＿＿＿＿＿＿＿＿＿＿＿＿＿

＿＿＿＿＿＿＿＿＿＿＿＿＿＿＿＿＿＿＿＿＿＿＿＿＿＿＿＿＿＿

＿＿＿＿＿＿＿＿＿＿＿＿＿＿＿＿＿＿＿＿＿＿＿＿＿＿＿＿＿＿

* Delete as applicable (price includes postage – airmail for Europe/world).

ORDER FORM 2

Qty.	Title	Price (incl. p&p)*			Total
		UK	**Europe**	**World**	
	Living & Working Abroad	£14.95	£16.95	£20.45	
	Living & Working in America	£14.95	£16.95	£20.45	
	Living & Working in Australia	£14.95	£16.95	£20.45	
	Living & Working in Britain	£14.95	£16.95	£20.45	
	Living & Working in Canada	£16.95	£18.95	£22.45	
	Living & Working in the European Union	£16.95	£18.95	£22.45	
	Living & Working in the Far East	£16.95	£18.95	£22.45	
	Living & Working in France	£14.95	£16.95	£20.45	
	Living & Working in Germany	£16.95	£18.95	£22.45	
	L&W in the Gulf States & Saudi Arabia	£16.95	£18.95	£22.45	
	L&W in Holland, Belgium & Luxembourg	£14.95	£16.95	£20.45	
	Living & Working in Ireland	£14.95	£16.95	£20.45	
	Living & Working in Italy	£16.95	£18.95	£22.45	
	Living & Working in London	£13.95	£15.95	£19.45	
	Living & Working in New Zealand	£14.95	£16.95	£20.45	
	Living & Working in Spain	£14.95	£16.95	£20.45	
	Living & Working in Switzerland	£16.95	£18.95	£22.45	
	Renovating & Maintaining Your French Home	£13.95	£15.95	£19.45	
	Retiring Abroad	£14.95	£16.95	£20.45	
	Rioja and its Wines	£11.95	£13.95	£17.45	
	The Wines of Spain	£13.95	£15.95	£19.45	
					Total

Order your copies today by phone, fax, mail or e-mail from: Survival Books, PO Box 146, Wetherby, West Yorks. LS23 6XZ, UK (☎/▤ +44 (0)1937-843523, ✉ orders@ survivalbooks.net, 🖳 www.survivalbooks.net). If you aren't entirely satisfied, simply return them to us within 14 days for a full and unconditional refund.

Cheque enclosed/please charge my Amex/Delta/MasterCard/Switch/Visa* card

Card No. _ _ _ _   _ _ _ _   _ _ _ _   _ _ _ _

Expiry date _____   Issue number (Switch only) _____

Signature _____   Tel. No. _____

NAME _____

ADDRESS _____

_____

_____

* Delete as applicable (price includes postage – airmail for Europe/world).

SURVIVAL BOOKS ON FRANCE

Buying a Home in France is essential reading for anyone planning to purchase property in France and is designed to guide you through the property jungle and make it a pleasant and enjoyable experience. Most importantly, it's packed with vital information to help you **avoid the sort of disasters that can turn your dream home into a nightmare!**

Living and Working in France is essential reading for anyone planning to live or work in France, including retirees, visitors, business people, migrants and students. It's packed with important and useful information designed to help you **avoid costly mistakes and save both time and money.**

The Alien's Guide to France provides an 'alternative' look at life in the 'Hexagon' and will help you to appreciate the peculiarities (in both senses) of its inhabitants.

The Best Places to Buy a Home in France is the most comprehensive and up-to-date homebuying guide to France, containing detailed regional guides to help you choose the ideal location for your home.

Lifelines books are essential guides to specific regions of France, containing everything you need to know about local life. Titles in the series currently include Dordogne/Lot, and Poitou-Charentes.

Renovating & Maintaining Your French Home is the ultimate guide to renovating and maintaining your dream home in France, including practical advice and time- and money-saving tips.

Foreigners in France: Triumphs & Disasters is a collection of real-life experiences of people who have emigrated to France, providing a 'warts and all' picture of everyday life in all parts of the country.

Order your copies today by phone, fax, mail or e-mail from: Survival Books, PO Box 146, Wetherby, West Yorks. LS23 6XZ, United Kingdom (☎/🖳 +44 (0)1937-843523, ✉ orders@ survivalbooks.net, 🖳 www.survivalbooks.net).